Criminal Justice

Recent Scholarship

Edited by
Nicholas P. Lovrich

A Series from LFB Scholarly

The Rule of Bureaucracy
A Reflection on Chinese Criminal Justice

Yu Zhang

LFB Scholarly Publishing LLC
El Paso 2016

Library of Congress Cataloging-in-Publication Data

Library of Congress Cataloging-in-Publication Data

Names: Zhang, Yu, 1975- (Criminologist) author.
Title: The rule of bureaucracy: a reflection on Chinese criminal justice system / Yu Zhang.
Description: El Paso : LFB Scholarly Publishing LLC, 2016. | Based on author's thesis (doctoral - Northeastern University, 2014), issued under title: Bureaucracy and law : a study of Chinese criminal courts and social media. | Includes bibliographical references and index.
Identifiers: LCCN 2016011893 (print) | LCCN 2016013181 (ebook) | ISBN 9781593328092 (hardcover : alk. paper) | ISBN 9781593328146 (e-book)
Subjects: LCSH: Criminal justice, Administration of--China. | Bureaucracy--China.
Classification: LCC HV9960.C53 Z43 2016 (print) | LCC HV9960.C53 (ebook) | DDC 364.0951--dc23
LC record available at http://lccn.loc.gov/2016011893

ISBN 978-1-59332-809-2

Manufactured in the United States of America.

Contents

List of Figures and Tables

Acknowledgements

I am grateful to those people who have inspired me in writing this book. This book is dedicated to my parents and my homeland.

Preface

In recent decades an increasing number of English language studies featuring multiple areas of focus on the Chinese criminal justice have been published, including some on imperial legal history (e.g., Bodde and Morris, 1967; Ch'ü, 1961; Cohen, 1968, 1969; Meadows, 1970; Watt, 1972), on the modern criminal justice system and court practices (e.g., He, 2013; Hegel, 2007, 2009; Leng, 1982; Lo, 1995; Lubman, 1999; McConville, 2013; Shih, 1999; Trevaskes, 2007), and on the topics of criminal court procedures and legal reforms (e.g. Lu & Miethe, 2002; Lu & Miethe, 2003). These studies have most assuredly provided important discussions regarding theoretical and conceptual framework of the Chinese criminal courts, but they rarely review Chinese courts and the Chinese criminal justice system within the broader framework of the long-established Chinese bureaucratic hierarchy. The Chinese variant of bureaucracy is heavily emphasized in this book because some of the particular characteristics of Chinese bureaucracy are directly relevant to the creation of the essential foundations of judicial independence.

What is the Chinese style of bureaucracy? Why is it important to explore the political bureaucracy framework in a study of Chinese courts? If we look back across the thousands years of Chinese history, it is clear that Chinese society has been deeply rooted not only in a hierarchical bureaucratic system, but also in a profoundly bureaucratic culture. If we do not consider this deeply founded bureaucratic context in Chinese court studies, we cannot understand why it is so difficult for China to advance toward the goals of judiciary independence and to ultimately achieve the rule of law.

This book looks into the underlying causes of the lack of genuine rule of law in China, and identifies the major barrier—namely, an omnipotent political bureaucracy. The long history of Chinese

Mandarin bureaucracy has given rise to the habituated practice of relying on executive authority for justice rather than providing for the pursuit of justice through a system of courts. The judiciary in China has to cope with both indirect and direct challenges from the all-powerful political bureaucracy, and it lacks the social and institutional standing to provide any genuine measure of judicial independence to act in defense of the rule of law. While change is taking place in the direction of judicial independence and the rule of law, that change is both slow in pace and progress made often comes at great cost to those brave lawyers advocating for it.

Introduction

Although concepts of judicial independence and rule of law may be treated as a matter of common course in most Western countries, they are far from self-evident when viewed against a tradition of hierarchical bureaucracy which has a legacy of thousands of years. The Chinese people have their own uniquely Chinese hopeful dreams regarding their history, as do all peoples on Earth. In regard to the tradition of Chinese political thought, these hopeful dreams tend to relate to bureaucracy rather than to individuals. The three principal Chinese dreams of direct relevance are: *wise Emperor*, *honest Official*, and *upright Knight* (Yi, 2010). Born in a culture of bureaucracy, Chinese people tend to rest their hopes of attaining justice and achieving a good life on the bureaucracy, on their emperors, and on their public officials.

They expect that there could be a good emperor who can bring a well-ruled dynasty in which people can live in peace and wellness. They expect local officials to be honest and to care about people. If these two dreams are unrealized, they expect that some brave knights would take action to save all of the poor people by bringing down the rich and powerful. None of these three traditional dreams is related to either the rule of law or to the provision of legal assistance to protect ordinary people. In existence of thousands of years, how these ideal dreams of justice in Chinese culture changed? Have the rule of law and the concept of democracy entered the Chinese people's thinking regarding justice? Have the Chinese people developed new dreams for justice for their future?

This book examines Chinese criminal courts and legal reform in the context of bureaucratic society in China. It presents both historical and cultural considerations in the review of contemporary legal reforms, and explores the reforms through a focus on social media. The book discusses the complex nature of the criminal justice system in China, investigating the potential for the Chinese judiciary to build its independent identity and contribute to the achievement of democracy. It is argued here that the Chinese judiciary arose within the political bureaucracy, and it has functioned as a bureaucratized system since its inception. The bureaucratized judiciary is more the heritage of Chinese history than an innovation arising after the revolution of 1911 or the national liberation of 1949. Criminal cases are used here to disclose the nature of the operations of the contemporary criminal courts in China. Also explored here is the potential for change in a global era revolutionized by advanced information technology and the Internet. A large amount of social media data is presented to showcase the dynamic legal community and online activism present in contemporary China.

This study weaves these historical, cultural and social media strands together to paint a vivid picture of a new era of informational politics framed in the criminal courts trapped within a deeply engrained and ubiquitous bureaucratic culture. The history and characteristics of Chinese bureaucracy have had a significant influence on the contemporary legal system, but the vibrant social media present have clearly given rise to an emerging force for potential change.

In chapter 1, the process of bureaucratization and its impact on the judiciary are discussed. Different from judicial bureaucratization trends present in Western countries, the Chinese judiciary was given birth as part of Imperial bureaucracy. It is argued that the bureaucratization of Chinese judiciary is a virtual birthmark of Chinese law; the bureaucratized judiciary was created at the outset of government rather than acquired as a reform on the road to democratization.

Methodology and data collection processes are set forth in Chapter 2. Although legal reform in contemporary China shows evidence of influence from the West, the Chinese judiciary remains a highly bureaucratized system and operates with a distinctively administrative as opposed to legalistic style. To obtain a clear understanding of the contemporary Chinese criminal justice system this book not only uses case studies to analyze the character of criminal case processing, but also investigates the contemporary Chinese legal professional community through their active presence on the Internet. Both criminal case narratives and social media texts are used here to expose what occurs behind the closed doors of Chinese criminal justice system.

The long history of China is presented in Chapter 3, focusing on the ambivalent state of the Chinese judiciary over the course of time. Being part of the imperial bureaucracy, the Chinese judiciary has never had the opportunity to build its independent identity. Around 1000 B.C. the bureaucracy system started to take shape in China, handling both executive and judicial affairs as though they were inseparable duties of governance. In the central and local governments alike (*郡jun and 县 xian*[1]), Imperial appointed officials possessed both executive and judicial powers. From that time on, this type of patrimonial bureaucracy has provided structure and staff to promulgate and administer law. As a result, no independent judiciary was ever established separate from the executive bureaucracy system. While the bureaucracy can increase efficiency in the judiciary in service to the public interest, it is undeniable that efficiency cannot override justice, and equally undeniable that judicial independence is needed to assure rule of law. In recognition of this unavoidable conflict in values between efficiency and justice, there have been several attempts to build a modern legal system and judiciary in China since the beginning of 20th century. Legal reforms were initiated in the late *Qing* dynasty and similar legal changes were introduced after the imperial dynasty system was overthrown in 1911. However, these attempts have all met stiff resistance from the bureaucracy, and floundered after a rather short period of operation.

The national liberation achieved by the Chinese Communist Party in 1949 led to revolutionary changes, including efforts to build a new legal system. However, the operation of the revolution-bred reforms led to a virtual train wreck during the 10 years of the Great Cultural Revolution. The reconstruction of the contemporary judiciary began after 1978, featuring both increasing legislation and conscientious institution building. Chapter 4 sets forth a review covering the past 30 years of legal reform, and it describes the major features of current state of the Chinese judiciary.

The criminal case narrative approach represents a storytelling way to capture those important cases which have had significant impacts on both the criminal justice system and on Chinese society. In Chapter 5,

[1]郡(jun) and 县(xian)are the administrative area of local governments.

twelve criminal cases are used to analyze the current criminal justice system in China. These cases will show how a culture of bureaucratization has not only affected the trial process, but also how it has shaped people's expectations with regard to criminal lawsuits. These illustrative case reveal how the highly centralized political bureaucracy leads to the exercise of absolute executive power, the exercise of which weakens the legal system. These twelve cases illustrate as well how the Chinese justice system can be manipulated by executive officials to pursue personal interests. Taken in combination these cases show how the judiciary lacks independence and the collective strength to distribute justice and resist intervention from the political bureaucracy.

A vibrant and vigilant civil society is required to hold a bureaucratized system accountable. The Internet presents possibilities for the creation of public space and civil surveillance for accountability. In Chapter 6, the development of a virtual civil society is discussed, exploring how a dynamic legal online community can add strength to offline legal activism and move legal reform forward. Using social media analysis tools, this book documents the importance of criminal courts and the criminal justice system in contemporary China; the performance of the system will influence the whole of contemporary Chinese society. The use of social media texts allows the creation of a vivid picture of current legal professionals who are courageously writing legal history in China. In Chapter 7, I provide a summary of the work presented in this book and discuss the current state of the Chinese criminal justice system with respect to prospects for the rule of law and the advent of democracy in China.

CHAPTER 1

Bureaucracy and Law

BUREAUCRACY

Our contemporary lives are dominated by private and public organizations organized as bureaucracies. Pervasive bureaucratization is part of the modern predicament. We have moved from a society of a finite number of individuals to a society of organizations acting upon the isolated individual. Human beings wake up to see that they must live and work with forms of authority that presuppose a highly structured world beyond human comprehension. Bureaucracy is a particular type of administrative structure which developed through the progressive development of what organizational scholars' term rational-legal authority (Weber, 1978).

According to Max Weber (1978), the ideal type construct of bureaucracy features these characteristics: clearly specified jurisdictional areas, with activities within these jurisdictions being defined as official duties; the organization structure follows the hierarchical principle; abstract rules govern all workplace decisions and actions; the means of production or administration belong to an office rather to any individual person; officials are selected on the basis of their technical qualifications, officials are appointed, not elected; and all officials are compensated by salary; employment within the organization is viewed as a career commitment and is protected by tenure of office upon good conduct vis-á-vis established rules and regulations. Bureaucracy entails more than formal structures; it also includes roles, policies, procedures, and even culture. It might be easy to pull down a structure alone, but once it is fully combined with all those roles, policies, procedures and culture, bureaucracy becomes the most resistant to destruction among all social structures (Weber, 1958).

As many scholars have noted since Max Weber's time, bureaucracy has great importance for modern society, and the history of the twentieth century is largely one of widespread bureaucratization (Fiss, 1983). Almost every phase of our life is dominated by large-scale, complex organization, and the very same trend toward bureaucratization has taken place in all the government powers, including those of legislative, judicial and executive offices. Weber specifically acknowledged that the legal processes of both England and America, as opposed to those of the European Continent, were not highly bureaucratic (Weber, 1958).

However, in more recent years, the bureaucratization of the judiciary in the U.S. has been largely criticized by many legal scholars (Fiss, 1983). For example, the U.S. Congress has 12 internal agencies, and already consists of about 24,000 employees in the year of 2000;[2] there are 20 committees, 68 subcommittees, and 4 joint committees in the U.S. Senate; there are 20 standing committees in the House of Representatives.[3&4] "Bureaucracy", a term which conventionally refers to the executive branch, now shows a highly similar pattern of development within virtually all government agencies. The bureaucratization of the judiciary in the Western countries signifies the full influence of modern life, and reflects the courts' commitments to the separation of powers in the Western democratic form of government.

BUREAUCRACY IN CHINA

Compared to the procedural and organizational bureaucratization of the judiciary in the U.S. and other Western countries, the judiciary in China is moving along a clearly different route. Although Max Weber argued that the ideal type of bureaucracy is most fully approximated in political and ecclesiastical communities which exist in modern societies

---

[2] http://legacy.c-span.org/questions/weekly35.asp.

[3] http://www.senate.gov/general/common/generic/about_committees.htm.

[4] The Committee System in the U.S. Congress, Congressional Research Service, Library of Congress. August 29, 1994, revised by the Senate Historical Office, September 2002.

and the most advanced institutions of capitalism, he fully acknowledged that Imperial China had already a developed, large and rather comprehensive governmental bureaucracy (Weber, 1958). The origins of Chinese bureaucracy are to be found in the governmental practices of the *Western Zhou* state (1045-771 BC), a period much earlier than would occur in Western societies (Hsu & Linduff, 1988).

Being an overwhelmingly agrarian society, China had a vast peasant social base largely without local governmental organization, and the merchant class was culturally looked down upon and lacked social autonomy. The Imperial officialdom present at the time had consistently held power over Chinese people for thousands of years. In addition, those imperial bureaucrats were typically specialized in dealing with human beings, utilizing the management technique of mutual supervision among the members of society with whom they dealt. The tradition of collective responsibility has become the principal practice for the imperial bureaucrats to avoid direct responsibility and shift their work obligations onto the shoulder of others. Confucianism, the Imperial state ideology, teaches respect and submission to the dictates of one's elders and social superiors, and as a consequence helps officialdom strengthen their authority of rule.

China has been deemed a "permanently bureaucratic" society, and the long duration of Chinese imperial bureaucracy has had a profound impact on nearly all aspects of Chinese social life (Balazs, 1964, p.13). Max Weber argued convincingly that organizational forms based on kinship and personal loyalty cannot deal with the diverse activities of large numbers of individuals found in modern day capitalist societies (Weber, 1978). The capitalist societies all turned to the increasing use of the legal/rational form of bureaucracy to maximize efficiency. It is clear from the case of China, however, that some ancient bureaucracies were quite effective even though they do not meet all of the criteria of Weberian bureaucracy.

Chinese bureaucracy differs from the Weberian rational bureaucracy ideal type in some respects (Whyte, 1973). It is known that Chinese bureaucracy is a Mandarin form of bureaucracy, and it places a focus on the distinctive "mandarin" concept of role obligation of officials in government. Mandarin, a word which originates from the Portuguese language, first was used in a Portuguese report about China referring to higher-level officials encountered in the country (Ferguson,

1902). A Mandarin bureaucracy is a bureaucracy composed of generalists in which recruitment to all positions is based on competitive examinations; training is geared toward faithfully serving the public; and the job environment offers near immunity from all social, political and occupational pressures based on widespread respect for officials within society (Khator, 1997).

The Chinese Mandarin bureaucracy was a powerful bureaucratic system in which generalist officials were selected and graded through an open, competitive, written, national examination system based primarily upon knowledge of the Confucian classics (Riggs, 1997). The exams given tested on whether a candidate had a proper understanding of social ethics and properly cultivated tastes rather than on any knowledge of the law or of any other form of technical knowledge. In stark contrast, the Weberian form of bureaucracy features a focus on technical knowledge and the skills associated with a specific organizational position. Without these specialties, how could Chinese bureaucrats have excelled in the system and gained such great power and influence over the course of thousands of years? It is most interesting to note that the source of power for a Mandarin bureaucrat remains expertise and knowledge. The knowledge these bureaucrats held was not about the skills related to their positional needs, but rather the administrative and people skills associated with effective governance. After gathering sufficient administrative expertise and experience, the Mandarins became virtually indispensable to the Imperial rulers and they became very powerful players in the political system (Khator, 1997).

Because the recruitment to service was through competitive examinations rather than political appointment, this method of selection gave bureaucrats a certain degree of neutrality. However, this neutrality also explains why many bureaucrats felt little sense of accountability. The system allows bureaucrats to escape from responsibility for outcomes because their performance is measured by the degree to which implementation has been carried out rather than the degree to which goals have been met (Khator, 1997). In addition, these Mandarin bureaucrats were paid very little by the state; they functioned within a tradition where "gifts" (referred to as "going through the back door" or using *guanxi*) were a socially accepted mode for influencing decision-makers (Dellapenna, 2005, p.370). Given these elements of the Mandarin system it is not surprising to see examples of abusive use of power and shameful corruption in such a Mandarin bureaucracy system.

With the advent of modern society, Chinese bureaucracy has seen a great deal of formal bureaucratization, with the all-pervasive communist party ruling over the political system. Weber argued that bureaucratization is an inevitable concomitant of economic development and modernization, in both socialist and capitalist countries alike (Whyte, 1973). Weber had predicted that future socialist societies would require an even higher degree of formal bureaucratization than would be the case in capitalist societies (Weber, 1968, p. 225). Weber noted that the traditional Chinese bureaucracy differed from the ideal type rational bureaucracy in important ways (Weber, 1968).

The modern Chinese bureaucracy shies away from the ideal type of Weberian bureaucracy, lacking a high degree of specialization and not achieving the development of occupational professionalism due to the dominance of party. The action of the bureaucracy is not only supposed to maximize internal efficiency, but to pursue certain revolutionary social goals or policy objectives, with the latter taking precedence in the case of any conflict (Whyte, 1973).

CHINESE BUREAUCRACY AND LAW

Different from judicial bureaucratization in Western countries, the Chinese judiciary originated as part of the imperial bureaucracy. For thousands of years, the Chinese judiciary has had no independent status and social identity separate from executive power, and imperial law was administrated by the Mandarin bureaucracy. As a result, the bureaucratization of the judiciary is a hallmark of Chinese law; the bureaucratized judiciary was an aspect of birth rather than acquired (Haque, 1997). The key question is how to control a strong bureaucracy, one which has deeply penetrated into virtually all aspects of the society, to create a rational-legal system which can effectively serve modern society and promote democracy. Which route to legal reform is to be preferred, a forceful revolution or a gradual evolution?

Moore (1966) has argued that all modernizing societies have undergone a version of one of three types of revolution—namely, bourgeois class revolutions (England, France and the United States), revolution from above (Germany and Japan), and peasant revolution from below (Russia and China). A revolution, mostly a violent rejection of the legal order of the past, entails the rejection of old laws and existing legal systems (Berman & Whiting, 1980; Salas, 1983; Kim, 1987).

Rebuilding a new rationalized legal system takes a rather long time after revolutionary destruction, and during the interim leaders rising from the revolution tend to rule the new regime based on their charisma. Although charisma is a source of primordial power, it typically entails much improvisation and often results in legal instability, inconsistency, and even the subversion of established orders (Gonzalez, 1983; Weber, 1978). If the leader cannot retain the prestige and the admiration of the population, the new system will not be secure (Valdes, 1976). In order for long-term survival and stable development, a highly predictable, consistent and stable legal system has to be established (Berman and Whiting, 1980; Weber, 1978). The impersonal rule of the modern bureaucratic state has largely replaced both traditional and charismatic pre-modern authority (Weber, 1978, p.245, Meyer & Rowan, 1977).

Legal–rational forms of governance have to establish their own identity over time. This generally requires a gradual evolutionary process. Revolution is tempered by evolution, and evolution is punctuated and accelerated by revolution (Watson, 1987). Evolution, a nonviolent revolution associated with peace and caution, is a more gradual and continuous development in morals and ideas without entailing some sort of catastrophe (Reclus, 1891). Because evolution is acceptable to people who look upon revolution with fear, it will win the largest amount of supporters on its way to the goal. Haste makes waste, and it is worthwhile to choose a road which takes a long time and avoids dramatic events.

The development of legal systems may well require an evolutionary process. The law is essentially discovered, not made nor "revolutionized" in its entirety. In its systemic discovery process, law reflects the experiences of all people over the course of history. Law, as a natural outcome of society, takes an evolutionary developing route (Younkins, 2000). It would be difficult to imagine indeed that a rational-legal system could be built in a tumultuous revolution. The idea of law includes rules of behavior, as well as institutions and devices for at once changing, clarifying, refining, and applying the rules. All of these actions require much time and effort, even generations. Building an effective legal system is a process of institutionalization by which legal organizations and procedures acquire value, social acceptance, and stability (Huntington, 1968, p. 12).

The Chinese criminal court system originated as part of the imperial ruling bureaucracy, and it has been seem as a reining tool for thousands of years. Although China has indeed experienced numerous wars and revolutions, it is surprising to find that changes to the legal system and bureaucracy have been slower to come about than people imagined. The Chinese Judiciary still features a bureaucratic structure following the Party's leadership and local government's wishes. The executive bureaucracy not only can issue and interpret their own rules, but they also can require the courts to enforce these rules and dictates. In the criminal justice area, the extensive power of the police, administrative offices, and the Chinese Communist Party over the criminal process still exists despite some signs of progress toward judicial independence (Lubman, 1999).

In addition, the Chinese legal system reflects its own historical heritage in many ways. For example, China has a tradition of written law, so it is much easier to adopt continental laws which are codified into a referable system than to emulate American or English common law legal norms and practices. A bureaucratized judiciary is clearly a heritage from thousands of years of Chinese history rather than a result of revolution. As noted above, the development of any existing legal system entails an evolutionary process.

The revolutionary movement of the Communist Party attempted to build a new social system and smash all old practices after 1949; such efforts led to a virtual train wreck during the 10 years of the Great Cultural Revolution. The reconstruction of the judiciary began after dramatic events in 1978, with both increased legislation and a commitment to institution building being strongly in evidence. The past 30 years of legal reform have established a comprehensive system of criminal law with a great deal of legislation, rules and regulations coming into being. However, an independent legal system is composed of more than detailed laws; it requires efforts from a judiciary which can make just decisions and act independently. Although the contemporary Chinese criminal law reform reflects some influence from the West, the Chinese judiciary is still a highly bureaucratized system and operates with more of an administrative style than a legalistic style. The deeply-rooted reasons of this fact come from Chinese history and originate in the nation's culture. In Chapter 3, the long Chinese history of bureaucracy which gave the birth to the Chinese judiciary is summarized. In Chapter 2, the research methods of the study are set forth in considerable detail.

CHAPTER 2

Methodology: Case Study and Social Media

The book seeks to describe the present Chinese judicial system and its operation and demonstrate how it reflects the impact of the country's political bureaucracy. Since it is very difficult to acquire direct information from the closed judicial system, the research conducted for this book uses the case study approach to examine court operations. In addition, social media analysis is used to showcase the development of a new virtual Chinese legal community coming into existence in the Internet era. Admittedly, research on the court and criminal justice system in China faces many challenges, but this combination of case analyses and social media pattern identification provides some important insights into that system.

The courts and criminal justice system represent important ruling tools used by the government. Previous research on Chinese criminal courts mainly focuses on legal reforms and judicial procedures. The existing literature on Chinese courts typically discusses theoretical and conceptual frameworks regarding criminal courts, and the scant empirical research done on Chinese courts is highly limited because the availability of data is extremely limited. In this chapter I first provide an overview of the methodology of previous research on Chinese criminal courts, and then I discuss the methods used in the current study in some detail.

PRIOR RESEARCH

One of the obstacles to Chinese court research is the difficulty of gaining access to reliable, accurate and meaningful data. The court documents of record are not easily obtained for research use, and any large-scale court observation process is out of the question given both facility limitation and administrative restrictions (Liang, 2008). Dutiful scholars, however, have made brave attempts at data collection and systematic research, and as a consequence tremendous progress has indeed been made over the course of the last two decades. The majority of studies have made use of diverse methods such as interviews of lawyers (e.g., Liu & Halliday, 2011), the study of lawyers' online discussions (e.g., Halliday & Liu, 2007), study of court documents (e.g., Lu and Miethe, 2002a), and the detailed study of online televised trials (Zhong, Hu & Liang, 2011).

Some research on criminal processing and sentencing entailed the collection of data such as legal rulings in particular areas of the law. For example, Lu and her colleagues have examined a series of case collections compiled over the course of the last decade (Lu & Drass, 2002; Lu & Liang, 2008; Lu, Liu & Crowther, 2006; Lu & Miethe, 2002). After examining legal defense issues with data on the prosecution and the subsequent adjudication of theft cases in a Chinese court, the researchers found that legal representation has little net impact on pre-trial detention and sentencing decisions, and some types of legal defenses were more likely to be accepted by judges than others. They also used a sample of 1,009 criminal court cases to examine confessions and criminal case dispositions in China. They reported that the majority of offenders confessed to their alleged crime, and that confession is associated with issuance of less severe punishments by the court.

Interviewing is another way of collecting data in Chinese court research. Liu and Halliday (2011) conducted 194 in-depth interviews with criminal defense lawyers and other relevant informants in 22 cities across China. They sought to test for the influence of politics in everyday legal practice using the case of Chinese criminal defense lawyers. They argued that lawyers' everyday politics have two distinct faces; on the one hand, lawyers potentially can challenge state power, endeavor to protect citizen rights, and pursue proceduralism in their daily work. On the other hand, they often have to rely on their political connections with state agencies to protect themselves and solve problems in their legal practice. Their interview data collected show that the Chinese criminal defense bar is differentiated along these two meanings of politics into five clusters of lawyers which could be usefully characterized as *progressive elites*, *pragmatic brokers*, *notable activists*, *grassroots activists*, and *routine practitioners*.

Numerous other studies on contemporary Chinese courts typically accumulate data through the news media. Liu and his colleagues systematically collected data from the journals of the police, prosecution, judiciary, and lawyers' associations over the period 1979 to 2005 and associated stories in newspaper stories and other popular periodicals (2009). They argued that Chinese lawyers' difficulties in criminal defense have deep roots in the recursive nature of the criminal procedure reforms which have been put in place since 1978.

Despite well-known difficulties to be faced, some scholars nonetheless tried to collect court data by means of direct observation. Susan Trevaskes compiled such first-hand grassroots court data in a court in Inner Mongolia (2001; 2003; 2004; 2007; 2010). She examined the politics, practice, procedures, and public perceptions of the *yanda* anti-crime campaigns taking place in the first 25 years of the post-1978 reform period. Trevaskes develops the concept of "campaign policing and justice" in China in order to describe the Chinese criminal justice practice of punishing criminals "harshly and swiftly" in response to a rising crime rate. This campaign has been in force since the start of the economic reform era in the 1980s (Trevaskes, 2010, p.163).

Along with the more open political environment and more mature status of China's social science research, more and more empirical studies are taking place in China through active cooperation between scholars from Chinese local parties and researchers overseas. The research of Mike McConville and his associates (2011) presents a survey of basic-level and intermediate-level courts by observing the criminal law process at work. They interviewed key actors in the daily operation of the courts from 2001 to 2006, with some additional follow-up interviews conducted in 2007–2009. McConville and his colleagues studied every stage in the formal criminal adjudication process at 13 courts spread throughout China where they had unmediated access to a total of 1,144 case files. Courtroom observations were undertaken in 227 cases.

McConville's team also conducted 267 interviews with judges, procurators and defense lawyers. The study focused on first instance cases in the Basic Court and in the Intermediate Court, giving an overall assessment with respect to each stage of the criminal justice process—namely, from the manner in which crimes come to the attention of authorities, through the collection of evidence, to the trial stage and onto the ultimate conclusion of a criminal trial. The McConville team noted the ambiguousness of some substantive criminal law provisions, underscoring how both the criminal procedure law and criminal law codes combine to obstruct the accused from effectively arguing their cases effectively. The authors argued that changing the law has not in any significant way changed the behavior of courtroom actors since the result, both in terms of verdict rendered and sentence issued, is almost invariably predetermined prior to a trial's commencement.

Phil He conducted a "*Legal Representation and Criminal Processing in District People's Courts: A Pilot Study in J Province*" (LRCP) during 2009-2011. The data collected in this study included four components: (1) a comprehensive questionnaire survey of *Fujian* lawyers, judges, procurators, and police officers (n=642); (2) more than three hundred full-length criminal court trial observations (n=325), conducted in two-thirds of the district people's courts (i.e., 55 courts out of a total of 82) in the Province; (3) a sample of complete criminal case dossiers (n=149, ranging from 1994 to 2010), collected from 10 district courts in five of the nine prefectural cities. This study obtained valuable empirical knowledge on how criminal defendants are represented in Chinese courts, especially at the lowest level district people's courts and demonstrates both the necessity and feasibility of conducting comprehensive empirical legal research in China (He, 2013). His book opens with a historical framework of the Chinese criminal justice system, featuring both Western and Chinese interpretations, and an overview of the current state of the system, using the data from ordinary criminal trials as primary evidence. He's study unveiled the day-to-day reality of criminal cases tried by the lowest level courts in China.

With the prevalence of computers and network technology, the Internet has gained solid grounding in most parts of the world. Since the mid-1990s, the Internet has revolutionized popular expression in China, enabling users to organize, protest, and influence public opinion in unprecedented ways (Yang, 2009). Data collection through the Internet started to attract the attention of scholars considering its advantages such as easy access and relatively low costs. Halliday and Liu (2007) looked into lawyers' online discussions from which they argued that China has enacted criminal and procedural law reforms which bear some resemblances to legal liberalism, and the nation has laid the primary foundations of an independent legal profession and an effective regulatory framework. However, researchers have noted that the formal law is not particularly descriptive of practice, and that professional regulation is scarcely self-regulation on the model of bar associations present in other countries. The legal profession in China appears to be a largely hapless victim in a larger drama where long-standing traditions, hostile ideology and intrusive political institutions remain powerful. They nonetheless remain optimistic and argue that even "hollow laws" in time, with changed circumstances, may become a solid foundation for the construction of political liberalism (Halliday and Liu, 2007, p.105).

Guobing Yang (2009) collected data through the Internet (online forum, discussion board, blog etc.) over the course of a decade and employed a variety of methods (mostly qualitative) in an effort to examine social movements, voluntary organizing, and Internet-based politics in China. Though Yang's research on online activism in China is not directly relevant to the criminal law field, it has significant methodological value from which legal research can borrow. Yang's research demonstrated that social change in China cannot be properly understood without appreciating the radical nature of critical thought and the scope of contested struggles being played out in China's cyberspace. Since the mid-1990s, the Internet has revolutionized popular expression in China, enabling users to organize, protest, and influence public opinion in previously unprecedented ways. Chinese cyberspace became an arena for creativity, community formation, conflict, and control **all at the same time**. It gave rise to a range of innovative contentious forms and practices.

Yang delineates a nuanced and dynamic image of Chinese online activism which leverages cultural and social resources from China's incipient civil society. The combination of online activism and civil society thus creates a vivid story of the immense potential social changes on the horizon, indicating a new era of digital information-driven politics. In addition, Yang's online data collection method serves a useful example for social media data collection in our criminal law field. For example, Yang registered his own account online to follow online forums, discussion boards and blogs, and he collected data from those various online texts. He then annotated the content of these texts to analyze the context and conditions of online activism. The current research also uses similar textual analysis to study the online legal community and the scope of characters engaged in legal activism in contemporary China. The results and insights gained from these analyses will be discussed in detail in chapter 6.

Part of Liu and Halliday (2009)'s three-year online ethnographic work involved the collection and analysis of a large number of written discussions from the official Internet forum of the All-China Lawyers Association (ACLA) regarding the professional work of Chinese criminal defense lawyers. Their research entailed data analysis based on 60 threads of messages on criminal defense in the ACLA forum. Through their unique data source, they were able to examine spontaneous interchanges among lawyers about problems encountered in the implementation of the Criminal Procedural Law that purport to institutionalize some basic elements of political liberalism. Because these exchanges were directly from lawyers without contamination by outside observers, the authors argued that such data could help contrast the "public voice" of the bar association journals with the "private voices" of its members (p.916). Their empirical analysis did demonstrate that these interchanges are linked in pairs and in sequence by interactions of the four component mechanisms of *recursivity* (indeterminacy of law, contradictions, diagnostic struggles, and actor mismatch) in both lawmaking and implementation.

This research based on this officially recognized online legal forum depicted an informatics insight into the Chinese legal profession sphere and demonstrated the potential for insightful future legal research to be done in an era of the Internet. Although the prospect of

Internet censorship in China may cast some doubt on the data collected online in terms of the amount of sample bias in opinions and the like, Liu and Halliday (2009) thought the forthrightness of opinions expressed in the forum indicate that official censorship and even self-censorship was **surprisingly restrained.** A detailed content analysis (Halliday & Liu, 2007) shows that lawyers participating in the forum spoke openly and forthrightly, and often very critically, about almost every aspect of legal practice, the courts, the police, the concentration of political power, and the absence of rule of law or democracy.

Through the study of those forum discussions, Liu and Halliday concluded that China's criminal and procedural law bears some resemblance to legal liberalism, and likely has laid the foundations of a legal profession and a rule of law regulatory framework for the future. However, the formal law "on the books" is too often not descriptive of contemporary legal practice, and legal professional regulation is not very close to self-regulation as would be required in a rule of law country. The legal profession in China appears to continue to be vulnerable to a larger drama where long traditions, hostile ideology and powerful institutions hold the upper hand. Important for their study, Liu and Halliday's research further refined the methodology of online data collection in the field of legal studies.

THE CURRENT STUDY

Research Questions

This book explores the development of criminal courts in a highly bureaucratized Chinese society, and in so doing faces many difficulties of data access. First, the opportunity to observe organization and bureaucratic practices of the criminal courts is mainly closed to outsiders. Second, the very concept of bureaucratization is quite abstract and is difficult to operationalize by empirical measures. Third, the bureaucratization process has to be understood in a dynamic way rather than in terms of static measures. Considering all these challenges, the current study uses both a set of illustrative case studies and social media analysis as the main methods to provide an informed depiction of contemporary Chinese criminal justice and court work. Legal case studies and social media analysis provide deep insights into the character of justice administration and the practice associated with criminal case processing in China.

The current study aims to explore the following questions. What is the major impact of the long history of political bureaucracy on the Chinese legal system? How does the current judicial system deal with political cases? If the political bureaucracy system obstructs criminal case processing, how do they do that? The following hypotheses guide the book as it develops its narrative:

1. The long history of the Mandarin form of bureaucracy has formed the *cultural habit of mind* of relying on executive authority for justice rather than pursuing justice through courts.
2. The judiciary as a social institution lacks independence and strength to distribute justice.
3. The judiciary has to face both indirect and direct challenges from powerful bureaucracy-based authority.
4. The rule of bureaucracy rather than rule of law exists in the Chinese criminal justice system.

Criminal Cases

Twelve criminal cases which gained nationwide attention were selected to permit qualitative analyses. Information regarding these cases was systematically collected from Chinese national news websites. All twelve of the cases have clearly discernible connections with the bureaucratized system of criminal court operation in contemporary China.

<u>Why Case Studies?</u>

I use criminal case studies to examine Chinese courts and legal system because of the rather unique situation of Chinese courts. As a part of a bureaucratic system, Chinese courts have rarely disclosed their inside operations to the public, and it is difficult to gain information as to their organizational structure and practices. For example, the Chinese Procurator system has published its organizational information each year with detailed numbers of offices and prosecutors at different jurisdiction levels, but the court system has never released official organizational information except for the total count of judges and trial courts in the country. In addition, it is difficult to collect court operation data due to strict control over such information, and as a consequence little previous research has been done on Chinese criminal court operations and organization. The case study method is needed to gather informed impressions concerning the criminal justice system given these constraints on researchers.

The case study method is an empirical inquiry that investigates a contemporary phenomenon within its real-life context; it is used when the boundaries between a phenomenon and its context are not clearly evident, and it is used in situations where multiple sources of evidence can be used (Yin, 1984, p. 23). Although some scholars have argued that the study of a small number of cases can only produce exploratory research, it is the case that carefully planned and systematically crafted studies lead to a successful description of real-life situations, issues, and problems (Soy, 1997). Using detailed contextual analysis of a limited number of events or conditions and their relationships, case studies can examine contemporary real-life situations and provide the basis for the application of ideas and extension of methods (Soy, 1997). In this book carefully selected criminal cases are used to describe the present situation of Chinese criminal courts, and document how the political institutions and Mandarin bureaucracy cultural legacy affect criminal court operations in contemporary China.

Case study research is particularly useful when the relevant behavior of interest cannot be manipulated and the investigator has little or no control over events (Yin, 1994, p.9). Case study research can involve single or multiple cases of a phenomenon viewed in their context and do not permit replication of the phenomenon in a laboratory or in controlled experimental settings. Criminal cases are just such phenomena. They represent a set of events which we cannot manipulate, and they provide a natural context to study. To understand Chinese criminal courts and to gain knowledge about the factors which have an impact on case processing within the real-life context, the book presents the results of twelve illustrative cases.

Sampling for Illustrative Value

The twelve cases were chosen based on national voting on the Chinese news system. In China, every year newspapers will ask their readers to vote on the most important news in different fields and there is a ranking list for rule of law events. I made use of these lists to select the most important criminal cases resolved during the period 2000-2013. After selecting twelve big cases, I searched out these cases on the Internet to obtain all of their respective news reports from the six major news websites. These are popular news websites engaged in the ongoing reporting of Chinese news. The list of websites includes: *Xinhua News, South China Morning Post, Sohu News, People Net, Chinanews.com* and *globaltimes.com*. I also selected five international news websites, which included Western sources – namely, the *New York Times, The Guardian, BBC news, Wall Street Journal,* and *CNN news*. Using news reports from these 11 news websites, all relevant information for the twelve cases was obtained, including information pertaining to case processing, investigation, evidence, legal representation, and trial hearing etc.

Because the case studies aim to study the context of these criminal cases rather than present a word analysis of the court dossier, these cases are described in a storytelling narrative style to convey the sense of a lived world. As a result, I generally paraphrase these news stories rather than replicate a written document. Of course there are some noteworthy limitations for the case study method. Since they entail limited samples purposefully selected, the findings noted cannot be directly generalized to the population from which the cases were drawn. Moreover, the criminal cases in question are complicated, and it was not possible to obtain all the information associated with each case. Finally, my analyses could be biased by my values and legal and social science training. For case studies, I may have developed subject sympathy feelings which may influence the analyses set forth here. What follows below is a listing of cases with a simple introduction of each cases and an account of their relationship with the Mandarin bureaucracy. These cases are grouped into seven categories.

<u>Case list</u>

1. The Case of Zhu ling

This case pertains to a 19-year-old unsolved poisoning case (1995-2013) in China which sparked a petition to American government, and the petition exceeded the 100,000 signatures necessary for an official response from the U.S. White House. This case again illustrates how

Chinese people have been acculturated to rely on an upper-level official to solve wrongs rather than resort to the process of law.

2. The Case of Wang Lijun, the Case of Bogu Kailai, and the Case of Bo Xilai

These three cases represent three distinct layers of a big case involving a CCP high level official, *Bo Xilai*. This major case exposed corruption deriving from the absolute power of the political bureaucracy, and involved high-ranking police officials becoming complicit in the corruption. The trials for these cases were conducted with unprecedented transparence, though noteworthy shortcomings characterized the legal proceedings in each case. This set of cases can be seen as an initial step for the Chinese judicial system to develop its own identity.

3. The Case of Zhou Yongkang

Zhou YongKang, who was one rank higher than *Bo Xilai*, was arrested and expelled from the Party in December 2014. *Zhou* was a retired member of the Politburo's all-powerful Standing Committee. He also was the Minister of Public Security (2002-2007) and the Secretary of the Central Political and Legal Affairs Commission (*Zhongyang Zhengfawei 中央政法委*) between 2007 and 2012. In other words, he had been in charge of Chinese legal and law enforcement affairs for 10 years. On June 11, 2015, *Zhou* was convicted of bribery, abuse of power and the intentional disclosure of state secrets.

4. The Two Season Case of Li Zhuang

Li Zhuang, a lawyer, was sentenced to eighteen months for perjury; this case discloses the plight of Chinese lawyers since the active enforcement of Article 306 of the 1997 Criminal Law regarding the crime of lawyer's perjury. This major case attracted the attention of lawyers across China who support *Li* and cried out for their own redemption. This case also gives a good example of the distorted "plea bargain" process used in some Chinese criminal cases.

5. The Case of Nie Shubin and the Case of Wang Shujin

These two cases shed light further on Chinese criminal justice system. *Nie Shubin* was convicted of a murder in 1994 and has executed. In

2005, *Wang Shujin* was arrested and confessed to four cases of murder and rape, including the murder of the person said to be the victim in *Nie Shubin*'s case. The Chinese courts have repeatedly dismissed *Wang*'s confession, and blocked the filing of an appeal from *Nie*'s family. In this case, Chinese courts again face a test with respect to the principle of 'innocent until proven guilty" (presumption of innocence).

6. The Case of Chen Yongzhou

Chen Yongzhou, an imprisoned Chinese journalist, confessed to wrongdoing on Chinese state TV. The prime media is essentially conducting a public trial and in the process violating the presumption of innocence as a foundational principle of criminal adjudication.

7. The Case of Yu Qiyi, the Case of Chen Qingxia, and the Case of Xia Junfeng

These three cases illustrate the fact of the existence of coercive measures used to influence court processes from outside of the criminal justice system. These coercive measures are effective extensions of the Mandarin bureaucracy's power and would be regulated under formal legal system if the rule of law were truly present.

Case Analysis plan

Case narratives will be presented and I will use a storytelling mode of discourse to explain the case based on an ordered timeline. In order to assure validity in each depiction, multiple sources are used to present the cases rather than reliance being made on single news website. The problems of each case will be analyzed, and the cause and effect elements of the case will be examined. In accordance with the theme of my book, the case studies will document how the executive bureaucracy casts shadows across these various cases. These qualitative analyses will show how difficult it is for an independent judicial system to arise from a powerful executive bureaucracy of the Mandarin legacy type present in contemporary China.

Social media data

Why Include Social Media Analysis?

By June of 2015 China already had 668 million the Internet users, and

China has had the world's most active social-media population. Chinese cyberspace has the potential to accelerate social change in this country, and social media has most clearly pushed the phenomenon of "online activism" to a very high degree. Social media in China is increasingly becoming both a reflection of public opinion and seedbed of new social forces. *Microblogging* in particular has become part of people's daily life with the rapid development of mobile devices.

The China Internet Network Information Center's report shows that there had been 204.32 million microblog users by the end of June 2015. The latest research from Data Center of China Internet (DCCI) shows that microblog users in China accounted for 88.81% of total Chinese netizens. Netizen is a new word created in the Internet era and means a person who actively uses the Internet, especially in a proper and responsible way according to Merriam-Webster online dictionary.[5]

Microblogs nowadays are very popular and attract all kinds of people in China. Legal professionals on microblogs are rather opinionated users with large personal followings, and they often express their own opinions on controversial issues. The people working in legal field, including professors, lawyers, judges, prosecutors, and police officers, mostly have college or above degrees and can use social media proficiently as a convenient tool for communication and expression of views on matters of public affair. Most legal professionals post discussions on legal issues, including legal reform, law revision, and important criminal cases and the like. They discuss legal issues on diverse online social media, including the legal web forums, blogs and microblogs.

The social media data assembled for this study were collected through these microblogs. Different from traditional social media, the tweets of a microblog can spontaneously involve a large amount of people in certain discussions, and taken in combination form a very responsive virtual community. Law professors, judges, prosecutors, lawyers, and police officers can respond to each other on diverse legal issues and present their own opinions "for the record" via the

[5] According to the Merriam-Webster online dictionary, netizen means a person who actively uses the Internet especially in a proper and responsible way; an active participant in the online community of the Internet. December 14th, 2013 retrieved from http://www.merriam-webster.com/dictionary/netizen.

microblog. Through this data source we can overhear, without contamination by outside observers, the spontaneous exchanges among legal professions about their issues of concerns and shared problems. The analysis of tweets can catch a highly interactive picture of the legal community. Since social media data analysis of this type has rarely been used in criminal justice research, the research reported here reveals valuable noteworthy findings and illustrates the potential for other applications of this analytical tool.

Data Collection

In order to collect social media data I registered for microblog accounts in *Sina* in which many legal scholars have opened their microblogs. *Sina Weibo* has an identity validation system, and most legal professionals have passed through this validation process so that their real name and actual profession can be verified. During May of 2012, I searched legal professionals on the *Sina* microblog by key words "judge, lawyer, police officer, prosecutor and law professor." The selection criteria for the people who I followed were: first, the person had at least 1,000 tweets. Because *Sina Weibo* was launched around 800 days from August 2009 to May 2012, tweets of 1,000 or more means that this person averagely tweets each day at least once. This criterion assures us that the accounts I follow are not fake, but rather are active. Second, at least 50% of the tweets are original. Although retweet and forwarding also reflect attitude, more original tweet content is required to serve as data to reflect individual opinions.

In the end I chose to follow 180 legal professionals on *Sina Weibo*, among are 87 lawyers, 37 judges, 24 prosecutors, 11 police officers, and 21 professors. Since the overwhelming majority of criminal law professors are also lawyers, I categorized those people who were mostly posting legal thoughts rather than commentary on specific criminal cases they are dealing with as law professors. Following the tweets of these 180 people on legal discussions in the legal community, including original, retweets and forwarded messages, provides for a rich source of data. Most people also have legal blogs besides their microblogs located in the same web platform, and I also collected articles posted on their legal blogs.

From May 2012 to November 2015, I collected 580 tweets, and 80 legal blogs entries. Among these are 393 items from lawyers, 101 items from Judges, 41 items from scholars, 25 items from prosecutors, and 20 items posted by Police officers. I use these data to analyze the impact of the microblog form of social media on legal reform in China chapter 6. It is interesting to find that lawyers and judges are more active and brave in talking about rule of law issues on microblogs than in most other forums. Prosecutors and police officers rarely talk about these issues, so that it is particularly difficult to collect relevant commentaries from them. Further, 8 of the tweets I collected from police officers on *Sina Weibo* accounts were later deleted by the officers themselves. All these tweets were translated from Chinese to English, and all are used in the analysis reported in this book.

Since social media data are rarely used in criminal justice research, no previous model can be found in literature to guide the analysis presented here. To the extent possible I incorporate traditional survey and interview methodology into my analysis. These social media data can be treated somewhat similarly as an interviewee's responses in traditional survey and interview studies. Since most microblog accounts names are conventional web names, I refer to them using capital letters such as A, L or S in my narrative, along with their Chinese original web names in order to identify each micro-blogger.

<u>Social Media Analysis plan</u>

Microblog texts are written by bloggers individually and take multiple forms, among them being: (1) descriptions of problems; (2) narrative stories; (3) analyses of situations; (4) proposals for remedies and solutions; (5) expressions of emotional encouragement; and (7) explicit promotion of collective actions to be taken by the legal community. These social media data can be subject to content analysis and intensive case study alike. Due to their different roles in the legal community, legal professionals present their varying opinions on certain legal issues of common concern; this is roughly equivalent to survey respondents answering questionnaire items or interviews responding to interview questions. Moreover, because the social media permit people to record responses to each other instantly, it is clearly more interactive than either the traditional survey or the face-to-face interview. Thus, I will use these social media data to describe the interactions among elements of the Chinese legal community and explore the trends of legal development documented in these interactions.

Any study on the contemporary Chinese criminal courts and criminal justice system confronts many obstacles, and lack of access to relevant data is one of the most serious difficulties. These obstacles are even more daunting if we want to go beyond pure theoretical discussion and probe into the deep roots of the system. The Chinese judiciary system was born within the Mandarin bureaucracy and has never moved to build its own independent identity. In order to better understand the courts in China we need to start from the beginning of the story. Chapter 3 looks into and provides highlights from the long history of Mandarin bureaucracy within which the Chinese judiciary arose as a social institution.

CHAPTER 3

Historical Perspective: Bureaucracy and the Criminal Court

THE ORIGINS OF BUREAUCRACY AND LAW

Despite major revolutions in 1911 and 1949, the contemporary Chinese judicial system is very much a heritage institution deeply grounded in Chinese history. Imperial China had a developed and large bureaucracy, and a highly centralized and bureaucratized political system to go with it. Within that governmental system a highly bureaucratized judiciary was created, one which was closely integrated with executive authority as opposed to viewing itself as rightfully independent of that authority.

Having the longest surviving civilization in the world, China is one of the best places to learn about the development of law. Chinese law originated from the need for order and predictability of the ruling political bureaucracy. Once the population increased and families aggregated in large numbers in the primitive society, social relations were transferred from a familial to a territorial foundation, along with the evolution of both legal principles and provisions of law. This type of fundamental change of social structure happened in China during the *Zhou* dynasty (1100-256 BC). I will first discuss the origins of bureaucracy and law in ancient China, and principal theory underlying the model of Chinese imperial law. I then proceed to describe how the imperial law came to be ruled by a combination of bureaucracy and politics. The tradition of law by bureaucracy continued all the way from the imperial times to the 20th century, and it even casts a great shadow over the contemporary Chinese legal system.

Irrigation, Colonialism or Social Unit Change?

When did the bureaucracy arise and law begin in ancient China? What are the stages of development of the Chinese feudalism-era Mandarin bureaucracy? Many researchers have proposed theoretical explanations for the character of development of early Chinese society. One type of approach that has been taken is that of the geographic-economic explanation. For example, Wittfogel's hydraulic civilizations theory argues that the system of rice crop irrigation, which required substantial and centralized control over land and forced labor, called for monopolized political power and dominance over the economy—resulting over the historical long haul in an absolutist managerial state (Wittfogel, 1957). Wittfogel thought the development of irrigation led to the use of mass labor and an organizational hierarchy was needed for coordinating and directing activities.

While tribal societies' form of government was usually personalistic in nature, in contrast irrigation needed to break out of the confines and limitation of kinship and required the establishment of a distinct and permanent all-inclusive institution. In time, an impersonal government capable of directing mass labor and proper distribution of the water was established, but only with the capable implementation of orders from the leadership by a capable officer class. Wittfogel believed that irrigation on a massive scale changed living styles; larger numbers of people agglomerated into towns and cities because of the increased food supply made possible by irrigation; armies were needed to protect populations; concentration of population increased the specialization of labor; the more complex economy arising requires records, writing and systematic knowledge accumulation (Wittfogel, 1957).

Another similar thesis holds that the major theme of early Chinese society was the interplay of forces between the principally agrarian society in central China and the nomadic society of China's northern periphery (Lattimore, 1951). The nomadic civilization in northern China was based on a mixed economy of hunting and gathering and fishing, and ongoing episodic food-gathering. Later on, when the domestication of animals took place and primitive cultivation agriculture was developed, irrigation became a crucial factor due to the seasonal irregularity of rainfall in northern China. Because informal organization was clearly insufficient for maintaining order and assuring timely water supplies a government of some type had to emerge which could assume the duty of regulating and initiating irrigation works. The booming of irrigated agriculture led to increased population and the accumulation of wealth which in turn brought about great social changes. When irrigation projects developed to such a large-scale that the feudal nobles had to act together, such politically larger combinations promoted the amalgamation of small states and formed a new kind of bureaucratic empire (Lattimore, 1951).

Theories of "irrigation" focus on geographic features to explain the origins of organized societies, but actually the link between irrigation and these features is not fully established because some of these features may appear without large-scale irrigation. Moreover, Chinese civilization began in the northern region of China, an area which did not require irrigation for the successful cultivation of wheat and millet. Some scholars have even argued that the irrigation projects were only one valuable by-product of some water projects featuring canals designed to secure strategic transportation routes; moreover, building real irrigation works usually came from the local populace and not the central government (Eberhard, 1970).

Archaeological evidence fails to support the theory that irrigation is the primary cause of the formation of coercive political institutions, and much of the complex system of irrigation even came after the appearance of cities and other conventional indicators of bureaucratic statehood (Adams, 1966; 1978). Moreover, some other countries which featuring similar conditions—they had large rivers and needed to control them for substantial food production and needed irrigation projects, e.g. India and Sri Lanka—evolved the decentralized caste-oriented state structure, not a tightly organized bureaucracy such as arose in China (Subramaniam, 2009). There is no doubt that geographic features have an important impact on politics, but we lack evidence to prove that they are the decisive factors to lead to the evolution of the political structure or bureaucracy.

Opposite to the geographic-economic perspective, the socio-political advocates approach describes the observed pattern of feudalism as a result of an explicit ethnic super-stratification characterized by expansion and proactive colonial activity. *Zhou* rulers came from Western China, accompanied by a group of militarily organized tribes, and conquered and then occupied East China. By means of purchases and other methods, the rulers probably gained much of the land originally possessed by the area's natives, and then built a complex web of new contractual landlord-tenant relationships (Eberhard, 1970).

This "colonial" thesis stresses the importance of human relations; however, conclusive proof of such relationships has not been found in archaeological records. Neither the geographic-economic theory, nor the socio-political approach has provided a fully satisfactory explanation for the initiation of feudal society in China. Both approaches neglect the momentous change in the basic units of society—namely, moving from a familial system to a territory-based system. This transformation may have exerted the most significant influence on the evolution of Chinese society, ultimately leading to the development of Mandarin bureaucracy and law in China. The radical social changes in question will be illustrated in the following account of the *Zhou* dynasty.

From Familial System (*Zu* 族) to Feudalism

A number of respected scholars have explored the transitions of human society from ancient times to the modern period. When investigating the origins of family and state in the *Anthenian state*, Marx and Engels described the decline of gentile society and the rise of the state as a result of land distribution and the intermixture of tribes (Engels, 1972). It can be argued that perhaps ancient China had a similar developmental trajectory. In the *Shang* dynasty (1600-1027 BC), *zu* (lineage) was the basic unit of society, and it was a consanguineous group of families with all of the people being descended from a single common ancestor (Liu, 1998). More than 200 *zu* have been distinguished from the oracle bone inscriptions (Ding, 1956).

Some large lineages were either independent or semi-independent polities, and they had developed norms which were recognized by their members but were not applied to members of other *zu*. These norms were probably the earliest precursors to law in China. After *Zhou zu* subdued the *Shang*, the geographic expansion and increasing population posed challenges for effective administrative control. *Zhou* government tried to build a united political authority through the strategy of *fengjian*, which was something like a dual pyramid.

Fengjian in Chinese means feudalism. As duly noted in the *International Encyclopedia of the Social Sciences* (1968), Feudalism conventionally denotes the type of society and the political system originating in western and central Europe and dominant there during the greater part of the Middle Ages, especially from the twelfth through thirteenth centuries (Sills, 1968, p.393). It often refers to a system of government in which a ruler personally delegates limited sovereignty over portions of his domain to vassals (Creel, 1964, p.163). The term feudalism in English is derived from a Germanic word “fehu-od” meaning "property in cattle" and, later, "tenure" or "property in land" (Sills, 1968, p.393). It stresses the importance of land tenure and the rights and privileges attached to it in the overall system. The King had the ownership of all land, and beneath him was a hierarchy of nobles, with the most important nobles holding land directly from the King and the lesser nobles holding land from prominent nobles, down to the seigneur who held a single manor (Sills, 1968). The seigneur granted peasants use of the land and his protection in return for their personal services and for dues. Weber considered feudalism as one type of "patriarchal authority" (1957, pp. 375-376).

There have been several types of feudalism over the course of world history. Feudalism in Western Europe emerged as a form of social, economic, and political organization after the fall of the Roman Empire, largely between 300 and 500 AD. The Romano-Germanic society saw the diminishing importance of cities as centers of administration and of specialized economic activities. Through migration and subsequent settlement, the Germanic tribes (*Sippen)* had loosened their tribal ties and a state structure able to take over and to fulfill its public duties (Sills, 1968, p.394). It is argued that the Japanese form of feudalism which developed at the end of the twelfth century may have had very similar feudal characteristics in the various institutional spheres to that of Western Europe. Local proprietors began to divide lands among family members or retainers, and vassal families in time became the basis of the social system. Different from Europe, however, the imperial center enjoyed continuous importance in Japanese feudalism and familistic rather than contractual elements were expressed in the relations between and among lords and vassals (Sills, 1968, p.399).

In Russia, the feudal (patrimonial) principality in medieval Russia was accompanied by certain immunity from political authority, conferred by private possession of land (Sills, 1968, p.400). The system was based on the absolute sovereignty of the Tsar, who, requiring service from any of his subjects with granting a *pomesfe* in return for such service (Szeftel, 1956). In the Byzantine Empire, giving lands to a person in *pronoia* is to give lands into his care. In practice it meant that estates were given for administration to high officers of the state or the army, to Russian Orthodox monasteries, and to private persons as a reward for services, and there was a predominance of economically independent small estates combined with a growing pattern of political decentralization (Sills, 1968, p.400). Chinese feudalism also featured a measure of such political decentralization. Many politically self-sufficient patrimonial units in the system of Chinese feudalism were in fact highly developed, but there was neither a fully developed system of vassal-lord relations nor a full-fledged social organization of either a military class or a political class.

Although there have been different types of feudalism in the world, they all arose from the dividing up of land. In China, politically self-sufficient patrimonial units in feudalism also developed with the distribution of the land. The land was distributed within the feudalism system through a systematic familial succession process. The King was not only the ruler of the country, but also the leader of his own royal *zu*. After he died, his eldest son would succeed him as both the King of the country and leader of royal *zu*. The other sons of the King were seen as minor descendants and were invested with land and people to build their small states, and they became princes of those states (the *zhuhou).* After these princes died, the same process would take place between their eldest sons and their minor descendants. The ministers and great officers applied the same succession principle among their sons, but their minor descendants would merely be given the title of officers; after these minor descendants died, their minor sons would become commoners, and so on (Zhang, 2014).

The *fengjian* (feudalism), a pragmatic device to control newly acquired territories and population, has produced significant influences on Chinese society. First, *fengjian* split the land into small units though lineage segments and allowed large room for a locality to grow. *Fengjian* was originally designed to attain the absolute authority of central government, but actually led to the opposite result and lead to the reduction of central power and advent of many local divisions. Driven by self-interest, local powers seemingly never tired of fighting for additional territory in ancient China, and the country was nearly always undergoing movement through an ongoing transition from united—divided—reunited—re-divided—newly reunited status again and again.

In order to attain effective central control, Chinese rulers had to rely on a systematic bureaucracy composed of elites and officials who are in a line of ranks from top to the bottom. The hierarchical system in some degree covers the real patterning of China—namely, a sheet of loose sand. In a word, feudalism laid a cultural foundation for the development of a powerful bureaucracy in China, and that same large bureaucracy foundation system has been kept intact during China's long national history. A powerful bureaucratic structure has been one very critically important cushion to reduce the social turmoil of ongoing regime change, but it has also constituted a very strong obstacle to progressive social reform (Zhang, 2014).

Feudalism also broke down the old residence pattern in which each *zu* lived in a separated place, and forced different *zu* to live together in a shared space. In order to solve the conflicts arising between different customary laws of various *zu* the *Zhou* government allowed *non-Zhou* peoples to use their own customs and their own customary laws continuously as far as "such a continuation did not pose a threat to the rule of the *Zhou* House" (Hsu & Linduff, 1988, p. 188). At the same time, however, the *Zhou* government started to design a series of *li* (rites) in an attempt to maintain the unity of *Zhou zu* and separate it from other peoples, such as *Wei(卫), Qi(齐), Lu(鲁), Yan(燕), Wei(魏)* etc. (Liu, 1998).

It is now clear, based on this brief retelling of Chinese history, how changes in the economic and commercial activities of the Chinese people and their associated social structures brought about the need for a powerful bureaucratic system. It is likewise clear how Chinese feudalism laid the foundation for the development of the Mandarin bureaucracy and ultimately Chinese law. During the *Zhou* dynasty, the state bureaucracy gradually started taking shape, with the initiation of feudalism as the cultural background.

The Rise of Bureaucracy and Chinese Law

The evolution of early Chinese law and the associated penal system occurred as a gradual process (Liu, 1998). In order to help readers understand this process, a chronology table of Chinese history is provided in appendix. In the *Shang* dynasty, people lived in *zu* and each *zu* handled its internal affairs according to their own customary norms; accordingly, the state organization was loosely knit and present only in the far background of daily affairs. The customary law of a particular *zu* was applicable only to its own members, and there was not a hint of a unified state law universally applied to the several *zu* (Liu, 1998). If a *zu* member infringed upon the norms in his/her *zu*, he or she would be punished. Based on the available historical records, most people agree that Chinese criminal law and the systems of punishment originated in the *Shang* or even earlier, and the earliest written legal code in China is *Zheng ren zhu xing shu* (Criminal Code of State *Zheng* 郑人铸刑书) (536 B.C.) (Legge, 1960).

In the Western *Zhou* period, the lord of the state maintained only a small government due to its rigidly stratified feudal structure, and he maintained contact with these nobles at different levels through a few liaison great officers (Liu, 1998). No clearly defined body of law existed, and this posed a problem for controlling the feudal lords and solidifying the feudal system. The *Zhou* dynasty then introduced a special code of law—the *li* (rites) *(禮)*. A series of rites were formulated to regulate the behavior of the nobles, and nobles disposed the affairs of their *zu* according to their own customary laws. These rites only applied to nobles, not to commoners, and there was still nothing that could be considered universal law applicable to all Chinese people (Liu, 1998).

The concept of *li* entailed the instilling in the people a set of social norms, and/or training them to develop a sense of propriety (Wu, 1982). Through the strict observance of norms, *li* tried to inculcate the concepts of high and low positions, the different ranks of the nobility, and the nearness and remoteness of relationships into the minds of all nobles. In this manner a hierarchical ranking system could be built and take root in Chinese society. However, the rigid *li* could not accommodate radical social change which was to come, and efforts of build stability based on *li* would encounter serious problems during the many periods of transition from united to divided authority. The *Spring and Autumn* period saw the advent of radical social change and social disorder, and after 770 BC the power of the *Zhou* King became progressively weaker.

During the following *Warring States period* (475-221 BC), states had to gain wealth in order to compete in the many territorial wars. They needed to build large-scale waterworks, to construct new walled cities, to raise local armies by conscription, and to levy taxes; consequently, a new administrative system was in great need of formation (Liu, 1998). The expanded territories and the heterogeneous population gained through constant wars also called for far more systematic management. A bureaucratic system filled with officials then emerged during this period, and an institution of legal codes correspondingly was also created to help consolidate the new social structure under development. These law codes were written, publicly enacted, and made equally applicable to all people in place of the various customary laws of the *zu* (Liu, 1998).

Although the bureaucratic system and new law codes encountered severe resistance from the strong *zu,* this type of reform continued. In *Qin*, the *Code of Qin* (*秦律* made by *Shang Yang*) was publicly enacted and made applicable to all people. The old system of land tenure was abolished, and land could be bought and sold by the peasants; land-owing tenants paid taxes directly to the state rather than to their immediate overlords. Various small towns and villages were organized under the *jun* (*郡,*commandery) and *xian* (*县* county) with their officials appointed by the lord of the state. At the grass-roots level, families were organized by the *shiwu* system which grouped between five and ten families together, and every family was equally responsible for the wrongdoing of every other family, and equally subject to punishment if one failed to inform the authorities of such wrongdoing in a timely manner (Liu, 1998).

Based on the *xian* and the *shiwu* system, the lord of *Qin* could effectively control the individual families, the basic units of society, through his officials in a bureaucratic system, according to the written codes (Liu, 1998). *Qin* became the most powerful Chinese state, and finally defeated all its rivals and established a unified empire—the first united imperial empire in Chinese history—the *Qin* dynasty. The *Qin* Empire later was replaced by the *Han* dynasty, and the *Han* regime continued and extended the *jun-xian* system. By the end of the first century, there were eighty-three *jun* and 1,314 *xian* with executive power located in the hands of the centrally controlled bureaucracy. According to historical records, there were 130,285 such officials under Emperor *Ai* (Bodde, 2014).

During *Zhou* times, a centralized bureaucratic system of administration which handled both executive and judicial affairs started to take shape, and this bureaucracy was later was established during the *Qin* and *Han* dynasties. The bureaucracy and attendant legal system have been complementing each other during the long history of China ever since then. The bureaucracy provided structure and staff to promulgate and administer law, while the law defined and promoted the bureaucracy. From the central to local governments (*jun郡 and xian县*),[6] salaried appointed officials possessed both executive and judicial powers by design. During the *Qin* and Han dynasties, the framework of imperial law, including the penal system and most of the important legal institutions, were laid out rather precisely. The earliest political and legal theories of traditional China emerged, the earliest written codes were promulgated, and some of the most important characteristics of traditional Chinese law were formed during this period (Liu, 1998). I next discuss the development of traditional Chinese legal theories, and seek to explain why law in China has always been a tool of governance rather than a foundation for the protection of citizens' rights or interests.

The Creation of Traditional Chinese Legal Theories

Along with the bureaucracy emerging in the *Zhou* dynasty, traditional Chinese law started to take shape and diverse legal theories were formulated in this period. During the following *Warring States period*

---

[6] Junxian system is a prefectural system referred to the division of the empire into artificial administrative jurisdictions such as prefectures and counties and their governance by centrally appointed, salaried and rotated professional officials (Rowe, 2010, p.60).

(475-221 BC), the whole stratified structure of the feudal system gradually collapsed, and the *li* which was used to regulate the relations between the *Zhou* King and his nobles became less observed and increasingly was either ignored or expressly violated. The tradition of *li* was no longer practiced in sacrifices, funerals and marriages. For example, only the Son of Heaven and the princes of states could make sacrifices to *Tai* mountain according to the *li,* but the chief of some big families also went to make sacrifices to that same sacred mountain[7] (Legge, 1960, p.154-156).

Though old *li* books were losing the regulating power, a new type of *li* was emerging in their place. At the end of the *Spring and Autumn* period, some learned scholar-officials attempted to define a *li* and relevant theories—and it is noteworthy that Confucius was the most famous scholar who completed a systematic theory based on such thought. Confucius was fascinated by *Zhou li (Rites of the Zhou)*, and he once said, "*Zhou* had the advantage of viewing the two past dynasties. How complete and elegant are its regulations! I follow *Zhou*." (Legge, 1960, p.160).

Confucius also observed and studied the various customs and usages in numerous *zu,* and tried to compile a type of new conception of *li* which would be applicable to all people and to all human relationships, treating all people as equal human beings (Creel, 1949; Liu, 1998). Confucius could well be one of the first scholars in Chinese history that recognized human beings as being equal, and this was due to the social situation in the *Spring and Autumn* period when the social unit shifted from the *zu* to the individual family. Old *Zhou li* was deserted, and new norms were needed to regulate human relationships. Confucius's *li* helped stabilize the new structure of society and human relationships, and his theories were then transcended into a distinct school of thought — *Confucianism* — with numerous works of his many followers later all contributing to that important school of thought.

As an example, in Book of Rites, Confucius emphasizes the significance of Rites and expresses his belief that the world can achieve a great union if the Rites are followed by everyone and viewed as law. I quote his words to this effect below:

---

[7] *Lun Yu,* Vol. 1, p.154-156.

> When the Grand course was pursued, a public and common spirit ruled all under the sky; they chose men of talents, virtue, and ability; their words were sincere, and what they cultivated was harmony. Thus men did not love their parents only, nor treat as children only their own sons. A competent provision was secured for the aged till their death, employment for the able-bodied, and the means of growing up to the young. They showed kindness and compassion to widows, orphans, childless men, and those who were disabled by disease, so that they were all sufficiently maintained.
>
> Males had their proper work, and females had their homes. (They accumulated) articles (of value), disliking that they should be thrown away upon the ground, but not wishing to keep them for their own gratification. (They labored) with their strength, disliking that it should not be exerted, but not exerting it (only) with a view to their own advantage. In this way (selfish) schemings were repressed and found no development. Robbers, filchers, and rebellious traitors did not show themselves, and hence the outer doors remained open, and were not shut. This was (the period of) what we call the Grand Union. (Book of Rites, chapter of *Liyun*)[8]

The spirit of law in ancient China was greatly guided by the philosophy of Confucianism, which served as China's state ideology from the early *Han* dynasty until the collapse of the *Qing* dynasty in 1911 (MacCormack, 1996a). The "rites" in Confucianism refer to the ideological institutionalization of social norms which include the regulation of social relationships connection rulers and their subjects, senior and junior, man and woman, the blood-related and the acquainted (Ren, 1997). If people can be located in structured individual relationships and use rites to regulate their behavior, the entire society will be in order (McKnight, 1997; Ren, 1997; MacCormack, 1996a). Confucianism views human nature as fundamentally good, and holds that criminals could be reformed

---

[8] Chinese text project, March 5th, 2014 retrieved from http://ctext.org/liji/li-yun.

through moral education; peace and happiness will result as long as the ruler can set a moral example for his subjects, instills them with virtue, works to eliminate social evils, and ensures the stability and prosperity of the state (Windrow, 2006).

Hierarchical relations are stressed in Confucianism as tools to mitigate deviancy, while formal laws are regarded as having only a slight legitimate function. Confucius exalted the value of "benevolence" (仁) as the one universal principle of ethics, and advocated "moral enlightenment and prudent punishment (明德慎罚)" in the Western *Zhou* Dynasty (16th century- 770 BC), for "moral enlightenment is primary while penalty is supplementary" (德主刑輔) (Liu, 2009). Although Confucius's *li* was similar in some respects to the Western conception of natural law, its basis was not law, and it was still framed in terms of rites. For Confucius, "law" is associated with punitive punishment, a tool of ruling, rather than being viewed in terms of the protection of rights. He acknowledged, however, that rites require the support of "law," including the use of punishment provided for under those law at times to reinforce adherence to the norms specified in rites.

Confucius's idea faced challenges during the early *Warring States* period. The competitor, the Legalist School, reflected the belief that the *li* (propriety), grounded in kin solidarity, could no longer regulate the political sector. Advocates of the Legalist School urged constructing a new political form distinguished from rule by propriety. The new political order simultaneously established a type of norms which was independent of the clan code, called the law, and which was viewed as a needed stabilization mechanism (Park, 2006). The laws developed were centered around criminal law and administrative law, and were simply seen as a means to govern more effectively rather than as a means to secure any rights and protections for individuals (Park, 2006; MacCormack, 1996a). The Legalist School advocates believed individuals' greed and selfishness inevitably led them astray, irrespective of education or social pressure, so severe punishment in the hands of the state was necessary to curb these human tendencies to deviance (Ren, 1997).

The rule by law called for in the Legalist School is different from the modern rule of law in the West where the law had a long history of growth and maturation in the civil society before being incorporated into the political state; in stark contrast, the law in imperial China was combined with politics from the outset. Unlike law in the West which assumed the task of regulating state power from the beginning, law in ancient China was used to complement the institutionalization of the Imperial political system. Politics and law in the minds of the Legalist School advocates defined and constituted each other, and both were externalized from society without supervision (Park, 2006). Legalist School advocates actually reaffirmed the idea present in Confucianism—namely, law is the ruling instrument of the ruler, and it even "completely rejected the traditional virtues of humanity and righteousness" (MacCormack, 1996a, p.4). The Legalist School reflected the belief that law should be made according to political needs, and further that risk of severe punishment and existence of harsh law can reduce crime and meet political needs simultaneously (Windrow, 2006; Park, 2006).

Thus both Confucianism and Legalist School advocate the law as a ruling tool, and punishment is viewed as a key aspect of law. This ideology was dominant in the spirit of Chinese law, and is likewise deeply rooted in Chinese culture. "Law" in the Chinese language also presents itself as punishment. *Shuo Wen Jie Zi* (《說文解字》), a dictionary compiled in the Eastern *Han* Dynasty (around AD 100-121), stated that "法 (*Fa*), 刑 (*Xing*) 也 (law is punishment)". The ancient Chinese character of "law" ("灋") can be split into three parts: "氵", "廌" and "去" (Liu, 2009). "氵" means "water" which represents "fairness, equality and justice" because when you pour water into a place, the surface of water keeps flat (fair). "廌" (*Zhi*), the unicorn, is a mythological animal with a single horn representing "justice" because *Zhi* will tell out the criminal suspect by hitting him/her with its horn. "去" means "to remove" the criminals and it represents "punishment".

Thus, "law" as it is viewed in the Chinese language and culture originally meant that the legal process exists to punish crime with fairness, equality and justice. To a great extent, the *Fa* (law) was synonymous with punishment (*刑 Xing*), and its fundamental role in society was to "stop violence and eliminate evil" (Zhang, 1999, p.68). Thus, the primary aspect of the traditional Chinese legal system was **criminal law**, with relatively little content reflecting civil law (Zhang, 2010). The important question which arises next is that of who is in charge of using law to punish? If the law is the water to bring justice, what kind of container can hold the water? The bureaucracy which controlled the application of law in China is the next topic of concern.

LAW BY BUREAUCRACY AND POLITICS

Both Confucianism and the Legalist School supported a highly centralized hierarchical bureaucracy, and both schools of thought were mainly concerned with the relationship which should exist between the state and its citizens. This political institutional development focus of attention led to a legal system in which civil law was largely overshadowed by criminal law and considerations of the most effective and morally appropriate forms of punishment of wrongdoing. An independent judicial system did not exist in imperial China, and the functions of policing, prosecution and trial court processes were all addressed by imperial bureaucracy officials rather than arising from an independent judicial system. In China the legal profession was generally despised, and people who pursued justice through lawsuits could even be prosecuted as opposed to being viewed as courageous advocates for justice. The independent identity of the judicial system clearly could not grow under these circumstances of absolute control of the imperial bureaucracy which retained exclusive power over the dispensation of justice.

Imperial Bureaucracy

The Legalist School is an element of Classical Chinese philosophy, one that emphasizes the need for order above all other human concerns and its associated political doctrine was developed during the Fourth Century B.C. (Schafer, 1967). Scholars of the Chinese Legalist School generally argued that a strong government and a carefully devised code of law were essential to public order (Lau, 1963). Both Confucianism and the Legalist School called for clear governmental hierarchies and steadfast adherence to tradition. Confucianism reflected a clearly optimistic view of human potential and advocated ruling benevolently, while the Legalist School was more focused on the occasional malevolence of human nature and emphasized the necessity of a robust policing force to stringently (but impartially) enforce rules and punish for even the most minor infractions as an reinforcement of good behavior.

Despite the emphasis placed on "benevolence" in Confucian thought, the followers of Confucius were aware that the maintenance of hierarchical relations requires the development of law and the power to enforce law when deviance occurs. Confucius believed that a too tolerant and overly lenient government would lead to people becoming negligent, an undesirable trait which must be "corrected with a firm grip" (Park, 2006, p.11). Confucianism advocated a centralized power system, in the form of a political bureaucracy, to support the law and the King or Emperor is on the top of that structure. The ideal governance arrangement in Confucianism is that the state should be ruled by a King who exemplifies the virtue "benevolence (*ren* 仁)" using "rites (*li* 礼)" to regulate people's behavior, with law and punishment (*xing* 刑) as only a complement to deal with malevolent acts and persons perpetrating them (Windrow, 2006; Park, 2006; Erie, 2003). The Chinese Legalist School also advocated centralization of authority in the ruler, and its specific ideas included the creation of extensive criminal legal codes, building a vast bureaucracy and implementing severe laws and administering stern impartial punishments for wrongdoing (Liu, 1998; Ren, 1997; MacCormack, 1996; Huang, 1996).

A good deal of depiction of the imperial Chinese bureaucracy is to be found in the literature on governmental practice associated with the Western *Zhou* state (1045-771 BC); this government has been referred to as the inventor of "modern-style bureaucracy" (Finer, 1997, p87-90). Max Weber's *pure type* of bureaucracy was based on modern Western governments which separate officials from the means of administration, describing how the "rational-legal" authority of the modern state promotes impersonal rules with a paralleling progress of modern democracy (Weber, 1958, p.225-226). Weber's conceptualization of bureaucracy can be characterized as a set of traits: division of labor, hierarchy of authority, extensive rules, comprehensive system of procedures, impersonality, separation of administration from ownership, as well as hiring and promotion based on technical competency (Weber, 1958; Hall, 1963; Pugh, Hickson, Hinings & Turner, 1968).

In the case of China, however, Chinese imperial officials were not separated from their positions, which could be characterized as either "fat" or "lean" in terms of their wealth accumulation potential, and officials could rightfully accumulate great personal wealth through their official work. Because of this aspect of the Chinese bureaucracy there was a general confusion between private and public resources associated with the Mandarin bureaucracy (Will, 2012, p. 10). The Chinese Imperial Bureaucracy, in contrast to the pure form of bureaucracy, is properly characterized as being among the class of "patrimonial bureaucracies" which are principally based on "traditional authority" (Will, 2012, p. 10). It has a major focus on the generalist officials recruited to service the "Mandarin," and is often referred to as Mandarin Bureaucracy in the organization theory literature (Ferguson, 1902). The officials employed were generalists, and they were qualified in terms of humanistic learning and selected through competitive examination, although they often lacked the management skills and technical proficiency in administrative work which they were recruited to accomplish (Riggs, 1997).

The Western *Zhou* government intended to manage its affairs on a day-to-day basis, and it started early on to build a permanent body of administrative officials rather than rely upon temporary appointments (Yang, 1984; Yang, 1999). Thus, a substantial body of clerical officials was recruited to do the work of routine governance and public services maintenance, and male and female servants were recruited to work under their supervision (Hsu, 1966; Huang, 1985; Shizuka, 1954).The general structure of the *Western Zhou* government was a clear hierarchy. On the top was a body of imperial officials associated with the Ministry (*qingshiliao, 卿事寮*), the most important segment; below it were the Many Intermediate Officials (*zhuyin, 诸尹*) and they were also officials of the central government; following them were District Administrators (*lijun, 里君*) who were local civil officials in charge of delimited areas directly controlled by the *Zhou* central government. Finally, hundreds of Craftsmen were at the bottom of the structure who worked in the government-operated workshops (Li, 2008). The regional rulers of various statuses such as *Hou (侯), Dian (甸)*, and *Nan(男),* who owned their states, were viewed as local leaders existing beyond the administrative control of central government.

General structural divisions of administrative roles and procedure already existed in the *Zhou* government. The Ministry, or the "Bureau" (*Liao,* 寮), a congregation of multiple relevant offices, had emerged, and it was routinely maintained by a collective management within an institutionalized structure at a particular location; certain definitions of roles, rules and standard administrative procedures started to develop (Li, 2008, p.53). The three most important offices were: Supervisor of Multitudes, Supervisor of Construction, and Supervisor of Horses, each with a role separated from the other offices. It remains unclear whether the judicial function of the *Zhou* government led to the creation of a distinct legal office. Bronze inscriptions have been located which showed that lawsuit affairs had been part of the Supervisor of Construction's function. However, it is argued by many scholars that the general trend to enforce the state legal system and to also promulgate written legal codes gradually took place in the *Spring and Autumn* period. The role of Supervisor of Lawsuits (*sikou,* 司寇) was frequently mentioned in the official records of that later period (Li, 2008). Some evidence suggests that the term *sikou (*司寇*)* should be translated as Supervisor of Criminals because they assisted high officials at the *Zhou* court in their various legal duties (Skosey, 1996).

The state *Qin* adopted the Legalist School theories and built the first Chinese imperial dynasty. *Qin*'s government was highly centralized and it ruled with a uniformed legal code. The *Qin*'s governance is characterized by an extensive apparatus of penal and administrative rules, together with an elaborate bureaucracy (MacCormack, 1996b; Grafflin, 1990). Its detailed, penal-oriented legal code and the vast, tightly regulated bureaucracy were later adopted by all of the successive Chinese dynasties (Lin, 1998; Ren, 1997; MacCormack, 1996a; MacCormack, 1990). The immense size and extremely long duration of the Chinese bureaucratic machine has led to the development of a deeply-rooted culture of bureaucracy, and the profound reverence for bureaucratic order remains an essential part of the contemporary Chinese culture.

In the year of 5 BC the total number of officials in the ancient Chinese empire reached 130,285 (exclusive of military officials), roughly twenty times more than those in the Roman Empire of the same period (Wang, 1983; Wang, 1949; Li, 2008). This trend toward greater cadres of officials keeps increasing up to the present time. The ratio of officials to civilians was 1:900 in the Qing dynasty, and increased to 1:26 by 1999. The ratio of officials in charge to staff is 1:0.84, compared to 1:1.17 in the U.S., and 1:3.6 in Japan (*International Herald Tribune*, 2005). The poorer the province in contemporary China, the higher the ratio of officials to civilians. In some places becoming a public official is the only way a person can live a good life (*International Herald Tribune*, 2005).

Imperial Law

Imperial law did not separate the civil code from the criminal code. This fact has led to the now discredited belief that traditional Chinese law had no civil law, much less a distinction between civil and criminal procedural laws (Park, 2010; Muhlhahn, 2009; Zihe, 2003). Civil law was quite largely overshadowed by the criminal law in the imperial legal system because the *li*-premised legal system was mainly concerned with the relationship between the state and its citizens (a vertical relationship); there was relatively little attention paid to civil matters (a horizontal relationship) (Zhang, 2010). In virtually every dynasty criminal law constituted the principal backbone of the legal code, but the same code contained both criminal and civil laws, always placing criminal violation punishment at the center.

Existing legal research shows that *Qing* officials systematically sorted cases into either "major" or "minor" categories and into different jurisdictions of origin (Zhao, 2003). In this regard, county/district courts can hear minor cases, including household registration, inheritance, marriage, land, irrigation and debt disputes if these minor cases do not involve death or grand theft; for major cases, county/district courts do have primary jurisdiction, but they have to report to the higher court for review (Zhao, 2003). For both types of cases the same legal procedures were to be followed.

Dynasties in ancient China generally pursued progressive codification of the national law. The *Qin* (221–206 BC) rulers had very harsh codes, the *Han* Dynasty had the "*Jiuzhanglü*" (*九章律*), and the *Tang* (618–907 AC) had the "*Tanglvshuyi*" (*唐律疏議*). The process of amalgamation of Confucian views and written law codes was considered complete by the time of the *Tang* Code of AD 624, and this code was regarded as a model of precision and clarity in terms of its careful drafting and clear structure. The codification with Confucianism revised form as state orthodoxy continued during the *Song* (960–1279 AD), the *Ming* (1368–1644 AD), and the *Qing* (1644–1912 AD) dynasties. The emergent traditional Chinese law cannon was primarily penal in nature, and it was largely in place by the time of the *Qing* dynasty (featuring only a handful of specific provisions dealing with civil and commercial issues) (Brockman 1980, p. 85).

Although successive imperial dynasties all tried to codify law, many legal scholars have argued that the rites (*li*) continued to dominated the Chinese legal system for a very long time in practice, and that all acts against ritual propriety were defined as criminal offenses (Muhlhahn, 2009; Keith, 1994). Since the ritual norms, maintained by tradition, are natural rules for people to follow, the Imperial law with rites as the core then did not require much of a special legal system for this aspect of rule enforcement, but relied instead on the discretionary judgment of the administrative bureaucracy (Fei, 1992). As a direct consequence the emergent legal institutions in ancient China were not particularly well developed, being located within a political administrative system wherein clearly judicial functions were carried out by administrative officers.

A genuinely independent judicial system did not exist in imperial China, and the administration of justice was often carried out by the Imperial bureaucracy with the judges being seen as officials rather than jurists (Gray, 1972). The Imperial legal system was actually primarily about "criminal justice," not about citizens' rights protection; the law was closely associated with punishment as a key element of justice in a society where order was highly prized. The core functions of policing, prosecution and conducting of trials had all been addressed solely by the Imperial bureaucracy for thousands of years as natural aspects of administrative governance. The legal profession was not honored in any way, with magistrates being widely seen as either the Emperor's agents or failed sages; people who help " manage a lawsuit" were often characterized as "litigation hoodlums" and could even be prosecuted (Jenner, 1992). The institutionalization of independent legal branches separate from the legislative and executive functions has no tradition in China. Instead, the Imperial bureaucracy, which represents the

Emperor, is seen to have the exclusive authority to develop and administer the Chinese justice system.

Judicial Bureaucracy in Imperial China

Lawsuits in the *Zhou* government fell under the Supervisor of Construction's jurisdiction. In the *Spring and Autumn* period the role of Supervisor of Lawsuits (*sikou, 司寇*) is believed to have emerged, and the trend to codify and enforce the Superior state legal system intensified. Officials dealing with all legal matters were always a part of the Imperial bureaucracy, and have never had a chance to gain their own independent identity. The magistrates were administrative officers, and their expertise was that of knowledge of Confucian classics rather than command of legal skills. The legal profession was virtually banned from existence, and the gradual institutionalization of an independent judiciary in China was not possible while Chinese magistrates were acting as layman judicial officials on a routine basis.

The Traditional Imperial Judiciary

Inherited from the Legalist School and Confucian lines of thought, Chinese law was primarily viewed as an instrument to control the people, and the legal system functioned as an integral part of the centralized administrative system as it matured over the centuries (Park, 2010; He, 2005; Alford, 1984). The fledgling Imperial judiciary, such as it was, prioritized criminal law and punishment in its work. No autonomous legal institution existed, rather the exercise of judicial power was actually part of executive power; administrative levels were a reflection of the "the judicial ladder," moving from county on up to the central government (Park, 2010; He, 2005; Alford, 1984). Since the advent of the *Shang* dynasty, the judiciary bureau situated at central court assisted the Emperor with all law-related affairs. In the *Zhou* dynasty, the central court had a judicial official called a Major [*Sikou (大司寇)*], and below him was a Minor [*Sikou (小司寇)*], and below them were staff functionaries. In both the *Qin* and *Han* dynasties, the judicial official was known as *Tingwei (廷尉)*, and *Yushi (御史)* took charge of a monitoring and management function (Zhang, 1999).

Over time the judiciary bureaucracy became substantially more systematic and specialized in its judicial function. There were three distinct legal branches at the central level of government: the Board of

Punishment *(Xing Bu,刑部)*, the Central Judicial Court *(Da Li Si,大理寺)*, and the Office of Censors, or *Censorate (Yu Shi Tai,御史台)* (Zhang, 1999).This three-branch format was established during the *Tang* dynasty, and subsequent dynasties largely adhered to it. The Board of Punishment was in charge of drafting and examining laws and regulations, and responsible for classifying criminal punishment. It also had the power to review judgments concerning both the death penalty and exile sentences. Being the top body of criminal law legislation and enforcement, it was the most powerful of the three branches (Zhang, 1999). The Central Judicial Court, much like the U.S. Supreme Court, was responsible for adjudicating all cases except for the death penalty and exile cases; these two special types of cases were exclusively subject to the Board of Punishment's review and approval. The Office of Censors dealt mainly with the supervision of officials working at the central and local level, but was also authorized to adjudicate certain types of cases (Zhang, 1999).

However, such a division between these branches did not signify a functional separation of powers, and the ultimate source of law remained with the Emperor who possessed all the powers of the legislative, the executive, and the judicial aspects of governances (See Figure 2.1). For some important cases, the three branches would sit together to try a major case, and such adjudicative conclaves were referred to as "joint hearing by three branches" *(San Tang Hui Shen,三堂会审)* (Zhang, 1999, p.520-521). No matter how the judiciary might change names or functions, the Emperor retained the ultimate power in all cases, and the Imperial edict was the supreme law of the land. The judiciary was never independent, either in principle or in practice, and was generally subordinate to the administrative executive officers in all of its activities (Zhang, 2010). Although the judiciary had three divisions at the central level, there were no local courts; an executive bureaucrat handled everything at the local level, including judicial affairs.

Beginning with the *Qin* Dynasty, the structure of local administration was divided into three levels: province, prefecture, and county. Each of these local administrative offices were known as *Yamen (衙门)* and they served as both the executive office and the courtroom for the jurisdiction in question. The executive officer thus was empowered with judicial authority, adjudicating both civil and criminal cases alike (Zhang, 1999). With this dual authority, he could greatly affect the life of any particular person; these officials were often venerated as "parental officer" *(Fu Mu Guan 父母官)* (Zhang, 1999, p.214). This combining of the public administration and the judiciary into one local office remained the practice throughout the feudal period of Chinese history, and the deeply imbedded practice had an impact on the post-Imperial era (e.g., Republic period). This system ensured that the nation's judicial power retained under the Emperor's control, but in so doing it made the executive office superior to the judiciary writ large. As a consequence, a tradition has existed since Imperial China that the executive could interfere and supersede all judicial proceedings (Zhang, 2010).

Figure 2.1 The Judiciary Structure in Imperial Times of China

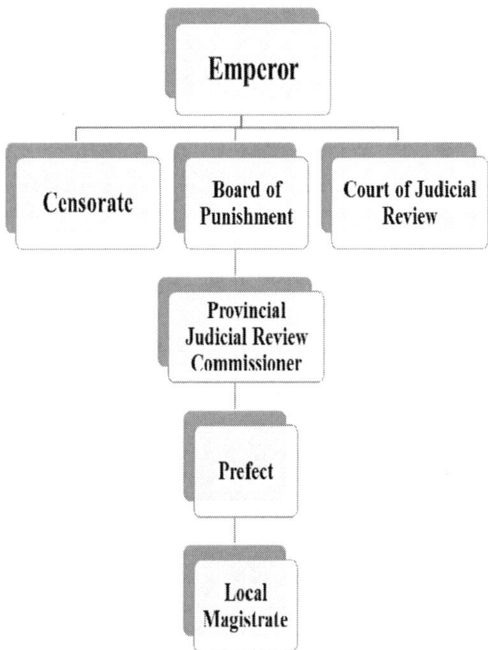

A Layman Judiciary Bureaucracy

The government structure in ancient China remained highly centralized and largely uncomplicated for a very long time (He, 2005). In most dynasties, at least four levels in administration existed, from lowest to highest, including: (1) county or district (*xian* 县); (2) prefecture (*fu* 府); (3) province (*sheng* 省), and (4) the central government (Park, 2010). The county officials, all appointed by the central government, exercised comprehensive responsibilities to include the enactment of rules (legislature), the execution of rules (administration), and the resolving of disputes (judiciary) (Park, 2010; He, 2005; Alford, 1984). The county official, named the *magistrate*, exercised jurisdiction as the judge of the lowest governmental tribunal (Park, 2010).

The formalization of the recruiting process for judicial officials dates from the *Shang* and *Zhou* times. It was broadly believed that a judicial officer should be good at administration and dispensing justice, and he must be both strict and fair (impartial) in legal practice. In the *Western Zhou*, a judicial officer was required to follow the law strictly in their work. The qualifications sought in recruitment was "*Sanjun* (Three requirement, 三俊)": the officer must respect and follow the law; judge by the law; and be cautious about the legal practice. *Qin*'s law was harsh, and its judicial officers were mostly recruited from low-level criminal justice clerk ranks. In time, criminal justice became more of a profession, and positions in criminal justice were even inherited by certain families. This tradition remained in force well through the *Han* dynasty.

Since the time of the *Southern and Northern Dynasties*, the *Wei* dynasty established the concept of the job position of *Lü Boshi* (Juris Doctor 律博士), a person who took charge of teaching law and educating legal officers. This was the earliest institution of legal education for Chinese legal officers. The *Sui* and *Tang* dynasties developed certain procedures to recruit suitable legal officers. For example, the *Sui* dynasty had legal courses taught by Juris Doctors and students who passed the exam could be entrusted with legal positions. Civil service examinations had already started as of the *Sui* dynasty, and people who wanted to become officials were required to take these civil service exams. Such exams required extreme familiarity with the ancient Confucius classical works, and examinees were required to give persuasive explanations underlying some Confucian views themselves. Thus, this process of recruiting officials was also called a process of Confucianization (He, 2005). Civil service examination may use "rule of knowledge" to complement "rule of man," however there is little doubt that knowledge of Confucian classics did not prepare people to handle administrative affairs—much less did it prepare them for managing judicial issues which required specialized legal knowledge (Ch'ü, 1962).

Civil service examinations actually produced a class of scholar-officials (or Mandarins), who held all the power and owned the largest amount of land were they resided. This elite enjoyed great prestige regardless of their heredity and formal education; the prestige derived from the function they performed—namely, their privileged position in the large state bureaucracy's hierarchy. This very special scholar-official class carried out and controlled all the functions of the state, and ordinary people had almost no role in any aspects of state affairs. Thus, both the country and people were under the control of the bureaucracy and the scholar-official class. A tentacular bureaucracy of this kind is argued to lead to a totalitarian state, in which the state has complete control over all activities of social life, and very limited social space can be left to the ordinary people (Balazs, 1971).

In late Imperial China, a single governmental official, the district or county magistrate, presided over some 200,000 to 250,000 residents, and had to deal with more than 10,000 cases in less than a year (Alford, 1984; Cohen, 1968). The district magistrate had to filter filed petitions to reduce caseloads. He had to deal with many administrative and fiscal tasks at the same time. County officials who were not legal experts had to hire consultants or assistants who had appropriate technical knowledge for handling the many legal issues requiring the attention of the state. The role played by office (*yamen, 衙门*) underlings and legal secretaries in these filterings should not be disregarded. The local tribunal usually consisted of officials' private secretaries, clerks who specialized in law, as well as a police force composed of constables and agents who carried out investigations and police duties such as detection, arrest, interrogation, torture, etc.

All the other people working inside the government served as the magistrate's assistants, and none had independent authority to check the magistrate's execution of power (Park, 2010; He, 2005). In the hierarchical bureaucratic system the county official was only subject to the supervision of higher level government officials. If local officials had to handle difficult criminal cases, they were permitted to request judicial review at the next level (Park, 2010). Performance of judicial duties was held to a standard by their superiors, and a magistrate could even be punished for his incompetence in managing their judicial function (e.g., could not effect an arrest of known criminals or took too long time to solve criminal cases) (Park, 2010).

Since there was no provision for the separation of powers and checks and balances, the county official held absolute power (judicial power included) without the supervision and check of any horizontal entity (He, 2005; Alford, 1984; Cohen, 1968). The county officials—the magistrates—had the combined power of detectives and judges, and they accumulated evidence, evaluated the evidence, rendered an official judgment, and passed sentence. Few restrictions for this kind of rule of man existed, and those which existed were mostly in the form of review and check from the higher level. For example, the *Tang* Code stated that higher-level officials were to review cases requiring punishment greater than a beating, and implementation of the death penalty necessitated Imperial review (Windrow, 2006).

Some dynasties did establish strict codes to punish crimes committed by officials; for example, the *Tang* Code had approximately 205 articles on criminal acts by bureaucrats acting in their official capacity, compared to 243 articles on criminal behavior among the general populace. However, the creation of a strict code could not compensate for the corruption arising from the absolute power of county officials. It was commonplace for potential defendants to pay bribes in order to dismiss pending enforcement or adjudication actions (Burke, Cutshaw & Krishna, 2006).

It was not so difficult for a judge to manipulate a case record in a subtle way to elicit either sympathy or disgust for defendants. The generation, age, sex, and mourning-period relationship between the criminal and victim affected the sentencing as well (Windrow, 2006). In order to attract the magistrate's attention in the case filtering process people needed professional help from a litigation master (*songshi*) for drafting petitions, otherwise petitions filed may not receive a hearing at the district magistrate's court (Susumu, 1993; Macauley, 1998).

Although the profession of law and lawyers were by-and-large banned, the legal professionals who "illegally" helped the people with lawsuits never disappeared entirely from the scene (Park, 2010; He, 2005; Burke, Cutshaw & Krishna, 2006).

These people not only wrote petitions for litigants, but also helped with litigation (*song*), and were called "litigation masters (*songshi*)," broadly considered to be a dishonorable business persistently banned by the government (McKnight & Liu, 1999). Most of those who were involved in this kind of business were relatively well educated *literati* who failed to climb the ladder of success through civil service examinations, and were self-trained in law. All of their work was done outside the court, and remained largely in secret for they could not represent clients and argue in court due to the ongoing illegalization of "lawyering" activities.

As a result of this situation He (2005) argues convincingly that "the traditional Chinese legal concept was a direct result of a judicial process dominated by laymen (p.97)". In ancient China, the magistrates had no training in law, and they dealt with disputes and cases as part of their administrative function. With Confucius-based knowledge and educational background, magistrates mostly applied the teachings of Confucianism or historical works in their ongoing trial and sentencing activities. Case decisions were based on the specific facts of the case, with little to no reference being made to precedents, much less any care for the continuity and coherence of the rules across cases (He, 2005). Without lawyers as adversary advocates the officials in the local tribunal setting dominated in the proceedings. As a result, many commonplace justice rules and theories could not be developed, such as Rules of Evidence, use of Neutrality and passive jurisdiction, and rights of accused parties, etc. (Gelatt, 1982; Cohen, 1968). The litigation business was condemned as "pettifoggery" and strictly banned, and its illegal status did not permit the nurturing of an honorable legal profession for promoting fairness and justice in civil and criminal adjudication.

Western history shows that the independence of the judiciary is directly related to the independence of legal professionals as a group. The independence of legal professionals as a group can lead to the building of legitimacy of the judiciary and cultivate support for legalistic justice through the progressive formality and clarity of legal professionals' work (Posner, 1995, p.35). For example, if judges follow strict legal procedures and make decisions without interference, their decisions will become unshakable. Legal professions consistently work for legal justice, and legal justice lays a strong foundation for the independence of the judiciary—a basic principle of Western legal thought. However, as was noted the Chinese legal profession was banned in ancient China, and the advocacy of an independent legal profession was nipped in the bud. The institutionalization of the judiciary in China could not receive the support of a group of informed legal professionals in Chinese Imperial history. In the Imperial legal practice we can see the clear disconnect occurring between the law as found in the books and the law as it works in reality.

Bureaucracy and Legal Practice

A bureaucratized legal system tended to set up detailed rules in legal practice. The traditional Imperial law structure featured four levels of trial, and a review process was provided for within the trial system. The bureaucracy also had a review and check system designed to promote justice. However, all these reviews and checks were done within the bureaucratic framework, and no effective outside review or supervision existed. The dictate of bureaucracy often presented more obstacles to the justice process than aides to the promotion of justice.

The Legal Process in the Books

The Imperial bureaucracy in ancient China was highly hierarchical, and it had very detailed rules in how it managed the legal process. Criminal cases entailing penal servitude and more severe punishments went through four levels of trial or review (county, prefecture, province and Imperial capital). The written law also featured detailed check and review stipulations over judicial actions. First, penal and administrative laws and regulations established comprehensive standards regarding matters including the apprehension, interrogation, trying, and sentencing of felons (Shiga, 1974; Metzger, 1973; Ch'ü, 1962). Rules to be followed by officials acting in a judicial capacity also prescribed that all persons accused of committing a single crime be confronted with one another collectively, specified in detail the type and degree of torture that could be applied in order to extract needed confessions, etc.

(*The Great Qing Legal Code,* 大清律). Magistrates would be punished severely if they were found to have violated these rules, and they would be tried as a common criminal if they ever went to trial (Ch'ü, 1962).

Second, based on bureaucratic hierarchy, the formal criminal justice process featured a so-called "obligatory review system." Magistrates could impose and carry out sentences only in cases involving a relatively minor sanction (Bodde & Morris, 1967). In cases involving more serious punishments, magistrates had to pass the case up to higher-level officials for their review. The heavier the sentence was to be, the more levels of official review it had to pass before it could be carried out. All death penalty cases had to come under the scrutiny of the Emperor himself (Shiga, 1974).

There was an appellate procedure in major cases after one's district level trial was complete; the accused could directly petition either those officials of the provincial government responsible for that district magistrate or specified entities in the capital; the Emperor could affirm or reverse the original verdict, he could dispatch a special commission to investigate the matter, he could order the Board of Punishments to reexamine the case itself, or he could refer the case to the appropriate provincial governor (Shiga, 1974).

Third, the bureaucracy had an internal check for district magistrates. The provincial superiors, circuit (*tao*) intendants, and censors were required to check on lower-level officials. Officials directly above the magistrate in the line of official authority not only heard cases arising through both the obligatory review and appellate systems, but they also had an affirmative legal obligation to uncover and report all wrongdoings committed by all officials beneath them (Metzger, 1973). Circuit intendants were empowered to conduct annual reviews of all cases heard at the district level (Shiga, 1974).

Fourth, there were the relatively independent Imperial Censors; these officials were responsible for ferreting out abuses committed by imperial officials and for making recommendations for appropriate actions to be taken by the Emperor (Metzger, 1973; Hucker, 1966). To foster their independence, Imperial Censors were not supervised by the Board of Punishments, but rather were allowed to communicate directly with high-level authorities, including the Emperor himself (Hsu, 2000).

The Legal Process in Reality

Although bureaucracy's legal processes were written in great detail, the rules and directions were not always followed in practice in the Chinese bureaucracy. First, the bureaucratic system featured prominent obstacles for the justice process. Because both magistrates and their superiors would be punished if alleged judicial errors were affirmed, the higher-level officials were typically quite reluctant either to accept or seriously reexamine the findings of their subordinates. Thus, the obligatory review system and appellate procedures were by-and-large pro-forma and constituted "empty promises" of accountability (Ch'ü, 1962). Also, reversal of a conviction led to an unresolved case and this could be a serious impediment to the bureaucratic advancement of superiors involved. In addition, most major appeals actually were directed back from the capital to local officials who had worked on these cases, and it was impossible to ask these officials to scrutinize themselves.

Second, a bureaucracy deeply rooted in politics could not avoid undue political influence into the formal criminal justice process. Political needs often led to the appointment of relatively unqualified individuals to official positions, thereby minimizing the likelihood that any well-connected officials would receive any type of official punishments, thereby reducing their incentive to follow closely the many rules designed to govern their behavior. Moreover, clearly undue political influence frequently prevented the correction of judicial errors. As if this wasn't enough, the formal criminal justice process also faced interference by the gentry. Conflicts between different political groups also delayed or disrupted the formal criminal justice process since legal or administrative issues were often transformed into full-blown political disputes within the bureaucracy (Alford, 1984).

Bureaucracy and Legal Reform

The prospects for legal reform in Imperial China were persistently poor, and this had to do with conflicts between different political groups. The highly centralized government bureaucracy, which held virtually all the military, legislative, judicial, administrative and taxation powers, was often an obstacle to the achievement of legal reform at the local level. First, any dissenting voice or act could be suppressed by the Imperial bureaucracy and be labeled as crimes of 'treason' or 'insurgency' (Ai, 2004, p6). Second, ministers and governors were reluctant to change for fear of losing power and benefits due to the reform (Ai, 2004). Third, the open recruiting system of bureaucracy was attractive to people. The bureaucracy had many ways to enroll members of society and hence carry favor with powerful segments of society, those being Imperial examinations (*科举*), recommendations (*贡监生*), inheritance (*荫袭*) or donations (*捐纳*). The advocacy of legal reform lacked a strong social foundation since people from the bottom would be reluctant to rise against the existing system (Ai, 2004). As a result of the combination of these barriers, few attempts at legal reforms were successful in imperial history.

For example, the first Chinese modernized legal reform in the late *Qing* dynasty was stymied by the bureaucracy and eventually failed. In the early 20th century, the late *Qing* dynasty was facing severe challenges in the form of invasion of the Western powers, as well as the rising dissatisfaction and protestation occurring within the nation. The Manchus, the corrupt leadership of the *Qing* dynasty, tried to maintain their rule through legal reform (Ai, 2004). They hoped that the revised legal code modeled after foreign laws might help get rid of extraterritorial privileges of Western powers and regain their ruling authority over the Chinese people (Ai, 2004; Li, 1989; Xu, 2008;). The Law Bureau within the Ministry of Law (*Fabu 法部*) was set and *Shen Jiaben* (1840-1913) and *Wu Tingfang* (1842-1922) were appointed to lead the drafting commission given the name Law Compilation Commission (*Fulü bianzhuan guan 法律编撰官*), which later was renamed as the Law Codification Commission, LCC (*Xiuding falü guan 修订法律馆*) (Xu, 2008; Li, 1989). Interestingly, the first step of this reform chosen was not the drafting of a constitution, but rather the writing of a criminal code; this again showed that criminal law, a ruling tool, was always the priority of imperial rulers. The drafting started in 1904, was to be ready by 1907 in order to solicit opinions from provincial governors before the fall of 1910. At the same time, work began on a civil code and this was the first attempt in Chinese history to separate civil matters from criminal matters.

Drafting was based on the "present situation of foreign relations and the legal codes of other countries" (Li, 1989, p.85). The draft criminal code was completed in October 1907. Under this code, punishments were limited to four types: the death penalty (by strangulation), imprisonment (*tuxing)* (term or life), detention (*juliu*) (under two months), and fines. Exile and corporal punishment were abolished, and it decriminalized illicit sexual intercourse with unmarried women in the old code. The draft also rejected the application of the law by analogy, and thus established the legal principle that any act that was not prohibited by the law constituted no offense (Xu, 2008). The draft code encountered vehement objections from high officials in the bureaucracy and was not formally announced (Xu, 2008). This draft code was later adopted as the Provisional New Criminal Code after the founding of the Republic of China.

Reformers attempted to promote the institutionalization of the legal process. First in this regard is the effort to promote procedural standardization. The Ministry of Law in 1907 proposed to standardize the judiciary, using standard complaint forms across the entire country. All issues regarding judicial administration, judicial process and legal interpretations in all provinces should be reported to and decided by the ministry (Xu, 2008). Second, the concept of due process was introduced, and torture during trials was proposed to be prohibited in most criminal cases (Xu, 2008). Although this provision did not go into practice until 1911, it persisted well into the Republican era. Third, the draft of criminal and civil procedural laws in light of foreign models was completed by April 1906, including the features of representation by lawyers and right to a jury trial (Xu, 2008). Because the draft was opposed by most provincial officials, it was not formally enacted.

The reformers also tried to institutionalize judicial independence by separating the judiciary from the administrative bureaucracy. In 1906, the existing Board of Punishment was refashioned into the Ministry of Law, which only took charge of judicial administration rather than the whole trial function. The General Procuracy was set up to function under the supervision of the Ministry of Law. The Court of Judicial Review (*Dalisi*) became the Supreme Court (*Daliyuan*), the final appellate court in the country. The Supreme Court and Ministry of Law then argued for creating a system of four levels of courts and three levels of trials. The four-level courts were township trial bureaus (*xiangyanju,乡研局*), district courts (*difang shenpanting,地方审判庭*), provincial high courts (*gaodeng shenpanting,高等审判庭*), and the

Supreme Court (Xu, 2008). The trial bureaus would take up criminal cases entailing flogging and penal servitude, and handle civil cases involving less than 200 *taels.*[9]

The appeal in such cases would go to a second trial at the district court, and end in a third trial at the high court. Criminal cases entailing punishments of more than penal servitude and civil cases involving more than 200 *taels* would first be tried at the district court, and appeals would go to the high court for a second trial and end with a final trial at the Supreme Court. This system was actually mirroring *Qing* practice in a way, but it was not implemented smoothly mainly because the bureaucracy was reluctant to give up part of its power. The court system plan was not completed before the *Qing* dynasty fell in 1911, and later this same system was inherited by the Republic. In 1912, there were a total of 345 courts at the provincial level, district courts existed in major cities, and court of first instance were in place at some counties, each with corresponding procuracies (Xu, 2008).

Traditional China did have a formal prison system. Prison system reform was launched in late *Qing* dynasty and a draft of the Prison Law was finished in 1910. It classified institutions of penal confinement into prisons (*jianyu,监狱*) (for offenders sentenced to imprisonment with labor), jails (*juliusuo, 拘留所*)(for imprisonment without labor), and detention houses (*liuzhisuo, 留置所*) (for criminal defendants waiting for trial); it provided for juvenile quarters, male and female quarters, and single cells within institutions of penal confinement. It emphasized a humanitarian spirit of prison management, and embodied the principle of both punishing wrongdoing and reforming convicts as the functions of incarceration by requiring work and moral education to be done within prisons. The draft law was not enacted, but it offered a blueprint for prison regulations under the Republic (Xu, 2008).

The late *Qing* legal reform did not win the battle over a thousand-year-old bureaucracy. Although the first constitutional document in Chinese history, *the Imperial Constitutional Outline,* was published in 1908, it was actually more of a powerful tool to protect the inviolable Imperial authority than a blueprint for progressive reform (Ai, 2004; Dai, 2009). There was not any actual alteration of the administrative bureaucracy, and the Imperial court still held the ultimate authority in

---

[9] It is a part of the Chinese system of weights and currency.

major issues (Ai, 2004). The nascent Chinese judiciary did not reach the goal of independence and enshrinement of due process, but it is no doubt that the judiciary has since started its likely long journey of self-identity seeking.

A series of modernized law drafts were later inherited by the Republic. Western legal thoughts such as judicial independence, due process and rule of law were introduced, and modern legal education was also initiated. Traditional Chinese law began to interact with other legal systems and legal scholars started to adopt some of their components. In 1906, the *Qing* court for the first time sent five ministers as government representatives to Japan, the U.S., Britain, France, Germany and Russia to study Western modern political and legal systems. Furthermore, some aspects of common law, continental civil law and Japanese law were introduced in this period, but in the end Roman civil law replaced the common law covering virtually all the newly-revised laws (Wang, 2006). Because almost every dynasty in ancient China had an exclusive set of codes, and it is easier for China to adopt a civil law tradition which is based on statutes as opposed to a common law tradition based on judicial interpretation (Wang, 2006). A new civil law tradition began to set its roots in the Chinese legal system.

CHINESE MODERN LEGAL SYSTEM AND CRIMINAL COURT

The Northern Warlords Government (Beiyang) (1911-1927)

Chinese legal tradition is based on the Confucian philosophy of social control through moral education, as well as the Legalist School's emphasis on codified law and criminal sanctions (Liu, 2009). As one of the oldest legal traditions in the world, it still has influence today. In addition, numerous external factors also affected the development of China's modern legal system, in particular persistent foreign interference, later Imperial legal reform against extraterritorial judicial privileges, influence from foreign legal system, and persistent abject poverty. The noteworthy achievements of the legal reform movement launched by the late *Qing* dynasty were maintained and continued in the Northern Warlords government (NWG)[10] from 1911 to 1928. The legal system reform effort taking place in this era was still motivated by two overriding related goals: to modernize China and to end extraterritoriality[11] (Xu, 1997). The laws enacted by the late *Qing* government were re-promulgated and put into operation without significant changes.

Following the 1911 Revolution, the Republic of China adopted a largely Western style legal code under the civil law tradition. The Republic inherited a series of draft laws in the late *Qing* legal reform and *Sun Yat-Sen*'s Provisional Government founded in 1912 enshrined the principle of judicial independence in the Provisional Constitution, with the separation powers of the administration, legislature and judiciary. The Provisional New Criminal Code (*Zanxing xin xinglu 暂行新刑律*) was issued in the same year (Yang, 1930). The following *Yuan Shikai* government (1912-1916) continued with the institutional formalization of the judiciary. Educational credentials were prerequisite for judiciary appointments, and there were judicial oversight officials to ensure that judicial officers upheld professional ethics (Xu, 2008; Meng, 1931). For example, magistrates were asked to cut their political ties to promote a public image of neutrality (*Zhengfu gongbao fenlei huibian, 政府公报分类汇编,* no. 36, 11, see Government Bulletin compiled in categories).

Although the Law on Organizing Courts provided a four-level court system (the Supreme Court, the high court, the district court, and the court of first instance), along with a three-trial process, provincial governors disapproved this plan and complained that it would take too much of their local budget. As a result, most courts of first instance had to be removed by 1914 due to the lack of funding. Instead, the County Judicial Office served as first instance court, and a trial officer (quasi-

---

[10] Although the years between 1916 and 1927 were politically unstable in the extreme, the government bureaucracy personnel remained unchanged and the central bureaucracy continued to function without disruption (Strauss, 1998, p.32).

[11] Extraterritoriality is the state of being exempted from the jurisdiction of local law, usually as the result of diplomatic negotiations. Extraterritoriality can also be applied to physical places, such as foreign embassies, military bases of foreign countries, or offices of the United Nations (see Quigley, 1926).

judge) and the county magistrate worked together to try cases. This was similar to what was done in the Imperial era, and represented a clear retreat from the goals of the separation of the judiciary and administration (Xu, 2008).

Because there was no legal guide to sentencing, the judges had very broad scope to impose punishment for offenses, leading to glaring inconsistency in sentencing practices. Another problem in the court was that judges and procurates could not speak in the local dialects where they served since the *rule of avoidance* prohibited them to serve in their own hometown. If they could not speak Mandarin either, they had to rely on court functionaries to speak to and deal with litigants (Xu, 2008). County functionaries might control the access to trials in order to squeeze illegal charges from litigants, and thus spawn irregularities and abuse in the trial process (*Zhengfu Gongbao,* 1927, no.4986). Clerks of the county offices controlled all paperwork and collected all fees, and knew nearly everybody in the area and were insiders at the county office, so they had various ways to squeeze money out of ordinary people who had to litigate or were being prosecuted for some offense.

The county magistrate, the assessor (*chengshen yuan*) and the secretary (*shuji*) were all-powerful persons in the county judicial process. They would decide when to hear a case or settle a suit, who should win and who should lose, too often depending on which way they could squeeze the most money from the parties involved (Xu, 2008). Because these officials were often associated with the local corrupt gentry, litigants had to pay money to the latter before they could hope that their cases would be won or even be heard. When it was a bandit case (*fei'an*), money could buy one's safety; otherwise, all kinds of tortures were used no matter what the result of the trial. Judicial police and gaol guards were equally highly resourceful in their respective manipulating, mistreating and extorting of ordinary people (Reed, 1995).

The formalization of process aspects of legal reform also met challenges. First, litigants were not well informed about the rules. Second, courts and procuracies saw the litigation fees as a ploy to increase state revenue rather than judicial revenue in order to operate the system. These two problems discouraged lawsuits (Xu, 2008). For the trial procedures, torture in trials was rendered illegal, and open trial was required. In 1912, the Ministry of Justice prohibited detaining civil defendants until trial (*Zhengfu Gongbao*, 1913, no. 33). The principle of legal defense was accepted, but lawyers only could represent defendants or plaintiffs in formal courts above the level of the county. Regulations on Lawyers ruled that lawyers could not appear at trials conducted by the magistrates at the county level (*Zhengfu Gongbao*, 1913, no. 280). Consequently, the people residing in most rural areas could not have legal representation in a trial.

Regulations on Trial Deadlines for Criminal Prosecution were enacted in 1915. Investigation of a criminal case was to be done within ten days of detaining the defendant, a pre-trial hearing was to be held within ten days of receiving the case file, and sentence was to be handed down within ten days of prosecuting (twenty days in cases of homicide and robbery) (*Zhengfu Gongbao*, 1915, no. 974). In 1918, new regulations of the Ministry of Justice extended an extra five days for each of these three deadlines (*Zhengfu Gongbao,* 1918, no. 851). Trial review for high courts and the Supreme Court was to be accomplished in ten days of receiving the case file. County magistrates should finish trying a criminal case within sixty days of receiving the case.

The check system for trial included a trial review and appeal process. The trial review from the Imperial period was kept. The 1912 regulations required trial review only for cases entailing five-year prison terms and above, and county magistrates then tended to give sentences just below five–year prison terms in order to avoid the stipulated review (Xu, 2008). The 1914 regulations required almost all criminal cases tried at the County Government Office to be sent for review within five days of case sentencing (*Zhengfu Gongbao*, 1914, no. 777). For the appeal process in criminal cases, the plaintiff could appeal within seven days if a procurator decided not to prosecute a case; the procurator could appeal within three days if a judge decided not to prosecute a case after a pre-trial hearing; either the defendant or the procurator could appeal within ten days after a trial for sentences heavier than detention and fine (Xu, 2008). Third trial appeal was limited to reasons that conviction and sentence contradicted the law. After the final decision, either party could file a special appeal to the

Supreme Court, limited to addressing the reason(s) why the trial was illegal.

For civil cases, litigants could appeal to a second trial court within twenty days of a first trial; appeal for a third trial was possible if the remedy sought was more than 100 *yuan*, within twenty days of a second trial (Xu, 2008). The challenge for the appeal process was that many counties were far away from district courts and were without convenient transportation, thereby being restricted in their access to appeal. The Ministry of Justice had to approve designating a county court as an appeal court for a neighboring county in such situations. In some areas, the administrator was even empowered with judicial responsibility to act as a court of appeal and to review cases tried in the counties (*Shi Bao*, 1914, December 24, p.5). This practice was a clear deviation from the formalization of process.

During the Northern Warlords government period the Ministry of Justice attempted to establish judicial independence and due process through setting judicial institutions and procedures, but its plans were often defeated by elements of the pervasive bureaucracy. The administrative bureaucracy exercised budget control over the judicial system, and often used this power to try to reduce the scope of the judiciary. The defects in the county level judiciary, such as the abuse of power of functionaries, squeezing litigation fees, the lack of legal representation, far from appellate court, etc. all work to limit access to justice for ordinary people. The effort to formalize the process and institutionalize the system usually had to cope with the realities of bureaucratic opposition, and major deviation from reform goals was commonplace.

Kuomintang Nanjing Government Period (1927-1949)

Different from the Northern Warlords government, the Kuomintang (KMT), which rose from a bourgeois revolution, had a distinctive party doctrine or ideology (*dangyi 党意*) to guide their state-building. On the one hand, it raised the idea of democratic constitutional government in the theory of Three Principles of the People (*Sanmin zhuyi 三民主义*); on the other hand, it emphasized that the long road to democracy had to experience three distinct stages: first was the military government (*junzheng 军政*), through tutelage government (*xunzheng 训政*), finally reaching constitutional government (*xian-zheng 宪政*). During the first two stages (starting from 1927), the KMT would exercise state power on behalf of the people and rule the country through the party (*yidang zhiguo 以党治国*). In other words, it was the KMT that controlled the political, administrative and judicial system of the country, and thus the country was called a Party-state (*dangguo 党国*).

The *Kuomintang Nanjing* governmental structure was divided into five core departments: legislative, executive, judicial, examinations, and control. The Department of Control had two main functions: impeachment and auditing, functions which were similar to those of the Board of Censors in the Imperial regime. The Department of Examinations was also closely associated with the political thought of the Imperial regime. The Nanjing government not only inherited the laws, civil regulations, and conventions enacted before, but also made some new laws. A new criminal code was enacted in 1928, followed by a criminal procedure law. In 1931, the first Chinese Civil Code was promulgated and it was based on the experience of civil legislation under Roman Law family countries such as Germany, Japan, and the Cantons of Switzerland. Collection of the Six Major Laws (constitutional law, civil law, commercial law, criminal law, civil procedure law, and criminal procedure law) finally took shape in China. This represents a process of the traditional Chinese legal system being replaced in some measure by Roman civil law, and a new legal tradition was finally established (Wang, 2006).

Under the *Party-state* ideology, the politicization of the judiciary was used as a weapon to strengthen political control. It was proposed that judges be trained in politics and party doctrine so that they could become at once efficacious and revolutionary. The prohibition of judges from joining political parties was abolished and no persons could be judicial officers other than those who were KMT party members (*Falü pinglun*, *法律评论*, 1927, No. 185). In addition, the jury had to be composed of KMT members selected by local party headquarters. The jury, however, had to be composed of KMT members selected by local party headquarters. The justification for this was that the KMT claimed to rule the country on behalf of society and the people, so the party was logically the soul body that should make and interpret law (*Zhonghuafaxue zazhi, 中华法学*,1930).

Under the influence of party ideology, categories of political crimes for the first time were created in Chinese history, so that the state could go beyond the regular legal system and process to eliminate people who were against the party's political control (Xu, 2008). These crimes classified people as "counter-revolutionaries" or "local bullies and evil gentry," colorful stigmatizing terms which were adopted in the Communist era later (Xu, 2008). Such classification undermined the formalizing of judicial institutionalization, and a host of political dissidents were incarcerated and executed outside of normal judicial procedures. Those "counter-revolutionaries" were detained in concentration camps and labor camps controlled by civilian and military secret services (Xue, 1985).

The principle of party dominance over the judiciary had a deep effect in the following years, and it is argued that this effect has continued into the judicial practices under the Chinese Communist Party (CCP) as evolved from the Soviet Republic era through the Maoist era to the present (Michels, 1962; Leng, 1967; Cohen, 1968; Cohen, 1969; Lotverit, 1973; Butler, 1983; Liao, 1983; Leng & Chiu, 1985; Ladany, 1992; Xu, 1997; Xu, 2008). Partifying the judiciary (*danghua sifa*) was clearly at odds with the principle of judicial independence, but the collective perception of KMT officials did not believe this was the case. They believed that judicial independence was a still an operative concept, noting the establishment of a judicial system which was independent of administration.

However, judicial independence entails not only an independent organizational existence, but also includes independent operation of the judicial system and judicial practice. The "partifying" of the system made the judiciary subject to party dominance, both simultaneously serving the purpose of the party-state (Xu, 1997; Xu, 2008). As for the court system, it was not established completely; local administrative officials continued to exercise judicial powers where no county judicial courts existed due to the shortage of both funding and qualified personnel. Lawyers were still prohibited from practicing and were not even allowed to work as legal consultants (*falü guwen 法律顾问*) at the county level (*Sifa xingzheng gongbao*, *司法行政公报*, 1932, no. 2; *Faling zhoukan*, *法律周刊,* 1932, no. 87-90; 1933, no. 148; Liu, 1934, p.34; *Sifa gongbao*, *司法公报*，1935, no.18). County magistrates were mostly educated at the post-secondary education level. There was an examination system to improve the competence of county magistrates, but this examination was not held consistently.

A detailed prescription of behavior for county magistrates existed, however the abuse of power and miscarriage of justice was a severe problem at the county level and magistrates often failed to follow judicial procedures required by the law (*Sifa gongbao*, 司法公报, 1935, no. 74). There was no consistent enforcement of the law, and encroachment upon the powers of the legislature and the judiciary by frequently changing administrative officers was commonplace. The military law and the military courts often imposed drastic penalties at the expense of the civil law and the civil courts (Keeton, 1937), further weakening the forces of uniform justice.

It was common for county magistrates to add a variety of fees in order to squeeze money out of parties to cases to cover their administrative costs. Both judicial officials and scholars agreed that such problems at the county level arose due to the fact that county magistrates held judicial powers (*Falü pinglun*, 法律评论, 1927, no. 215; 1929, no. 31; *Zhonghua falü zazhi*, 中华法律杂志, 1934, no. 5). At the county level judicial personnel were appointed by the magistrate, and had no way of conducting the judicial process independent of the magistrate. Additionally, the local gentry could exercise influence on the county judicial process since they could deny or provide important forms of support to administrative affairs depending on their preferences regarding how the county's judicial powers were being exercised.

The KMT Nanjing government tried to build a judicial system more clearly separated (not necessarily independent) from administrative bureaucracy from the capital down to the county level, focusing on properly trained and disciplined judicial officers guided by the rule of law and supportive of the principle of judicial independence. However, this progressive court system was never fully implemented due to shortage of funding and lack of qualified personnel, and as a result the judicial function was still carried out primarily by the administrative bureaucracy at the county level. The funding problems in turn led to the abuse of power and exercise of undue influence on justice on the part of the local gentry.

Moreover, a pervasive political ideology began to impose its influence on the judiciary during this era, and that politicization had a severe adverse impact on the development of the Chinese legal system. First, the theory of "partifying" the judiciary made the concept of judicial independence a distant goal without application to practice. Second, the idea that the party should control the judicial system rather than judicial independence was implanted in people's minds as a self-evident reality; unfortunately, one negative outcome was that the judiciary lost its spirit and self-identity as the reform process unfolded. Judicial independence as a clear goal of reform was transformed into a party-dominated social control model of court operation. The judiciary during this era could be best characterized as an "incomplete" court system burdened with a legacy of ideological subservience to political party control. This is most certainly a rather substantial deviation from a modernized judiciary exalting in its independence.

Chinese Communist Party Government (1932-1949)

During most of *Kuomingdang* governance time, the Chinese Communist Party also had its own government in its territory. In November 1931 a Chinese Soviet Republic was established in *Ruijin, Jiangxi* province. Its central government promulgated the Constitution, issued currency, and designed a national flag. An Interim Supreme Court, the highest judicial organ of the Chinese Soviet Republic, was set up in 1932, and at all levels of government magistrate divisions were also established. The quality of legal practice encountered challenges due to the lack of formal education and paucity of legal knowledge in the judiciary of the time. During this period, law had been taken as a weapon of dictatorship dedicated primarily to the establishment of a new revolutionary order.

The People's Commissariat of Justice developed more than 10 individual criminal laws and associated regulations to punish counter-revolutionary behaviors. Judicial procedures were under development, and certain formal process were set up, including: trial records, judgments, summons, warrants, pre-trial records, work reports, search records, etc. Seven major systems were initiated: (1) a public trial system and the Circuit Court; (2) a collegial system of trial and the jury system; (3) a defense system; (4) the rule that judges of the avoidance system with the families and relatives of the accused have ties or personal relationships, regardless of whether the trial or jury, shall not participate in the trial of the case; (5) the appeal system in the prescribed appeal period, the defendant may appeal to the higher judicial organs; (6) a death penalty review system; and (7) a People's Mediation System. The Jiangxi Soviet Republic was the first Communist government in China, and its legal practice could be seen as the predecessor of the socialist legal system of today (Li and Yang, 2004).

Due to the failure of the fifth anti-encirclement campaign, the Chinese red army was forced to begin its long march, and the Chinese Soviet Republic moved to the *Shan-Gan* soviet area. In 1937, the Chinese Soviet Republic changed its name to *Shaanxi-Gansu-Ningxia* Border Region Government. The government established the Supreme Court featuring 8 divisions—namely, a procuracy, a criminal court, a civil court, a secretariat office, a general office, a production office, a secretary, and a jail. Each county and town had a judicial clerk (Feng, 2007). The justice system was gradually set up, including law-making and law practice, substantive law and procedure law, legal institutions and systematic recruitment of judicial officials. The court during this time not only inherited the seven major legal systems featured in the *Jiangxi* Soviet Republic model, but also developed increasingly more systematic and efficient legal institutions and practices. The most popular system was the simplified trial procedure and practice of unified leadership in the judiciary.

In 1949, the People's Republic of China was officially founded by the Chinese Communist Party (CCP) and the legal system turned a new page in its development. The simplified trial procedure increased the efficiency of trials and later was fully incorporated into the legal system of the People's Republic of China after 1949. This type of unified leadership was also adopted in PRC legal practice. Although the unified leadership in the judiciary was a useful transitional measure developed in war time, it actually exerted a negative influence on the justice system later on as the system came to deal with a modern economy and engagement in the global marketplace. Chapter 4 discusses the current nature of Chinese courts and the Chinese criminal justice system.

CHAPTER 4

The Court and Criminal Justice System in China after 1949

During the last three decades a profound economic transformation has taken place in China, including opening up of the country to foreign investment, and permission being granted for internal trade and the widespread facilitation of start-up businesses. It has brought about both vibrant economic growth and dramatic social change. High social mobility, rapid and large-scale urbanization, social stratification and inequality changes provide ample opportunities and incentives for the occurrence of crime. All these conditions call for a robust justice system able to provide formal legal rights protection for individuals and maintain political legitimacy. However, legal reform in China lags far behind economic development reforms, and there is no genuinely independent judicial system to check the power and/or abuses of governmental actors or public agencies (Lubman, 1999). The Chinese judiciary is still more like a highly bureaucratized administrative branch operating under the Party's monitoring and government system rather than an independent judicial organ.

Similar to the highly centralized Imperial dynasties, the structure of Chinese courts largely remains as a hierarchical system parallel to both the government and the Chinese Communist Party. The judiciary is part of the civil service system and judges are employees of a quasi-executive branch. Diverse division offices are set up within each court to oversee different types of cases. The court is under the leadership of the Chinese Communist Party. It is highly localized because it has no centralized budget and is basically funded by local governments and court-imposed fees. The court and criminal justice system in China has gone through a long arduous process of progressive formalization and is now in an important transition phase.

COURT INSTITUTION IN PRESENT CHINA

Legal System after 1949 (1949-present)

In 1949, the People's Republic of China was founded officially by the Chinese Communist Party (CCP). The new country did not maintain the old laws in effect at the time, and indicated very clearly that "Under the democratic dictatorship of the proletariat, Collections of the Six Major Laws of the *Kuomintang* should be abolished" (Wang, 2006, p76). In classical Marxism, law is seen as a tool of the ruling class and the newly established political regime of the proletariat must dismantle the old state apparatus and establish its own legal system and social order (Wang, 2006). Hence, the Collection of the Six Major Laws of the *Kuomintang* was then abolished and socialist laws and judicial principles started to be enacted. Judicial work should be based on laws, orders, regulations and resolutions in the new democratic policies, and the judicial organs should also study and fully master the statist and legal perspectives implicit in Marxism, Leninism, and the Thought of Mao Zedong, as well as take into proper consideration the guiding principles of the CCP (Peking University Law Department, 1980).[12]

China started to build its Communist legal system from the outset. It adopted an overall format for the legal system from Soviet law, including public ownership of the means of production and subordination of the legal system to the Communist Party (Liu, 2009). Not only the 1954 Constitution, the first formal Constitution of the PRC, but also the late-1950s legislative work undertaken were designed to draft the basic civil, criminal and procedural codes to be adopted by the new China – all borrowed extensively from the Soviet model.

---

[12] The constitution of People's Republic of China, page 1, says the following: "Both the victory of China's new-democratic revolution and the successes of its socialist cause have been achieved by the Chinese people of all nationalities under the leadership of the Communist Party of China and the guidance of Marxism-Leninism and Mao Zedong Thought, and by upholding truth, correcting errors and overcoming numerous difficulties and hardships."

Development of the socialist legal system occurred in two distinct stages. The first stage, going from 1949 up to 1976, witnessed China creating a legal and court infrastructure following the Soviet approach pretty much to the letter, but that new infrastructure rapidly succumbed to political fanaticism which finally ended in the spectacle of the Great Cultural Revolution, a ten-year period of extreme domestic turmoil that largely paralyzed the legal system. The second stage of China's legal system development began after Chairman Mao's death in 1976, along with the advent of comprehensive economic reform. Beginning in the late 1970s China entered into a period of rebuilding its legal system by enacting progressive laws and developing associated regulations and adjudicative processes at an accelerated pace (Xin, 1999; Jones, 2003).

Over the period 1979 to 2008, the National People's Congress (NPC), the nation's top legislative body, promulgated over 230 new laws, and the State Council enacted more than 600 derivative regulations (Office of the State Council of China, 2008). In the White Paper released by the Office of the State Council of China in 2008, China claims that the foundation of the modern Chinese legal system was laid long ago, and this foundation is described as consisting of one core element, three levels of courts, and seven categories of law available to handle all major matters in serious dispute in society. At the core is the 1982 Constitution that has been amended four times through 2004.

Under the Constitution, there are three levels of legislation, representing the hierarchy of legal sources. At the top is "law," which is passed by the National People's Congress; the second level is the legislation made by the State Council and Provincial People's Congress termed "regulations"; the third level is made up of the aspects of central government legislation which are adopted by the various government ministries/agencies and by local government termed "rules or decrees" (Office of the State Council of China, 2008). The seven categories are the recognized branches of law, which are those of: (a) Constitution and related law; (b) civil and commercial law; (c) administrative law; (d) economic law; (e) social law; (f) criminal law; and, (g) litigation and non-litigation procedural law. In addition, local people's congresses passed over seven thousand local regulations, and various central government ministries and regional governments have issued multiple rules and official decrees (Xin, 1999).

After 65 years, a brand-new socialist legal system has been formed, but traces of the Roman law tradition still can be found. First, the legal tradition of the former Soviet Union is in fact in many aspects heavily influenced by Roman law (Quigley, 1992). Second, law is always established on the basis of the original legal tradition. The socialist Chinese law cannot avoid the influence from civil law tradition which had existed for 3 decades before 1949 (Lin, 1995). However, legal tradition is facing change in recent years. In the early 1990s, along with the collapse of the Soviet Union, the influence of the Soviet law tradition is diminishing in China. After 30 years of economic reform, China's economic system is now changing from a socialist planned economy to a socialist market economy. A comprehensive overview of the many complexities of the Chinese legal tradition is beyond the scope of this book, and more of the most noteworthy details can be found in the works of other authors (e.g, Cao, 2004; Chen, 1992; Diamant, Lubman, & O'Brien, 2005; Huang, 2001; Jiang, 2005; Ren, 1997; Andy, 2007).

Different from the relatively simple economic relations present in a planned economy, the increasing international trade and vast scale of contemporary domestic transactions taking place today calls for greater capacity for regulation to designate genuine property rights, oversee transactions and purchase orders, and enforce rules of the marketplace. The legal system has to be adapted to these changes and protect the market economy. In addition, the increase in global economic cooperation also requires that the Chinese legal system get closer in its operations to those which prevail in the international system, and international laws have clearly exerted their impact on the promulgation of law in China.

Literally thousands of Chinese students are starting common law study overseas, and then bringing back new legal concepts. Although the common law system, which is based principally on precedential cases and rules, is not inherent in Chinese law, the increased volume of foreign trade has required more common law elements to come into use. In addition, Hong Kong and Macao both retain their respective legal systems and laws after reversion to China, so that China now has three coexisting legal systems: Roman-law-based socialist law (mainland), common law (Hong Kong), and Continental Roman law

(Macao). Along with the pressures of globalization and international cooperation, not only civil laws but also public laws are facing challenges and pressures to change. The criminal law, and criminal procedure law in particular, have become the topics of greatest concern and most broad discussion in Chinese legal reform.

Court Development After 1949

The founding of the People's Republic of China in 1949 signaled a new era in China's judicial system, and around 1949 the number of people's courts reached a high (around 1900). On October 1, 1949 *Shen Junru* was appointed as the President of the Supreme People's Court, and on November 1, 1949 the Supreme People's Court began its work. Some local courts, such as provincial courts and county courts, were also set up. For example, the court of *Harbin* city was set up in 1946; the court of *Jilin* province was set up in 1948. Other local courts were established after taking over the judicial offices of the nationalist government. The Court of *Beijing* was set up on March 18 of 1949; the Court of *Shanghai* was set up on August 11 of 1949. Most of these early courts only had three units, these being the administrative office, the criminal trial unit, and the civil trial unit.

The process of the establishment of new courts was still in high gear during the 1950s, but a national campaign in mid-1952 disrupted the process. That campaign sought to apply the mass line to legal work and build a large nationwide mediation system rather than build a strong judiciary (Lubman, 1999). The police took on the major tasks of administrating law and carrying out sanctions imposed on wrongdoers. The Court and Procuracy figured little in governmental decision-making, and these offices were used primarily to formalize the most serious punishments being meted out. Mass line justice, rather than judicial procedures, was emphasized in public pronouncements and governmental actions (Lubman, 1999). As a direct reflection of the faith in mediation being displayed at that time, the courts in China usually started with mediation in cases brought to the court (often in the courtroom itself) rather than moving directly to adjudication.

Formal steps were taken to further regularize the legal system after 1953. In 1954, at the very first session of the first National People's Congress (NPC), a new Constitution was enacted, and the *Organic Law of the People's Courts* was adopted which systematically set out the nature, functions, organization and activities of the courts of China. A tripartite division of functions was established: the police were to investigate suspected offenses and make those arrests that had been approved by the Procuracy; a formally independent Procuracy was established outside the courts; the courts were to determine guilt in public trials before one judge and two citizens acting as jurors, trials in which the accused had a right to defense (Lubman, 1999). This represented a promising beginning, with the actual number of courts being newly established in 1954 being quite large (around 600). These new courts came into existence across most of the country.

After 1955, however, substantial political campaigns were launched putatively to "suppress counter-revolutionaries." These campaigns generally entailed the direct involvement of police sanctioning and the courts promoting specific policies rather than acting as neutral institutions seeking truth through a fair adversarial process. The formal criminal procedures and tripartite division among the police, procuracy, and courts on the disposition of cases were largely disregarded during the course of these campaigns launched to root out counter-revolutionaries. In most cases, the procuracy and courts relied on a file assembled by the police, and only confirmed the police recommendation for case disposition (Lubman, 1999). For example, during the infamous anti-rightist campaigns of 1957-1958, close cooperation among courts, procuracy and police was urged by the Chinese Communist Party and established formal procedures specified in existing law were again largely disregarded. The three agencies continued to work together and apply the mass line[13] into their legal work. Statutes were promulgated to authorize the police to administer minor punishments on their own judgment without need of judicial or procuracy involvement; the diminution of the status of Chinese courts increased as the role of the police grew (Lubman, 1999).

In figure 4.1 below we can see that in 1959 and 1964 the number of courts built was around 100, and in contrast in 1969 the number was only 36. During the period of the Great Cultural Revolution, the already

[13] It is the political, organizational and leadership method developed by the Chinese Communist Party which means applying correct ideas that the masses gain in everyday life.

fragile fledgling judicial system was very nearly completely paralyzed (1966-1976). Few courts were built due to the disruption of legal work which occurred during the Great Cultural Revolution. The Procuracy had been abolished in the late 1960s, and the function of courts had been disrupted and usurped, while the public security organs—the Police—took on a predominant role at the direct expense of both the Procuracy and the Courts. Later, the People's Liberation Army (PLA) intervened to end the chaos created by the Great Cultural Revolution, and the PLA also handled many criminal cases in which they had an interest without any participation of the courts whatsoever (Chiu, 1992).

The number of courts being built started to increase once again after 1974. Sadly, the 1975 Constitution once more confirmed the subordination of the judiciary to the administrative organs of government; that document officially abolished the Procuracy, whose function was transferred to the public security organs in existence at each corresponding level of government (Chiu, 1992). The judicial system was assigned a minimum role to play, and it ranked last in the status ranking of the three legal branches (police, procuracy, and court) (Liang, 2008). The Chinese courts throughout the 1950s, 1960s and 1970s dealt predominately with criminal cases, which accounted for approximately half of the caseload of the courts before 1979.

In 1978, the 11th Central Committee 3rd plenary session of the Chinese Communist Party officially acknowledged that the current principal contradiction is between the growing material and cultural needs of the people and the relative backwardness of systems of economic production (Leng & Chiu, 1985). Economic development rather than the class struggle becomes the government's priority concern. The Central Committee officially declared that a strong legal system was in fact imperative for China's long-term economic development. [14] The 1978 Constitution revived the Procuracy and established the right to a legal defense in criminal cases. The Criminal Law and Criminal Procedure Law were enacted in 1979. The number

---

[14] Communiqué of the Third Plenary Session of the 11th Central Committee of the Communist Party of China, Xinhua Radio Broadcast, Dec. 23, 1978 (in English), transcribed in U.S. Foreign Broadcast Info. Serv. Daily Rep.: People's Republic of China, Dec. 26, 1978, at E4, E10 (No. 78-248).

of new courts built was around 200 in 1974, around 300 in 1979, around 400 in 1984, but was down to around 100 in 1989.

In 1993, the Chinese Communist Party set the creation of a socialist market economy as a major target of legislative reforms, and the first Session of the Eighth National People's Congress amended article 15 of China's Constitution to read "the state practices socialist market economy." The transition to a socialist market economy inspired a tremendous amount of progress in legal system development and reform of the Chinese criminal justice system. The reform first started with the creation of the rural contract responsibility system which greatly enhanced farmers' incentives and increased agricultural production; the gross output value of farming outputs increased more than 16-fold, from 111.76 billion *yuan* in 1978 to 1.96 trillion *yuan* in 2005. The economic reform also expanded into industrial sectors, leading to the reemergence and rapid growth of the non-public-owned sector which contributed more than 50% of China's total GDP annually by 2005 and 2006 (Liang, 2008). The number of courts built increased to around 200 in 1999 reflecting the close tie between economic reform and the effective enhancement of the judiciary.

In 2001 China gained admission to the World Trade Organization (WTO) and this event spurred the development of new legislation and the marked expansion of governmental administration and the judiciary alike in China. The market economy was formally adopted by the government for domestic and foreign commerce, and the legal system was improved in order to facilitate the promotion of economic growth. A series of revisions to laws and regulations were made on foreign trade and intellectual property, and requirements for transparency in administration and rule-making were put into place in preparation for entry into the WTO. It is widely agreed among scholars that the massive change that economic reform brought to the Chinese economy created a need for similarly massive change in China's legal system.

In the beginning of the reform and opening period, the main task for the judiciary was to establish an institutional system of People's courts and Procuratorates, and carry out the creation of the relevant trial courts and prosecution system. About 2,000 courts were established nationwide after the founding of the new China, and in order to meet the increasing need after economic reform the number of courts was increased to more than 3,000; that number has stabilized at 3,500 during the 1990s (Liang, 2008). After examining the trajectory of court establishment, the key role of political factors in court development is quite evident. For example, the advent of new governance priorities or announcement of new public policy pronouncement often involves calling for more courts to be built. However, the process of court development can be arrested when political tides change, as was seen during the Great Cultural Revolution. This development pattern of the Chinese judicial system finds its root causes in the intimate connection of the courts to the political bureaucracy system, a system within which the Chinese judiciary was born. The Chinese judiciary, nurtured for a very long time within a political bureaucracy, has never gained its independence from that system. The judiciary cannot decide its own course of development; it must rely on the powerful bureaucracy system, which itself can be overridden by the Chinese Communist Party.

With the expansion of the Chinese judicial system the internal structure of the court system has become more specialized and the number of people working in courts at all levels has increased greatly. In order to cope with evermore diverse types of cases, specialized divisions were duly established within the court system. The primary units created have been the economic disputes division, the administrative litigation division, and the criminal litigation division. (Liang, 2008). On the heels of economic reform the legal system in China was greatly expanded into the economic, political, and social domains of Chinese society. The Criminal Law and Criminal Procedure Law were enacted in 1979; the Civil Procedural Law (CPL) took effect in 1982; and in 1990 the new Administrative Litigation Law (ALL) was enacted and the State Compensation Law became effective in 1994. The burgeoning market economy and associated new social developments at the time made reforming the judicial system a high governmental priority. The Chinese courts became front line social institutions in the nation's effort to resolve new social conflicts, and in the process the judicial system was required to meet many new challenges.

Figure 4.1. The relationship between the numbers of new courts established each year and the political events (1949 to 2004)

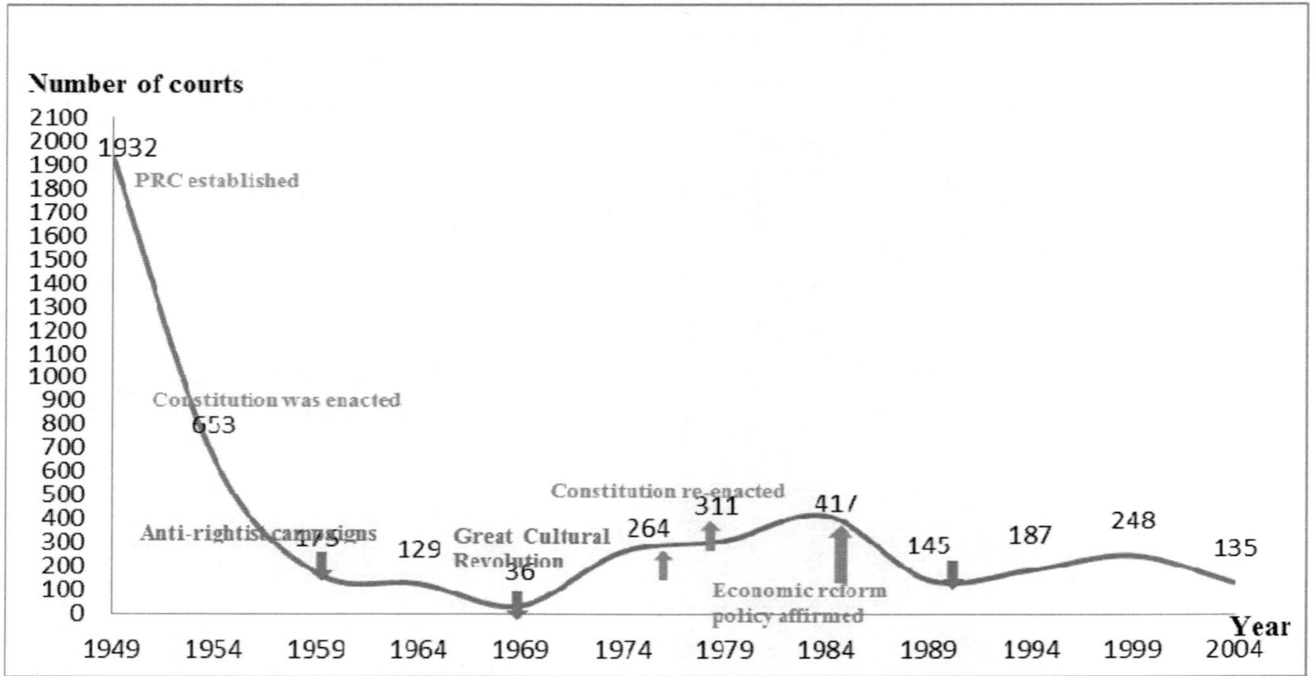

The total number of cases accepted by the courts in 1978 was only 447,755, but the number of cases reached 5,161,170 by 2005, an increase of more than tenfold in 27 years! The distribution of court case types also changed dramatically in this same period, with criminal cases representing more than 30% of all cases in 1978 but later representing only about 13% of total cases in 2005 (Liang, 2008). While great growth in the judiciary did occur, it nonetheless became obvious that the judicial system had not kept up fully with momentous social and legal developments occurring in modern China. The problem becomes more serious after 2005 as the pace of economic growth and urbanization continued to outstrip the enhancement of capacity in the Chinese judiciary.

According to statistics reported by the Supreme People's Court, there were 190,000 Chinese judges in 2006, and the number of cases processed was 8,555,000; there were 189,000 judges in 2007, and the number of cases was 8,551,000; there were 189,000 judges in 2008, and the number of cases was 9,839,000; there were 190,000 judges in 2009, and the number of cases was 10,545,000; there were 193,000 judges in 2010, and the number of cases was 10,999,000 (Zhang, 2014). This set of statistics indicates that the number of judges has kept relatively stable over this time period, but the number of cases has increased quickly. The chart below shows how the increase in the number of cases is much greater than the increase in the number of judges.

In addition, I collected population, economics and employment data from the Chinese Statistics yearbook (2006-2010)[15] for the same period. Table 4.1 compares the number of judges, number of cases, and GDP. Although the number of court cases, the national population, and the GDP are increasing, the number of judges has not increased correspondingly. Under such circumstances, the *administrationalization* of court trials is the most expedient way to handle a large number of cases with a limited number of judges. The administrationalization of court trial refers to the replacement of the content of the judicial system with administrative goals, structures, approaches, principles and effects, thereby turning it into a judicial system which is operating in a primarily administrative rather than adjudicative mode (Long & Yuan, 2014).

In order to meet the practical needs for efficiency and celerity, the progressive bureaucratization of the judicial system becomes the

---

[15] http://www.stats.gov.cn/english/statisticaldata/yearlydata.

current destiny for Chinese courts working in a country with a long history of centralized and hierarchical bureaucracy. Interestingly, each person growing up in China inevitably has to bear such a birth mark, and the court cannot avoid this aspect of Chinese culture. As part of state administration, courts are managed like any other of the many government departments situated within a hierarchical structure (Keith, Lin & Hou, 2013). How do the bureaucratized Chinese courts and the criminal justice system deal with this subservient status in criminal cases? The case studies set forth in chapter 5 will illustrate the long shadow of bureaucratization cast over the law and court trial processes in contemporary China.

Court Structure

Chinese courts are organized to precisely parallel the hierarchical structure of both the government and the Chinese Communist Party. The all-important Organic Law of People's Courts of the People's Republic of China (OLPC)16 was revised in 2006, and in that revised form states that the judicial authority in China is exercised by the following courts: local people's courts at various levels; military courts and other special people's courts; and Supreme People's Court (Article1 and 2 of OLPC). Special people's courts are tribunals set up by special institutions for deciding special cases such as military courts, maritime courts, railway transportation courts, and special courts of agriculture, forestry, oilfields and seaports. These special courts include only basic and intermediate levels of adjudication.

At the top of the court system is the Supreme People's Court (SPC), the highest judicial organ of the State. It supervises the administration of justice by the local people's courts at various levels and by the special people's courts, but it has no administrative authority over lower courts (Article31 of OLPC). The Supreme People's Court handles the following cases: cases of first instance assigned by laws and decrees to its jurisdiction and which it considers it should itself try; cases of appeals and of protests lodged against judgments and orders of higher people's courts and special people's courts; cases of protest lodged

---

[16] The English translation of OLPC is from lawinfochina.com, retrieved at 2/2/2012 from http://www.lawinfochina.com/display.aspx?lib=law&id=5623.

Figure 4.2, Number of Judges and Ruled Cases in Chinese Courts (2006-2010)

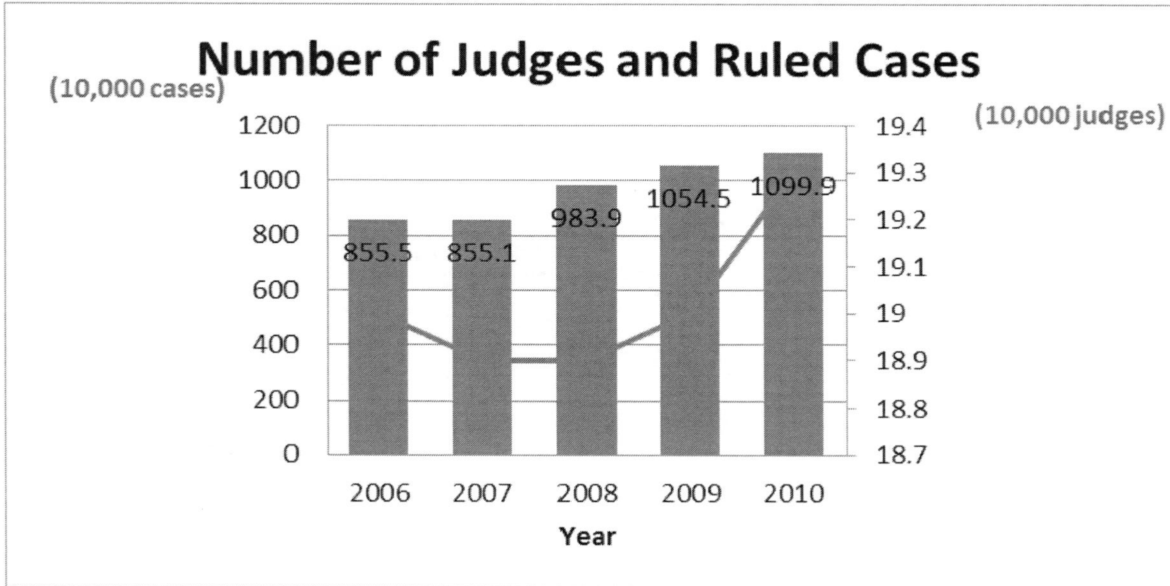

Table 4.1 Comparison of number of judges, number of cases, population, and GDP in China, 2006-2010.

Year	Judge number ×10,000	Case number ×10,000	Population ×10,000	GDP ×100 million *yuan*
2006	19	855.5	131448	216314.4
2007	18.9	855.1	132129	265810.3
2008	18.9	983.9	132802	314045.4
2009	19	1054.5	133450	340902.8
2010	19.3	1099.9	134091	401202.0

by the Supreme People's Procuratorate in accordance with the procedures of judicial supervision (Article 32 of OLPC).

Local people's courts at various levels are divided into basic people's courts, intermediate people's courts, and higher people's courts (Article2 of OLPC). The judicial work of lower people's courts is subject to supervision by the relevant people's courts at higher levels (Article17 of OLPC). The higher people's courts include higher people's courts of provinces, higher people's courts of the autonomous regions, and higher people's courts of municipalities directly under the Central Government. A higher people's court handles the following cases: cases of first instance assigned by laws and decrees to their jurisdiction; cases of first instance transferred from people's court at lower levels; cases of appeals, and of protests lodged against judgments and orders of people's courts at lower levels; and cases of protests lodged by the people's procurorates in accordance with the procedures of judicial supervision (Article 28 of OLPC).

Intermediate people's courts are established in the prefectures of a province or autonomous region, in the municipalities directly under the Central Government, in the municipalities directly under the jurisdiction of a province or autonomous region, and in autonomous regions (Article23 of OLPC). An intermediate people's court handles the following cases: cases of first instance assigned by laws and decrees to their jurisdiction; cases of first instance transferred from the basic people's courts; cases of appeals and of protests lodged against judgments and orders of the basic people's courts; and cases of protests lodged by the people's procuratorate in accordance with the procedure of judicial supervision (Article 25 of OLPC). When an intermediate people's court considers that a criminal or civil case it is handling is of major importance and requires trial by the people's court at a higher level, it may request that the case be transferred to that court for trial (Article 25 of OLPC).

Basic people's courts are on the lowest level of the contemporary Chinese court system, including county people's courts and municipal people's courts, people's courts of autonomous counties, and people's courts of municipal districts (Article18 of OLPC). Except for cases otherwise specifically provided for by laws or decrees, a basic people's court adjudicates criminal and civil cases of first instance (Article 21 of OLPC). When a basic people's court considers that a criminal or civil case it is handling is of major importance and requires trial by the people's court at a higher level, it may request that the case be transferred to that court for trial (Article 11 of OLPC). Besides trying cases, a basic people's court undertaking the following tasks: settling civil disputes and handling minor criminal cases that do not need to be determined by trials; and directing the work of people's mediation committees (Article 22 of OLPC).

The Staff System of People's Courts

The task of the people's courts is to try criminal and civil cases and, through judicial activities, to punish all criminals and settle civil disputes. In principle, the courts shall exercise judicial power independently, in accordance with the provisions of the law and shall not be subject to interference by any administrative organ, public organization or individual (Article 3 of OLPC). In order to carry out this function, the people's court has a staff system which includes a judge, a clerk, the judicial police, and administrative staff.

Judges as Civil Servants

In the U.S., people normally get appointed as judges only after a successful career in some other branch of the legal profession, such as in private practice, in prosecution, in public defense, or in law school teaching (Posner, 2005). In contrast, the Chinese judiciary is part of the civil service system and judges are "managed" as are all other government civil servants. Law school graduates freshly out of school can be employed by the court as a law clerk, and can expect to rise to assistant judges and higher as he or she gains professional experience (Posner, 2005). As employees of a quasi-executive branch Chinese judges are periodically elected and subject to recall by the NPC or local people's congress; they have no greater job security than any other governmental appointee (Clark, 2008). Moreover, the NPC supervises the courts' work by requiring them to submit annual reports, and the NPC deputies may also submit questions and queries to the courts.[17]

---

[17] Article 17 of the OLPC reads: "The Supreme People's Court is responsible to and reports on its work to the National People's Congress and its Standing Committee. Local people's courts are responsible to and report on their work

The Supreme People's Court is composed of a president, elected by the National People's Congress. Its vice presidents, chief judges, associate chief judges of law divisions, and judges are appointed or removed by the Standing Committee of the National People's Congress (Article 27 and 34 of OLPC). A higher people's court and an intermediate people's court are both composed of a president, vice presidents, chief judges and associate chief judges of divisions, and judges (Article24 and 27of OLPC). A basic people's court is composed of a president, vice presidents and judges (Article19 of OLPC).

Presidents of local people's courts at various levels are elected by the local people's congresses at corresponding levels, and their vice presidents, chief judges and associate chief judges of divisions, and judges are appointed and removed by the standing committees of the local people's congresses at the corresponding levels (Article 35 of OLPC). People's courts at all levels may, according to their needs, be staffed with assistant judges, persons who shall be appointed or removed by the people's courts themselves (Article 37 of OLPC). People's courts may also have elected people's assessors; these are lay citizens who are members of the divisions of the courts in which they participate, and enjoy equal rights with the judges during the period of the exercise of their functions in the people's courts (Article 38 of OLPC).

Other Staff

People's courts at all levels have clerks to keep records of the court proceedings and to take charge of other matters concerning the management of trials (Article 40 of OLPC). Local people's courts at various levels have Marshals to carry out the execution of judgments and orders in civil cases, and carry out the execution, in criminal cases, of the parts of judgments and orders concerned with property. Local people's courts at various levels have access to forensic physicians, and the people's courts at all levels have a certain number of judicial policemen working for the court (Article 41 of OLPC).

---

to the local people's congresses at corresponding levels and their standing committees. The judicial work of people's courts at lower levels is subject to supervision by people's courts at higher levels."

Functional System

The basic trial unit is the collegial panel. Cases of first instance in the people's courts shall be tried by a collegial panel of judges, or of judges and people's assessors; simple civil cases, minor criminal cases, and cases otherwise provided for by law may be tried by a single judge (Article 10 of OLPC). Appealed or contested cases in the people's courts are always handled by a collegial panel of judges (Article 10 of OLPC).

Collegial panels belong to different divisions within the courts. Different from the U.S. court system, Chinese courts feature diverse divisions, e.g. criminal division, civil division, economic division, etc. The Supreme People's Court , higher people's courts and intermediate people's courts all shall set up a criminal division, a civil division, an economic division, and such other divisions as are deemed necessary (Article 32, 27, 24 of OLPC). A basic people's court may set up a criminal division, a civil division and an economic division, and each division has a chief judge and associate chief judges (Article19 of OLPC). A basic people's court may set up a number of people's tribunals according to the conditions of the locality, make-up of the population and nature of cases heard (Article19 of OLPC).

Along with the advent of economic reform and the dramatic transition to a socialist market economy, the people's courts have become the major mechanism to channel social conflicts and disputes arising from dramatic social changes. In order to deal with diverse new issues, courts started to build various divisions as the total number of lawsuits in the courts in China since 1979 continued to increase in number and scope of issues brought for resolution. Since the OLPC states that the courts can establish divisions as are deemed necessary, the court divisions in question have become increasingly refined and complicated and often unique in make-up across the networks of courts. New divisions include such units as case-filing divisions, administrative divisions, juvenile divisions, intellectual property divisions, etc. In addition, some court divisions have established branches within them; for example, Shenzhen intermediate court has two economic divisions, and the 2nd economic division only deals with economic cases involving foreign trade. Some courts have set up sub-division; for example, the economic division may have a sub-division for real estate.

Besides the multiplication of divisions and subdivisions, the people's courts also set up many types of offices, including administrative offices, human resource offices, supervision offices, facility center offices, veteran cadres offices, etc. The Chinese Communist Party also set up branches across all levels of the court. Since 1995, the people's courts have been building a judicial police system which is in charge of court security and the enforcement of court decisions rendered. Judicial police now also carry out the death penalty on the rare occasions of its use. Along with the more detailed job division in the people's court, the number of staff working in the courts has increased dramatically, going from a mere 59,000 in 1978 to over 300,000 in 2008 (Liu, 2009).

From a positive perspective, the high degree of job specialization and diversity in the people's court can lead to improvement in judicial capacity. By expanding the courts' organizational capacity with more staff bringing a wide range of knowledge and skills, their capacity for action is increased. However, more divisions do not always increase the capacity of courts; the added offices and subdivisions may cause overlapping of functions and avoidable overstaffing. Courts have had to establish more administrative and supervision offices for the management of the division system, and divisions and subdivisions may develop jurisdictional conflicts (Liu, 2009). Due to the disassociation of adjudication from petition filing and from enforcement, cases often have to be examined multiple times by different divisions of the court; this can increase judicial costs (He, 2009). Over-refined division structures can lead to inefficiency and ultimately to a weakened judiciary.

JUDICIAL SYSTEM WITH CHINESE CHARACTERISTICS

Under the Leadership of the CCP

Article 126 of the 1982 Constitution (as amended in 2004) proclaims the principle of judicial independence from any interference by administrative, public, and individual organs. It holds that:

> The people's courts shall, in accordance with the law, exercise judicial power independently and are not subject to interference by administrative organs, public organizations or individuals.

However, it is not clear whether the Chinese Communist Party is included in the list as one of those organs that possibly can interfere with the independence of the Chinese judiciary. The Constitution upholds the single party ruling system and emphasizes the leadership of the CCP. According to the Constitution, the CCP possesses all powers of the nation, including the military. In reality, the CCP is found to have influence over the judiciary and the Party has continued to influence the nature of the judicial reforms to promote its interests (Qiao, 2005). People's courts set up local entities of the CCP and the courts are led by the committees of CCP of the corresponding districts. The judges are cadres who are selected, trained and managed by the CCP. The appointment of judges, especially high-ranking officials, is under the charge of the Party's local committees located in the jurisdiction of the courts.

In addition, the Constitution does not provide for checks and balances for such power, and the internal check system within the CCP has yet to prove effective. The CCP leadership not only determines the character of legal development in China, but the Party also affects how Chinese law is made, interpreted and enforced. It is argued that this phenomenon is reminiscent of traditional Confucian philosophy in that the success of the country depends on a leader rather than on a system, though in this case the rule of man (King or Emperor) is replaced by the rule of Party (Wang, 2008). The leadership of the CCP is structured from the central level down to the grass-roots level, secured through so-called "party branches" or party committees on the site of particular work units (Zhang, 2010). In almost every employment sector throughout the country, including major businesses and universities, behind the titular executive head there is a corresponding party chief who actually exercises ultimate control. In order to achieve party control over the practice of law, the Ministry of Justice (MOJ) makes it imperative that each law firm form either a party branch or set up some type of a quasi-party organization (Zhang, 2010).

The leadership of the CCP applies to both the legislature and the judiciary. Chinese jurisprudence is still framed in forms of the doctrine of Marxism, a doctrine which states that the law is a manifestation of the will of the ruling class, and holds that legislation is the process of turning that will into the will of the state (Yu, 2001; Shen, 2004). As China is a socialist country, the dominant class in the constitution is the Proletariat, and the CCP is deemed as the sole representative of the Proletariat. It is argued that the law in China is actually the expression of the will of the Party and the propositions of the CCP become the will of the state primarily through the legally constituted legislative process (Wu and Li, 2007). In China, the CCP holds the real legislative power; the legislature, the NPC and its Standing Committees must all follow the leadership of the CCP in their work (Zhang, 2010).

For example, in the legislative arena it is an unyielding principle that the Central Committee of the CCP must examine and approve all drafts of major laws of national importance. This principle was unequivocally announced by an internally circulated official document of the CCP's Central Committee (CCP Central Committee, 1991; Zhang, 2010). Virtually all laws passed by the NPC were pre-reviewed and ultimately approved by the Central Committee of the CCP (CCP Central Committee, 1991). In addition, the NPC is required to make maximum effort to ensure that all candidates recommended for various government posts by the CCP are both elected and duly appointed (Wu, 2009). The CCP also controls elections of delegates to the NPC. The direct election of delegates only takes place at the county level, and all other delegates are elected from the candidates recommended by the CCP (Zhang, 2010). Another provocative point is that among the delegates of the NPC, a vast majority are the members in good standing of the CCP, and all delegates who are CCP members must vote for whatever proposals the CCP has made for the NPC (Xia, 1998).

All courts in China are bound by a stated principle that the judiciary's work must adhere to the leadership of the CCP (Wang, 2009). A common practice in the early 1980s was that any case handled by either a people's court or a people's procuratorate would need to get approval from the party committee of government at the same level before a decision was made. This practice was repealed in September 1979 under the CCP's Instruction on the Firm Assurance of the Earnest Implementation of Criminal Law and Criminal Procedure Law (Wang,

2008; Wu, 2008). The lack of judicial independence affects the public confidence in the legal system because the general public still doubts that the current Chinese legal system is able to provide an unbiased result (Woo, 1999). Political and legal commissions (zhengfa weiyuanhui, 政法委员会) continue to exist in every security and judicial organization (public security, state security, justice, procuratorate and court) at every governmental level. These commissions are empowered to intervene in the major and most sensitive cases and court precedents, and adjudication committee leaders are tempted to consult with them before making difficult decisions (Cabestan, 2005).

Many presidents of the courts, if not all, are political appointees, and some do not even have the slightest legal background. A most recent survey reveals that among thirty presidents of provincial people's courts, fourteen are government officials with little or no legal training, fourteen have some work experience in legal areas (a few are formally trained lawyers), and two are from academia (Zhang, 2010). People's courts at all levels are directly under the supervision of the political and legal commissions of the CCP at their corresponding levels, and all major cases must be reported to such committees before a court judgment is rendered (Zhang, 2010). The Supreme People's Court recently adopted the "Three Supremacies" as its own guiding principle for all of the nation's courts: "the Cause of the Communist Party Supreme is supreme, the Interest of People is Supreme, and the Constitution Law is Supreme" (Hu, 2007; Zhang, 2010).

Localized Judicial system

Since there is no provision for a plea bargaining process, most criminal cases in China go to trial. This requires a significant deployment of public resources and is extremely costly to the nation as the number of cases brought to the courts continues to climb (Sheng, 2003). Since the Chinese judicial system has no centralized budget and financial allocation of its own, the courts are basically financed by the local governments within which they operate (Zhu, 2007). Consequently, the financial allocation for infrastructure, facilities, administrative fees and salaries of judges in people's courts at various levels competes directly with all other local and provincial government needs. The precarious financial condition logically requires courts to take into consideration relationships that are not laid down by laws, including possibly illegal relationships with the administrative organs at the corresponding level. The appointment of judges in local courts is also affected by local executive offices (Zhu, 2007). In addition, according to legal procedure laws, executive organs have the obligation to help accomplish the item relevant to law suits mandated by courts, so it is difficult for the trial and other activities of courts to strictly obey the provision of the Constitution as "not interfered with by any administrative organ" (Institute of Law of Chinese Academy of Social Science, 2001).

In recent years, the costs of the judiciary have increased beyond the allocation of money received from the local governments upon whose support the courts rely. As a result, many courts have established and implemented litigation fees to make up for their funding gaps, and some courts in remote areas have even sought to increase litigation fees by discouraging parties from withdrawing lawsuits, by stretching out or even ignoring jurisdictional rules, and by preventing parties from joining in class action suits so as to charge each plaintiff a separate filing fee (Peerenboom, 2008). The Chinese government is experimenting with a system whereby all litigation fees are sent to the provincial and central level, and then are redistributed through the finance bureau and high-level courts, and it has also increased central funding to the courts to a limited extent (Peerenboom, 2008).

Since 1999, the Supreme People's Court (SPC) started a five-year plan for reforming China's courts. The 2005 (covering 2004-2008) plan raises the topic of centralized financing of courts, but proposes no specific steps to be taken towards this goal. On Nov. 28, 2008, a proposal by the Central Legal-Political Commission to centrally fund all People's Courts was endorsed by the Chinese Politburo. If this proposal were to be implemented at some point in time a very important step in creating a more independent judiciary in the PRC would most certainly take place. Unhooking the Courts from the power and influence of their current paymasters, the local governments and Party organs where they sit, would provide for a substantially more independent judicial branch (He, 2009). This proposal has not been put into law as of this writing.

Institutional Dilemma of the People's Courts

Based on the Chinese Constitution, different levels of the people's courts are formed through appointment by corresponding strata of the people's congresses. However, the localized nature of China's courts also brings judges under the simultaneous influence of local enterprises and higher courts; local courts and their judges are often buffeted on all sides affected by the trials they conduct (Qiao, 2005). First, the courts' reliance upon funding and enforcement on the administrative system leads to their deep localization, and too often the local government departments, public enterprises, or private enterprises and influential individuals which provide services to the courts can intervene in the court trial (Qiao, 2005).

To make this issue even more complicated, the Chinese laws of litigation prescribe that the higher court can either order the local court to conduct a re-trial, or it can directly change the verdict rendered in the case (Article 136 and 138 of CPL). According to China's litigation regulations, if the re-trial or change of verdict is due to misjudged cases, the originating court's judges and chief judges will then be held responsible.18 The judicial system actually has to respond not only to the National People's Congress and higher court supervision, but also to various local government departments, enterprises or even well-situated individuals of social or political standing. This problem of judicial vulnerability to localized interests reflects a major constitutional issue which presents institutional obstacles to the unification of China's judiciary and the accomplishment of judicial independence at some future point in time (Qiao, 2005). The contemporary judicial system in China lacks an effective supervision mechanism, and it is very difficult for the Supreme People's Court to monitor compliance with procedural requirements in the country's local courts.

There are also internal pressures present in many judicial decisions. First, each court has a judicial committee which is provided

---

[18] In 1998, the Supreme Court made The people's court judges' accountability measure for illegal trial (人民法院审判人员违法审判责任追究办法（试行）). The people's court trial disciplinary measure (人民法院审判纪律处分办法（试行）).

for in Article 11 of OLPC. The task of the judicial committees is to sum up judicial experience and to discuss important or difficult cases and other issues relating to judicial work. The members of judicial committees of local people's courts at various levels are appointed and removed by the standing committees of the people's congresses at the corresponding levels, upon the recommendation of the presidents of these courts. The members of the Judicial Committee of the Supreme People's Court are appointed and can be removed by the Standing Committee of the National People's Congress, upon the recommendation of the President of the Supreme People's Court. The presidents of the people's courts preside over meetings of judicial committees of the people's courts at all levels within the system; the chief procurators of the people's procuratorates at the corresponding levels may attend such meetings, but they take part without voting rights (Article 11 of OLPC).

The internal managerial system in the court also discourages judicial independence (Clark, 2008). The president of each court is both the chief judge and the designee of the chief executive officer of the local government in question. The president has the power to influence the promotion and demotion of any particular judge serving on the court, and to actively supervise all judges through a formal reporting system. In most cases, the local people's court president is a political appointee designated by the local government. In addition, though cases are tried by a collegial panel, the panel's decision is subject to review by the adjudication committee consisting of the president, vice presidents, and division directors. Thus, the ability of the judge or collegial panel to reach an independent decision on a case is clearly very limited.

The Relationship among the Court, the Procuratorate and the Police

The Court, the Procuratorate and the Police constitute the three major agents in the criminal justice system of China. According to article 135 of the Constitution, the people's courts, the people's procuratorates and the police, in handling criminal cases, divide their functions, each taking responsibility for their own work. They are directed to coordinate their efforts and check each other to ensure the correct and effective enforcement of the law. Under the adjudicative model set forth, detention decisions must come after a trial in the court with all parties, including prosecutor, defendant, legal counsel, witnesses, experts and victims taking part. All parties have their opportunity to present their own aspect of the case before the court. However, adjudicated suspects are handled primarily by administrative bodies working under the authority of administrative rules rather than court procedures. Consequently, the detention decisions arrived at are typically a matter of policy, subject to social, political or economic exigencies rather than a matter of consistent application of rules as would be reflected in independent court decision (Yu, 2006).

The Public security organs (police) authorized by law possess a comprehensive type of power within the whole body of executive powers. Because Chinese courts have to rely on administrative organs for funding and trial decision implementation, public security organs often have much more power than their counterparts in other countries. The court is not the only state power in China which can take a suspect into custody, and there are a great many instances of lengthy administrative detentions. Administrative detention refers to any arrangement whereby an administrative official, rather than a judge, decides to detain a person in physical custody under a process not governed by the Criminal Procedure Law (Yu, 2006).

In China, there are 6 different types of administrative detention, including: (i) administrative detention up to 15 days (xingzheng juliu) under the Security Administrative Punishments Regulations (SAPR); (ii) re-education through labor (laodong jiaoyang or laojiao for short), which has received most of the attention abroad and within China, and was announced to be abolished over time in 2013; (iii) detention for education (shourong jiaoyu); (iv) compulsory drug treatment (qiangzhi jiedu); (v) forced detention in psychiatric hospitals; (vi) detention of juveniles in juvenile centers who commit criminal offenses (shourong jiaoyangsuo) or detention of juvenile troublemakers in work-study schools whose actions do not amount to criminal offenses (gongdu xuexiao); and (vii) stop and question (liuzhi panwen), whereby suspects may be detained for up to 48 hours of questioning (Yu, 2006).

In November 2013, the Third Plenum of the 18th Central Committee of the Chinese Communist Party (CCP) pledged to promote judicial openness and enhance human rights protections. The pledge states that China will optimize the allocation of its judicial functions and powers, improve the mechanisms whereby judicial organs share responsibilities, cooperate with and check up on each other systematically, as well as strengthen and regulate the legal and social supervision of judicial activities[19]. The third Plenary Session of the 18th CCP Central Committee also proclaimed that China will abolish the entire "re-education through labor" system.[20]

In summary, the preceding section has painted a picture of the courts in present China, including their structure and functional responsibility. Chinese courts are contained within a hierarchical system which is under the leadership of the Chinese Communist Party. Trial courts are localized, and operate without a budget allocation from the central government. Due to the lack of centralized fiscal support and the existence of both external and internal management systems, judicial independence cannot be said to exist in practice. Compared to the strong executive agencies in government, the Chinese judiciary is far from an equal branch of the state. Without court involvement administrative detentions can take place and an accused person can be detained in physical custody under a process not governed by the Criminal Procedure Law. Some noteworthy steps have been taken to reform the Chinese criminal justice system, and next I will discuss these in the context of a criminal justice system in the midst of a transition era.

CRIMINAL JUSTICE IN A TRANSITION ERA

Over the course of the last three decades China has carried out profound economic reforms, and the nation's GDP average yearly increase was 9.47% from 1978 to 2003 (Liu, 2005). This prolonged period of vibrant economic growth has undermined not only the economic planning apparatus of the past but also the associated social organizations which were part of the planned economy (Fu, 2011).

---

[19] Liu, Qiang. November 21th, 2013. China serious to honor judicial reform commitments. December 2, 2013 retrieved from http://www.china.org.cn/china/third_plenary_session/2013-11/21/content_30665686.htm.

[20] *Xinhua News*, November 19, 2013 retrieved from http://news.xinhuanet.com/english/china/2013-11/15/c_132891921.htm.

Rising crime rates are to be anticipated during periods of such dramatic social change due to the breakdown of traditional values, or heightened incidence of anomie in society (Durkheim 1893; 1897). High social mobility, urbanization, stratification and inequality provide ample opportunities and incentives for crime. Official statistics reported a more than three-fold increase of total crime, and a ten-fold increase in serious crime over the period 1979 to 1990 (Curran, 1998; Liu, 2005; Rojek, 1996; He, 2013). In 1978, the crime rate was 55.91 per 100,000; it reached 355.5 per 100,000 in 2005 (Zhang, Messner & Liu, 2008). This trend of rising crime rates has been steady over the course of the past 30 years. In this context of pervasive social change, a balanced criminal justice system is sorely needed, both to provide formal legal rights protection for individuals and to maintain political legitimacy. A series of legal reforms has been undertaken to address these public order and social dislocation problems.

Historical Development of Criminal Justice System after 1949

Chinese legal traditions are deeply rooted in history, pervasive in the culture, and social environment, and continue to influence the current legal system even though previous laws and judicial practices have been abolished by revolutionary change. The vicissitudes of dynastic transitions in Chinese history did not greatly affect imperial legal traditions wherein moral education rather than rule of law enjoyed priority attention; the court has traditionally not enjoyed independent judicial authority, but rather acted as a division of the imperial administrative Mandarin bureaucracy. The contemporary Chinese criminal justice system is heavily burdened with this long-established and deeply engrained tradition, imbued with a spirit of "partifying" during the KMT era and then with party direction continued into 1949. The Chinese criminal justice system in the Maoist period (1949-1976) was most clearly an instrument of social control, and there was neither a criminal code nor a criminal procedural code, let alone lawyers capable of providing for the defense of accused. In this period lawyers were virtually non-existent during that time period (Chiu, 1992).

Chinese courts throughout the 1950s, 1960s, and 1970s were predominately dealing with criminal cases. Crime, more than a violation of the criminal law, was viewed as a direct manifestation of class struggles between the Proletariat and the Bourgeoisie, and represented a challenge to the political order (Fu, 2011). Thus, the criminal law had long been an instrument used by the "people" against their enemies. Courts, as places and instruments of dictatorship, were used to fulfill the function of class struggle and class-based repression under the auspices of the Dictatorship of the Proletariat. Punishing counter-revolutionaries, both real or imagined, was the core judicial function during this period. Courts, as organs of the dictatorship, were directed to make certain that the work of the proletarian dictatorship would not be diluted and diminished (Fu, 2011).

During the period of the Great Cultural Revolution (1966-1976), the procuracy was abolished in the late 1960s and the functions of the court were usurped; the public security organs—the Police—increasingly took on the role of public order guardians at the expense of both the procuracy and the courts. Eventually, the People's Liberation Army (PLA) intervened to restore order and end the chaos created by the Great Cultural Revolution and adjusted many criminal cases without any direct participation of the established courts (Chiu, 1992; Ma, 2000). The 1975 Constitution confirmed the subordination of the judiciary to the administrative organs, and officially abolished the procuracy – transferring the prosecutorial function to the public security organs at the corresponding levels of government (Chiu, 1992).

In 1978, the 11th Central Committee 3rd plenary session of the CCP officially acknowledged that the current principal contradiction was between the growing material and cultural needs of the people and the backwardness of the nation's social production process (Leng & Chiu, 1985). Economic development rather than the class struggle was identified as the government's priority, and it was also officially proclaimed that a strong legal system was imperative for China's economic development.[21] The economic reform initiative first started with the advent of the rural contract responsibility system which greatly promoted farmers' incentives and enhanced agricultural production.

---

[21] Communiqué of the Third Plenary Session of the 11th Central Committee of the Communist Party of China, Xinhua Radio Broadcast, Dec. 23, 1978 (in English), transcribed in U.S. Foreign Broadcast Info. Serv. Daily Rep.: People's Republic of China, Dec. 26, 1978, at E4, E10 (No. 78-248).

The gross output value of farming increased more than 16-fold, from 111.76 billion yuan in 1978 to 1.96 trillion yuan in 2005. The reform next expanded into the industrial sectors, leading to the reemergence and growth of the non-public-owned sector which came to contribute more that 50% of China's total GDP annually, according to the official government data by 2005 and 2006 (Liang, 2008). Along with the vast scope of economic reform and dramatic improvement of the Chinese economy, the legal system in China started to revive and develop and mature as a social institution. The 1978 Constitution revived the procuracy and proclaimed the right to legal defense in criminal cases.

It was in 1979, after the 10-year "Great Cultural Revolution" that the Criminal Law and the Criminal Procedure Law were enacted. The Chinese Criminal Law and the Criminal Procedure Law of 1979 ended the history of handling criminal cases only according to police actions, public policies, special laws and regulations, and even experiences, or replacing law entirely by personal actions of individual with capacity to take action without relating to existing law or policy (Chen, 2010). Nonetheless, the Chinese legal system was extremely underdeveloped at that time, and both laws were enacted under general and simple principles. The 1979 Criminal Procedure Law consisted of only 164 provisions, with many issues not being precisely addressed. These laws still retained certain political elements of the past. For example, the concept of Marxism, Leninism, and Mao Thought were to be taken as a guide, and criminal punishments were to be used to promote the struggle against all counter-revolutionary and other criminal acts in order to safeguard the system of the people's democratic dictatorship and assure smooth progress along the course of socialist construction.

In alignment with the strictly planned economy and the highly centralized administrative model of governance, public security organs and prosecution organs were given strong powers and controlled the key functions of investigation and prosecution, with extensive and flexible authority to carry out those functions. With respect to defendants, the already weak accused parties were restricted in their ability to counter the strong investigation and the prosecution organs. Moreover, three divisions of the criminal justice system—the public security, the procuracy, and the courts— were all explicitly placed under the direction of the CCP party committee at the corresponding level of government. The party committees in question, appointed by the CCP's political-legal committee, in practice makes decisions as to arrest, prosecution, and sentence in all major cases (Chiu, 1992). To some extent, it is difficult to distinguish one criminal justice institution from the other in the jurisdiction handling the case since judgments about that case might have been made far before the official public trial by the political-legal committee in question (Chen, 2010).

In the 1980s the CCP acknowledged that China's socialism was still in a rather preliminary stage, and that the market was going to move from a supplement to the planned economy to become an organic component of the socialist economy. In 1993 the CCP set the creation of a socialist market economy as a major target of the party's reforms, and the first Session of the Eighth National People's Congress amended article 15 of China's Constitution, stating that "the state practices a socialist market economy." The transition toward a socialist market economy inspired a tremendous amount of progress in the Chinese legal system. In 1996, the Criminal Procedure Law and the Criminal Law were amended in line with democratization and scientification of the criminal procedure system, with reinforcement of the protection of personal rights. These reforms of criminal law and criminal procedure law signal noteworthy improvements in the criminal justice system of China.

The amendments introduced some adversarial justice elements into the Chinese criminal justice system. For example, the court no longer conducts or participates in any pre-trial investigation, and it is the Procuratorate that is held responsible for the validity of the evidence and for carrying the burden of proof. Under the revised CPL, the court's pre-trial role is limited to a procedural review of the materials submitted by the prosecutor, instead of a thorough pre-trial examination of the substance of the case. The court thus takes a decidedly more passive role, and the principal burden of producing evidence and arguing the case will now be assumed by the prosecutor; moreover, the defense counsel will have access to this evidence to frame a proper defense. However, some important issues remain unsolved. The presumption of innocence is not fully recognized, and there are not adequate safeguards against the use of evidence gathered through torture or any other illegal and improper means. Appeals are often more ritualistic than genuine, and the observance of defendants' rights is often at the discretion of the law enforcement bodies themselves without effective remedies for abuse of those rights.

Revised Criminal Law

The 1979 Criminal Law (刑法) was revised on March 14, 1997, explicitly in order to promote the democratization of Chinese criminal law and to strengthen the rights of criminal defendants. Certain progress toward democratization was made, though the effect on day-to-day practices which occur in the Chinese courts is still limited. The revisions have been depicted as a battle between individual rights protection and state power; between judicial power and executive power; between the judiciary and other agencies (this trend also exists in the revisions of Criminal Procedure Law). The Criminal Law has been revised through eight substantial amendments on December 25, 1999, August 31, 2001; December 29, 2001, December 28, 2002, February 28, 2005, June 29, 2006, February 28, 2009, and February 25, 2011.

These amendments add new types of offenses to control new criminal behaviors arising in the transition to a socialist market economy, and clarify crimes and gradation of criminal offenses. The death penalty has been eliminated for 13 offenses, and people of 75 years of age or older are excluded from death penalty consideration unless the accused caused the death of another person by extremely cruel means (Art. 17A, Art. 49, CL). Another amendment allows mitigation of punishment for defendants who did not initially voluntarily surrender, but who later confess truthfully, especially if serious harm is thereby prevented (Art. 67 CL). Another amendment eliminates a public record of conviction, with penalty of less than five years, for youth who commit a crime when under the age of 18 (Art.100 CL). Yes another amendment adds to criminal punishment with provision for community correction and prohibitions regarding engaging in certain activities, going to places or contacting particular people, parole regulations, an increase of minimum sentence requirements, and regulations affecting recidivists (Art. 38 CL).

One big point of progress in the revision of Criminal Law is the de-politicization of the Criminal Law; crimes such as acts of counter-revolution were replaced by crimes endangering national security.

Similarly, certain political terms have been removed; for example, references to Marxism-Leninism-Maoist Thought and the people's democratic dictatorship led by the proletariat and based on the worker peasant alliance have been removed. In March of 1999 the highly term loaded term "counter-revolutionary activities" was also removed from Article 28 of the Chinese Constitution and replaced by the phrase "crimes endangering national security."22 However, it is argued by some legal scholars that virtually all of the previous offenses coming under the heading Counter-revolutionary Crimes have been retained as Crimes of Endangering National Security, except for some minor changes, so that the term change is only a superficial one (Dobinson, 2002).

Second, the revision eliminated the practice of prosecution by analogy and stipulated that only acts which are clearly defined as crimes by the law shall carry criminal liability. This change reflected a genuine success of rule of law advocacy against rule by policy, and emphasizes the supremacy of law. By direct reasoning it means that everyone, including the Party and the Chinese State, is required to obey the law as written and in force. However, notwithstanding this noteworthy step forward punishment without law is still possible by the police through the mechanism of the Security Administration Punishment Regulations in China. The police in China are authorized to maintain social order through criminal detentions and arrests; they are also empowered to use administrative coercive means to either detain or shelter a person, or sentence a person to labor camp, all without resort to judicial procedures (Dobinson, 2002).

Third, the principle of all people are equal before the law appeared in the revised Criminal Law in 1997. Nevertheless, de jure inequality still existed in the 1997 Criminal Law. One example of such inequality is the difference between white collar crime and blue-collar crime. Officials who are charged with either corruption or embezzlement where the amount is between 5,000 and 10,000 RMB ($600 and $1,200 U.S.) may receive a lesser punishment, or even no punishment, if they return the money (Article 383 of 1997 CL); no such option is given to

---

[22] Six Amendments to the Chinese Constitution, People's Daily Online (Mar. 17, 1999), retrieved at http://english.peopledaily.com.cn/1999/enc_990317001002_TopNews.htm.

those that engage in blue-collar crimes such as fraud or robbery (Come, 1997).

In addition, such positive reforms as have taken place often have been largely undermined in practice due to deeply ingrained police and prosecutorial attitudes. For example, suspects may be allowed to meet with a lawyer as required by law, but either police are present in the room or the time provided is far too short to make the meeting meaningful for the lawyer preparing a defense. According to Article 306 of the Criminal Law, defense lawyers themselves are subject to criminal liability if they introduce false evidence at trial or assist in the fabrication of evidence. Statistics reveal that the percentage of criminal cases in which defendants are represented by counsel has been declining despite a continuing increase in the number of lawyers in China! According to the Beijing Bar Association, only 9% of criminal defendants in Beijing are represented by counsel, leaving the majority of the criminally accused largely fending for themselves in court (Sources: Beijing Youth Daily, July 2, 2003 and October 23, 2002).

Revised Criminal Procedure Law

In March of 1996 China's national legislature revised the Criminal Procedure Law (CPL), effective on January 1, 1997 (Zeldin, 2012). The first improvement made in the revised CPL pertains to pre-trial detention provisions (Luo, 2000). The administrative measure "shelter and investigation" which was used widely now is incorporated into the criminal procedure law with a maximum of thirty-seven days and formal arrest must be upon prior approval by the prosecutor. Nonetheless, the Police still have enormous discretion to hold suspected criminals and the courts play no role in issuing or reviewing detention orders. Only one among five pre-trial detention options is subjected to external check, that being arrest, which must be approved by the prosecutor. In practice, pre-arrest detention can in some instances last for more than a month. Detainees have no right of habeas corpus and bail, and the requirement to notify detainees' families of their whereabouts can be waived if, in the view of the police, this notification of family might hinder their investigation. There are still five distinct types of administrative detentions which are subject to no type of external review whatsoever.

The second improvement made is the expansion of the function of defense lawyers in criminal proceedings, especially at the pre-trial stage (Article 32-41 of CPL). Under the revised CPL, all suspected criminals are to be notified of their right to counsel when cases are transferred from the police to the prosecutor for a formal decision on whether or not to seek a trial, allowing more time for defense lawyers to prepare and present a more effective case on behalf of their clients. Courts are now required to appoint counsel for all defendants facing the death penalty. However, the police have the unreviewable power to block a suspect's access to counsel in cases involving ill-defined "state secrets" and the police can be present at meetings between suspects and their counsel. The revised law continues to allow closed trials in cases involving so-called "state secrets." Defense lawyers remain at a clear disadvantage relative to the prosecutor in terms of their ability to review case materials, gather evidence, and call witnesses notwithstanding these advances in the Criminal Procedure Law.

Third, the role of the court in the trial is strengthened, and now it is up to the trial court itself, rather than outsider, e.g. the court president in the prior law, to decide whether it needs to refer a case to this higher body. More importantly, the revised CPL eliminates the term "exemption from prosecution" and only a lawful court verdict can determine whether a person is guilty or not. However, the discretion of judges is limited by establishing maximum terms of imprisonment (Turack, 1999). The judiciary is not independent in terms of recruitment and funding, which are under the control of administrative offices and the CCP (Hecht, 1996; Peerenboom, 2005). A major form of non-judicial determination of guilt, "re-education through labor," is still beyond the courts' control. The good news on this front is that the third Plenary Session of the 18th CCP Central Committee in November 2013 decided to abolish "re-education through labor" over an indefinite period of time.

Despite clear signs of improvement the current criminal justice system in China, the system still features serious limitations. First, not enough financial resources exist because the courts are financed basically by local governments. Second, institutional capacity, especially with respect to judicial resources, is quite limited given the large number of criminal cases processed each year.23 The criminal justice process is more like an assembly line than a deliberation process in which quality control is greatly constrained by severely limited judicial resources (Fu, 2011). Finally, the extent of institutionalization of China's criminal justice system is far from ideal. The judicial process is still under the control of a political executive authority; the leadership of the CCP is above the law; the criminal trial is still a judge-led event with lawyers playing a relatively minor role, and the protection of for the rights of defendants remains weak.

With these serious limitation duly noted, it is important to acknowledge that positive factors also exist in the overall picture. First, judicial autonomy is growing; the criminal court is developing a professional identity and institutional interests which will enhance its ability to resist external interference into the judicial process over time (Fu, 2011). Second, judicial autonomy also inspires competence within the criminal justice system; the court and other institutions, such as the prosecution and the police, are developing higher standard rules on evidence produced at trial and gained through proper procedures rather than coercion, and they increasingly comply with these more firmly established rules. Third, the increasing competence of criminal justice institutions improves the fairness and overall commitment to due process through challenging the interest of the government to better protect the rights of the defendant (Fu, 2011). Fourth, the development of civil society institutions in China also contributes to the ongoing promotion of due process in the Chinese criminal justice system.

The legal system in China has some unique characteristics. The present Chinese courts are organized to precisely parallel the hierarchical structure of the government and the Chinese Communist Party. There is likewise not much difference between the judiciary and civil service in China; judges are civil servants and they are appointed and promoted by merit. However, signs exist of growing judicial autonomy, the development of a professional identity in Chinese courts, increasing competence within the criminal justice system, and a nascent civil society arising in China. All these developments contribute to the

---

[23] In 2009, Chinese courts accepted 768,507 first instance criminal cases (*Chinese Law Yearbook 2010*)

fairness and due process aspects of criminal justice in contemporary China. That said, it remains the case that the effort to achieve much fuller institutionalization of the Chinese criminal justice system faces many additional formidable obstacles, with the Chinese bureaucracy of a very long history being one of them. The case studies presented in chapter 5 will illustrate the ongoing impact of bureaucracy and pervasive influence of the bureaucratic culture on criminal case trials in contemporary China.

CHAPTER 5

The Chinese Criminal Court: Case Studies

The Chinese legal system was born within a powerful hierarchical bureaucracy. During Imperial times, the administrative officers took charge of all powers at their offices, including the judicial power. In modern times, political parties have replaced the Chinese Emperors, but this change in ultimate authorities did not fundamentally change the bureaucracy and the ruling system's influences in the judicial system. The Chinese judicial system, being so closely affiliated with the political bureaucracy system, cannot fully decide its own fate as it moves toward a more independent status. This chapter explores how the long history and culture of bureaucracy have greatly influenced the court and the processing of criminal cases. The method of case study analysis is used to develop insights into the administration of justice and criminal case processing in contemporary China.

CASE STUDIES

As discussed briefly in chapter 3, there was no separate judicial system in the Imperial era and executive officers held absolute power, including the judicial power. As a consequence, the Chinese people have been accustomed to seeking justice from executive officers rather than an independent court. In this chapter, twelve cases are discussed which all have gained national attention in recent years. These cases will illustrate the following key points:

1. How a culture of bureaucratization has not only affected the trial model, but also shaped the thinking of people involved in

criminal lawsuits (Case 1). The highly centralized political bureaucracy leads to absolute executive power which further weakens the legal system. The justice system can be manipulated by corrupt executive officials to pursue their personal/institutional interests (Case 2, 3, 4, 5). The judiciary lacks independence and strength to distribute justice and diverse forms of intervention on the part of the political bureaucracy persist (Case 6, 7, 8, 9).

2. Diverse types of actions emanating from the political bureaucracy can exert extra-legal coercive measures beyond criminal court control (Case 10, 11, 12).

What follows is the storytelling surrounding the cases, a legal summary of the case, and then an analysis of the significance of the case with respect to insight into the functioning of the criminal justice system of contemporary China.

Case 1—Zhu Ling

Summary

People who are deeply interested in the Chinese legal system would be wise to view a movie entitled "The story of *Qiuju*" made in 1992; the film was directed by *Zhang Yimou*. The movie depicts a Chinese village woman's attempt to use the legal system to seek justice for her family. Not satisfied after using the village or legal system to get justice for her husband, the woman whose name is *Qiuju* travels from one authority to another asking for someone to force her husband's attacker, the village chief, to apologize. Her futile attempts appear comedic to Chinese audiences, but leave American audiences scratching their heads in utter confusion.

Qiuju's pursuit of justice through executive authority rather than law is a rather normal Chinese phenomenon, the roots of which can be traced way back to ancient Chinese society. A fair and nice officer to distribute justice for ordinary people is one old Chinese dream, and Chinese people refer to this type of officer as "*Qing Tian* (青天)," literally meaning "blue and clean sky." The superior "blue and clean sky" is like a mirror to reflect the humble social status of ordinary people who only can kneel down to beg for justice from the authority.

Thousands of years have passed since this conception of a good authority came into being, but the thinking of ordinary people in China has not changed all that much. The culture of bureaucracy not only presents significant organizational barriers for the development of the rule of law in China, but also acts to color people's thinking. Most Chinese people today still rely on authority figures for justice subconsciously, and the Case of Zhu Ling is an example of this type of thinking. In this case, people failed to obtain justice from Chinese administration and then appealed to the distant administration of the U.S. The culture of bureaucracy has affected Chinese people deeply, even when they seek justice in another country. I start this story by quoting from a petition to the U.S. White House.

In May 3rd, 2013, an almost two-decade-old unsolved poisoning case (1995-2013) which happened in China has sparked a petition to the American government, and the petition exceeded the 100,000 signatures necessary for eliciting an official response from the White House. The petition reads as following:

> WE PETITION THE OBAMA ADMINISTRATION TO:
>
> Invest and deport Jasmine Sun who was the main suspect of a famous Thallium poison murder case (victim: Zhu Lin (g)[24]) in China.
>
> In 1995, Zhu Ling as a Tsinghua university student was found out to be purposely poisoned twice by lethal chemical: Thallium, which leads to her permanent paralysis. It was indicated that Sun, her roommate, had the motive, and access to the deadly chemical. Jasmine Sun was investigated by police as suspect in 1997. But resources show that the case was mystically closed due to her family's powerful political connections. Resources also show that she changed her name and entered USA by marriage fraud.[25]

---

[24] "g" is missing from the original text.

[25] October 12th, 2012 retrieved from white house website https://petitions.whitehouse.gov/petition/invest-and-deport-jasmine-sun-who-

The petition demanded the deportation to China of a woman who was investigated but not charged in connection with the case, and over 140,000 persons have signed this petition. This petition has been described as "hasty" and has been criticized for containing factual and grammar errors, and even the name of Zhu Ling was misspelled once in the title. Zhu's parents in China said that they do not support this petition and they still believe it is possible to resolve this case through normal channels. One of the normal channels in question which Zhu's parents have pursued for 19 years is to have the police, the Beijing Public Security Bureau, disclose its investigation file of this case.

The police investigation started in May of 1995 and continued until January 2006. The Beijing Public Security Bureau revealed to the media after repeated inquiries that their initial investigations had yielded a possible suspect. However, no one has yet been formally charged in connection with the case, and no official explanation has been given for the delay in releasing this information. The primary investigator, *Li Shusen*, told a correspondent from *Southern People Weekly* in a January 2006 phone interview that investigators have in fact reached some important conclusions regarding the case, but that the information was too sensitive to be released to the public at that time. Unable to pursue the justice they want from Chinese authorities, more than 100,000 Chinese people felt bad enough to petition to the U.S. government on the White House petitions website.

Analysis

Interestingly, as of June 2013 five of the six latest petitions on the White House petitions website related to China. Another such petition from Chinese web users demanded the Obama administration "remonstrate" with the Chinese government about a paraxylene (PX) project in *Kunming*, Southwest China's *Yunnan* Province[26]. There was a joke on Chinese twitter that the U.S. President Barack Obama had

---

was-main-suspect-famous-thallium-poison-murder-case-victimzhu-lin/Rd8C54p1.

[26] *Global Times News*, Chinese turn to White House website for help with petitions, August 10 2012 retrieved http://www.globaltimes.cn/content/780009.shtml#.UfA1g7HA8gA.

become the "head of China's petition office."[27] Some Chinese netizens stated that the opaque judicial system and a lack of credibility have caused people to petition the U.S. White House instead of resorting to Chinese legal channels; the U.S. petition website becomes an outlet for the public's long-term dissatisfaction with their government's internal policies.[28] At the same time, this type of petitioning also shows the traditional Chinese mindset for justice -- that is, rely on governmental leaders and the bureaucracy rather than a neutral judicial agent.

"*Chen Guangcheng* Escape" is a similar event related to appeal to U.S. authority. *Chen* is a blind Chinese civil right activist who had organized a landmark class action lawsuit against local authorities over the excessive enforcement of the one-child policy. He was arrested and went on trial. However, all three of his lawyers were detained by the local police and none of them can be present in the court to offer a defense for *Chen. Chen* was sentenced to four years and three months for "damaging property and organizing a mob to disturb traffic."[29] He was released from prison in 2010 after serving his full sentence, but remained under house arrest with ongoing police surveillance.[30] In April of 2012 *Chen* evaded security forces surrounding his home, escaped to Beijing, and found refuge in the American Embassy. *Chen*'s escape to the American Embassy is another example illustrating how Chinese ordinary people seek justice from authority, and the U.S. government serves the figure of "Blue and Clean Sky" in these cases.

---

[27] *Deutsche Welle News,* White House becomes the Petition Office and Obama is too Busy. August 10 2012 retrieved from http://www.dw.de/白宫成洋信访办奥巴马很忙/a-16798820.

[28] *BBC News,* May 6th, 2013, China poisoning case sparks White House petitions flurry. November 18th, 2013 retrieved from http://www.bbc.co.uk/news/world-asia-china-22445379.

[29] *BBC News,* August 24th, 2006, China Abortion Activist Sentenced. November 18th, 2012 retrieved from http://news.bbc.co.uk/2/hi/asia-pacific/5281440.stm.

[30] Chris Buckley, April 30th, 2012, China security chief down but not out after blind dissident's escape. November 19th 2012 retrieved from http://www.reuters.com/article/2012/04/30/us-china-politics-security-idUSBRE83T06J20120430.

Chen and those people who petitioned to the U.S. White House have been acculturated in the Chinese bureaucracy culture and it becomes natural for them to beg justice from a high administrative source. This case also shows that the Chinese judiciary lacks high authority and status. Even today's criminal court which is the beneficiary of some noteworthy improvements in status and capabilities is still affected by this habit of seeking out executive power. Next, three political cases are discussed which show how the processing of political cases is often handled through criminal trials in present-day China.

Cases 2, 3, 4—Wang Lijun, Bogu Kailai and Bo Xilai

The criminal justice system has been an effective ruling tool over the course of China's very long history; it has been used to control ordinary people rather than inhibit the exercise of power by high-level officials. As written in Confucius's *The Book of Rites*, criminal law cannot be applied to senior officials and the etiquette prescribed cannot be applied to common people (Liu, 1998). As a result, laws were to be enforced discriminately during the Imperial era. Since the 1970s three decades of ongoing reform and continuing opening up of society have not only brought great economic development, but have also occasional progress toward establishing the rule of law. However, people in China often complain that laws do not apply equally to everyone, and that law enforcement is often used to serve political or other purposes and is not associated with the promotion of public order or the fair dispensation of justice (Wu, 2009).

It is useful here to review cases involving high level officials and investigate the impact of politics on criminal case processing. First, we can see whether formal legal procedures have been followed in case processing. Second, we can see if there is a gap between the current criminal justice system and how these cases would be handled in the presence of the rule of law. In this section, I bring in three trials related to the *Bo Xilai* case which has attracted very wide public attention, both within China and abroad. On the one hand, it is a positive thing to see that some political cases now follow the formal legal procedure and that big cases which involved very high-level officials are becoming more open and transparent. On the other hand, the impact of politics on criminal cases can be documented clearly in those cases. The first case is that of *Wang Lijun* which represents the fuse bringing out the whole scandal. The second case is that of *Bogu Kailai*, *Bo Xilai*'s wife, who was convicted as a murderer. The third case is that of *Bo Xilai* which involved the trial of the highest level communist leader in three decades.

The First Chapter-- Wang Lijun

Summary

Before the blind activist *Chen*'s escape to the American Embassy another Chinese citizen entered the U.S. consulate, and that event started the biggest political scandal in China in recent years. On February 6, 2012, *Wang Lijun*, the former *Chongqing* police chief, went to the U.S. consulate in *Chengdu, Sichuan* province and spent more than 24 hours there. He reportedly revealed to U.S. officials details of corruption and murder involving his boss *Bo Xilai*, the Communist Party leader of *Chongqing*, a nearby city.[31] Among the shocking news that emerged was that *Bo*'s wife, *Bogu Kailai* (maiden name as *Gu Kailai*), had poisoned the British businessman Neil Heywood in a Chongqing hotel in 2011.

The Chongqing city government's news department said on its micro-blog site that *Wang* had gone on a lengthy leave during this time. The tweet reported that "It is understood that Vice Mayor Wang Lijun, who has suffered overwork and immense mental stress for a long time, is seriously physically indisposed. After agreement, he is currently taking holiday-style medical treatment."[32] It was reported that people had seen a large number of police officers who set up roadblocks outside the consulate.[33] After talks with Chongqing Mayor *Huang Qifan* inside the consulate, *Wang Lijun* left the building and was

---

[31] Lafraniere, Sharon, April 10th 2012, Death of a Briton is Thrust to Center of China Scandal. October 10th, 2012 retrieved from http://www.nytimes.com/2012/04/11/world/asia/detained-party-official-facing-ouster-from-politburo.html?_r=0.

[32] Bristow, Michael, February 9th, 2012, Chongqing policeman Wang Lijun mystery deepens. October 10th, 2012 retrieved from http://www.bbc.co.uk/news/world-asia-china-16958981.

[33] Ibid.

detained by Chinese security agents.[34] As indicated by the U.S. state department spokeswoman *Victoria Nuland*, *Wang* "left of his own volition."[35]

Wang Lijun became associated with *Bo Xilai* while *Bo* served as governor of *Liaoning* province and *Wang* followed him to *Chongqing*. On July 10 2009, *Bo* launched the *Chongqing* crackdown Campaigns against gangs, with *Wang* serving as his top enforcer.[36] During these crackdown campaigns, 1,544 suspects were arrested, including wealthy businessmen, government advisers, crime bosses and even some senior police officers (P. Wang, 2013).[37] This campaign had greatly helped raise *Bo*'s national and international profile, which promoted his potential political career in the Chinese central government.

Wang Lijun had a close relationship with both *Bo* and his wife *Bogu Kailai* until November 2011 when *Bogu* revealed to Wang that she had murdered the British businessman *Neil Heywood*. Though *Wang* recorded the conversation, he assured *Bogu* she will not be implicated in the case and tried to cover it up. In January, *Wang* told *Bo* that his wife is a key suspect in *Heywood*'s death and Bo responds angrily, slapping *Wang* in the face. *Wang* asks his officers to compile evidence related to the case, including blood extracted from Heywood's heart. A week later, *Bo* ordered the arrests of several assistants of Wang and reassigned Wang to a lower position. Fearing retribution from *Bo*, *Wang Lijun* went to the U.S. consulate on February 6th, 2012.

---

[34] Jeremy Page, *Wall Street Journal*, March 6th, 2012, Chongqing Mayor Reveals Role in Drama Outside U.S. Consulate. October 10th, 2012 retrieved from http://blogs.wsj.com/chinarealtime/2012/03/06/chongqing-mayor-reveals-role-in-drama-outside-u-s-consulate/.

[35] Michael Bristow, February 9th, 2012, Chongqing policeman Wang Lijun mystery deepens. October 10th, 2012 retrieved from http://www.bbc.co.uk/news/world-asia-china-16958981.

[36] Tatlow, Didi Kirsten, February 10th 2012, Gang-Busting Cop is One for the History Books in China. New York Times. October 10th, 2012 retrieved from http://www.nytimes.com/2011/11/03/world/asia/03iht-letter03.html?_r=0.

[37] Zhai, Keith and Choi, Chi-yuk, August 22th 2012. Focus: the Rise and Fall of Bo Xilai. October 10th, 2012 retrieved from http://www.scmp.com/news/china/article/1298386/rise-and-fall-bo-xilai.

Wang Lijun's case processing followed the formal criminal procedure to the letter. The National People's Congress Standing Committee announced the termination of *Wang*'s post as a deputy to the 11th NPC on June 30 2012. On July 22 Wang was arrested by the State Security Bureau of *Chengdu* for defection after the *Chengdu* Municipal People's Procuratorate approved the arrest. On Aug. 2, after the investigation was completed, the case was handed over to the *Chengdu* Municipal People's Procuratorate for examination before prosecution. On Sept. 5, the *Chengdu* Municipal People's Procuratorate filed charges against *Wang* with the *Chengdu* Municipal Intermediate People's Court. The *Chengdu* Municipal Intermediate People's Court held a closed-door trial for *Wang* on the charges of defection and abuse of power, because they touched on state secrets, and held an open trial on the charges of bribe-taking and bending the law for selfish gain.

Prosecutors and members of the defense counsel questioned the defendant in court. Prosecutors presented a good deal of material and documentary evidence, witness testimonies, defendants' statements along with incriminating video and audio recordings. The defendant and his defense counsel questioned the evidence. The prosecution and defense teams also debated issues, including facts, evidence and proper application of the law. Although this trial was not broadcasted live, state news agency *Xinhua* later published an article to report the details of *Wang Lijun*'s trial.[38] *Wang* was sentenced to 15 years' incarceration and deprivation of political rights for one year. However, *Wang Lijun*'s alleged abuse of power during the crackdown campaigns has not been investigated, and it is reported that those campaigns entailed routine lack of due process and observance of fair trial rights. In case 6, I will discuss a case in which a lawyer had gone through a distorted plea bargain process.

Analysis

The *Wang Lijun* case exposed several aspects of the contemporary Chinese legal system. First, the current legal system is under the control of local officials. *Wang* had to turn to the U.S. consulate for protection

---

[38] *Xinhua News*, November 19, 2012 retrieved from http://news.xinhuanet.com/english/indepth/2012-09/19/c_131861108_3.htm.

after he offended the local official.[39] Second, the magnitude of power that local law enforcement has is really broad and can be used to cover up crimes because no effective supervision exists. Third, local officials and their family members can manipulate law enforcement agencies and command the personal loyalty of police officers. These revelations show that an independent judicial system that can make horizontal and vertical checks on power does not truly exist in China.[40]

The Second Chapter – Bogu Kailai

Summary

As discussed in the *Wang Lijun* case, *Wang* had tried to help cover up the murder carried out by *Bogu Kailai. Bogu Kailai* (maiden name was *Gu Kailai*), the wife of *Bo Xilai*, the former party leader of *Chongqing*, was tried at the Intermediate People's Court in the eastern Chinese city of *Hefei, Anhui* province on Aug. 9, 2012. She and her household aide, *Zhang Xiaojun*, were accused of murdering *Bo* family associate *Neil Heywood*. The trial was attended by 140 people, including relatives and friends of the two defendants, relatives and friends of British victim *Neil Heywood*, diplomats from the British embassy and consulates in China, media representatives, members of China's legislature and political advisory body, as well as some members of the general public.[41] Prosecutors presented evidence and summoned forensic experts to testify, while the defense counsels of *Bogu Kailai* and *Zhang Xiaojun* conducted briefings for them, respectively. Legal representatives for the victim's family also presented their opinions.

---

[39] Hewitt, Duncan, September 24th, 2012, Wang Lijun's 15-Year Sentence May Clear Way for China's Leadership Transition. October 10th, 2012 retrieved from http://www.thedailybeast.com/articles/2012/09/24/wang-lijun-s-15-year-sentence-may-clear-way-for-china-s-leadership-transition.html#url=/articles/2012/09/24/wang-lijun-s-15-year-sentence-may-clear-way-for-china-s-leadership-transition.html.

[40] Ibid.

[41] *Xinhua News*, August 20th, 2013, Bogu Kailai and Zhang Xiaojun's Murder Case was Convicted. September 12th, 2013 retrieved from http://news.xinhuanet.com/legal/2012-08/20/c_112780986.htm.

Neil Heywood moved to China in the 1990s and met *Bo Xila,* the mayor of the *Dalian* city. *Heywood* introduced foreign firms to key officials, and helped the *Bo* family manage affairs in Britain where *Bo*'s son, *Bo Guagua* studied at Harrow. As *Bogu* stated in court, *Heywood* demanded millions in compensation for a deal he assisted with and had gotten into a dispute with *Bo Guagua* concerning the money. *Bogu* believed *Heywood* was a threat to her son's safety and she then lured *Neil Heywood* to a hotel in the southwestern mega-city of *Chongqing*. On the evening of November 13, 2011, *Bogu* drank with Heywood until he was intoxicated and then she poured poison into his mouth with the assistance of *Zhang Xiaojun.*[42]

After Heywood was dead, *Bogu* told *Wang Lijun*, the city's police chief, what she had done. *Wang* and his aides had tried to cover up this crime for her, but *Wang* recorded *Bogu*'s admission that she had killed *Heywood*. Four police officers from *Chongqing* went on trial in *Hefei* on Friday for assisting in covering up her crime. *Wang* confronted *Bo* with allegations against *Bogu* and soon received a demotion. Feeling threatened, *Wang* then fled to the U.S. consulate in *Chengdu* and this action unleashed the whole scandal of *Bo Xilai*. The trial lasted for about seven hours and was closed to international media. On August 20th, 2012, *Bogu Kailai* received a suspended death sentence, and *Zhang Xiaojun* was sentenced to nine years in jail.

Analysis

The *Bogu Kailai*'s murder case presents some implications about the criminal law process in China. First, she received help from a local police chief to cover up her crime due to her special status—namely, that of the wife of a local executive official. This shows that executive officials and their family members can get privileges in many perspectives, including in the legal system, most likely because the executive bureaucracy still can ride over the legal process. Second, four high-ranking police officials assisted with covering up *Bogu*'s crime, faking written testimony, hiding evidence, persuading *Heywood*'s family to accept the conclusion that he died of an alcohol-triggered heart attack, and cremating the body without an autopsy. *Bogu* herself was a well-versed lawyer. It is astonishing to see lawyers and police

---

[42] Ibid.

officers' defiance of the law and there is a lack of timely supervision over agents in the legal system. Third, although the trial was portrayed as being open, the detailed processing of evidence was not available to the public except for the brief news report issued. Because what the court describes as "solid evidence" is unavailable to the public to inspect, some court observers still had doubts on some of the details about the murder. The lesson to be learned is that cases involving high-profile officials should have more openness not less. In *Bo Xilai*'s trial, it is good to see the unprecedented openness permitted, though greater transparency could have been achieved.

The Third Chapter — Bo Xilai

Summary

July 25th, 2013, *Bo Xilai*, former Communist Party of China (CCP) chief of *Chongqing* Municipality, was delivered to the *Jinan* City Intermediate People's Court, *Shandong* Province and he has been charged with taking bribes, embezzlement and abuse of power, according to Jinan City People's Procuratorate.[43] *Bo*, 64, also formerly served as mayor of the city of *Dalian*, governor of northeast China's *Liaoning* Province, and China's minister of commerce. It is alleged by some political analysts that these charges are relatively narrow; for example, *Bo*'s anti-corruption campaign during his time in *Chongqing* government used the courts to stifle opponents and others, but this did not even get mentioned in the released charge statement.[44]

This case also followed the legal process as it progressed. *Bo* and his wife, *Bogu Kailai (Gu Kailai)*, were detained after *Bo*'s former police chief and close confidante *Wang Lijun* fled to the U.S. consulate in the nearby city of *Chengdu* and detailed for American diplomats a

---

[43] Wang, Yamei July 25th, 2013 Bo Xilai charged with bribery, embezzlement, power abuse. October 1th, 2013 retrieved from http://news.xinhuanet.com/english/china/2013-07/25/c_132572920.htm.

[44] Spegele, Brian, July 25th, 2013, China Indicts Former Senior Official Bo Xilai in Corruption Case. October 1th, 2013 retrieved from http://online.wsj.com/article/SB10001424127887323971204578627730368509700.html.

litany of allegations against the couple on February 6th of 2012.[45] *Bogu* was accused of being involved in the death of *Neil Heywood*, a onetime close family confidante who was found poisoned in a *Chongqing* hotel room. On March 15th *Bo Xilai* was been removed from his post as party chief in *Chongqing*; on October 26th *Bo Xilai* was expelled from parliament and this action removed his immunity from prosecution.[46]The Supreme People's Procuratorate passed the *Bo Xilai* case on to the *Jinan* People's Procuratorate on April 10, 2013; the *Jinan* People's Procuratorate instituted a public prosecution against Bo on July 25 on the three charges of bribery, embezzlement and abuse of power.[47]

Bo was alleged to have taken advantage of his position as a civil servant to seek gains for others, as well as accepting bribes worth about 21.8 million *yuan* (about 3.5 million U.S. dollars) directly or jointly with others; he was also alleged to have embezzled five million *yuan* of public funds and abused his power, causing major losses to the interests of the state and people.[48] *Bo* was informed of his legal rights and was interviewed by prosecutors and met with his defending counsel. According to the prosecution, *Bo*'s conduct violated Clause 1 of Article 385, Article 386, Clause 1 of Article 382, the first entry of Clause 1 and Clause 2 of Article 383, and Clause 1 of Article 397 of the Criminal Law of the People's Republic of China and he should be held criminally responsible for the three charges and be punished accordingly.[49]

Bo's trial started on August 22, 2013 and concluded on August 26 after 5 days, three days longer than expected. It is agreed that the trial followed the legal procedure and the defendant's legal rights were observed. The court approved all applications by *Bo* and his lawyers, guaranteeing them sufficient time to express their views. Neither judges

---

[45] *BBC News*, November 11st, 2013, Bo Xilai Scandal: Timeline. December 12nd, 2013 retrieved from http://www.bbc.co.uk/news/world-asia-china-17673505

[46] Ibid

[47] Ibid.

[48] *Xinhua News,* Xinhua Insight: Details of Bo Xilai's trial, October 1th, 2013 retrieved from http://news.xinhuanet.com/english/indepth/2013-08/28/c_125260515.htm.

[49] Ibid.

nor prosecutors ever interrupted or stopped *Bo* or his lawyers from speaking; even *Bo* agreed that the judges were fair and the trial procedure was both humane and civilized. When the investigation phase was complete, the prosecution and defense debated the facts, evidence and charges. Both sides expressed views on the facts, the evidence and the law, and both sets of attorneys questioned the defendant.

During the trial, *Bo* not only denied the evidence, but overturned his handwritten confession. The prosecutors stated that the charges were filed on the basis of a large body of factual evidence, rather than solely on his confession. Prosecutors observed that the defendant failed to provide evidence that could help refute the facts regarding his charges and expressed numerous conflicting statements during his defense. Based on the 7th Amendment and judicial interpretation regarding corruption by using the influence of public officer (2009),[50] the crime of taking a bribe can be prosecuted if factual evidence proves that the bribers have given the bribe to *Bo*'s family even though he denied he knew this.

It is not credible that *Bo* described his pre-trial confession to accepting massive amounts of money as having been obtained through unjust pressure and improper coaxing.[51] He might forget the torture cases found among *Chongqing* crackdowns on organized crime and the "anti-black" (*da hei, 打黑*) activities which took place while he was as the local communist party leader from 2009 to 2011. For example, one of the *Chongqing* torture victims, *Fan Qihang*, had been driven to attempt suicide by months of pre-trial torture.[52]

Analysis

Bo's five-day trial displayed the elements of neutrality and transparency. The trial was unprecedentedly open. First, about 110

---

[50] The Complement Regulation on New Crime Names, October 1th, 2013 retrieved from http://www.law-lib.com/law/law_view.asp?id=299478.

[51] He, Wefang, August 29th, 2013, Bo Xilai trial was a satire, but still helped to further rule of law in China, October 1th, 2013 retrieved from http://www.csmonitor.com/Commentary/Global-Viewpoint/2013/0829/Bo-Xilai-trial-was-a-satire-but-still-helped-to-further-rule-of-law-in-China.

[52] Ibid.

people attended the trial in the actual courtroom. Second, the court kept updating the trial and trial transcript on its official *Weibo* (Chinese microblogging site) where over 100 people were hearing the trial in the peak time. The court had tweeted more than 110 *Weibo* posts, including many transcripts, pictures and audio and video files of evidence, and many of those posts were re-tweeted thousands of times.[53]

Second, it is the first time that a Chinese court published its trial transcript for the public to inspect. This used to be considered a trial secret and even the lawyers arguing the case could not make a copy. Although some screening of content was done, it appears that most of the utterances made in court were published.

Third, significant witnesses testified in court and their testimony and videos of witnesses were also posted for the public to see. It is rare to see witnesses testify in bribery criminal cases in court; *Bo*'s trial presented a good model for witnesses to testify in court. Witnesses *Xu Ming*, chairman of *Dalian Shide Group Co. Ltd.*, *Wang Zhenggang*, then director of the *Dalian* municipal bureau of urban and rural planning and land, and *Wang Lijun*, former vice mayor of *Chongqing*, appeared to testify in court. Both the prosecution and defense cross-examined the witnesses. Compared to the *Hefei* trial of *Bogu Kailai* and the *Chengdu* trial of *Wang Lijun*, this was a major improvement. Prosecutors played video recordings of *Bo*'s wife *Bogu Kailai* and *Tang Xiaolin*, general manager of *Dalian* International Development Co. Ltd., and presented evidence including documents and audio-video materials, witnesses' testimony, and the confession and arguments of the defendant.

Fourth, the major parties of the trial, including the judges, the public prosecutor and defense counsel, behaved professionally and the defendant's right to speak in his own defense was protected to a considerable degree. It is fair to see that this trial showcased a high level of professionalism of the principal agents in the Chinese legal system.

---

[53] *Xinhuanet News*. August 24th, 2013. Microblogging Bo's trial hailed as historic transparency. December 3, 2013 retrieved from http://news.xinhuanet.com/english/china/2013-08/24/c_132659965.htm.

However, some noteworthy drawbacks are also obvious from a review of this case. First, the scope of crimes indicted by the Procuratorate of *Jinan* was constrained by the Commission for Discipline Inspection in terms of strict adherence to legal criteria. For the same reason, the public prosecutor and the collegiate bench judges were not able to investigate certain issues thoroughly and the proceedings blurred when these issues arose during the trial. For example, the defense lawyer argued that *Heywood* had demanded 14 million pounds from *Bo Guagua* (*Bo Xilai*'s son) as a commission on a project, and this was unrelated to the house involved in the case. This actually is a very good clue to investigate the *Bo* family's other alleged financial crimes, to find what kind of a transaction could generate such a huge commission and further to find the true motives behind *Bogu Kailai*'s murder of *Neil Heywood.* All these questions should have been thoroughly investigated in accord with strictly legal criteria, but the public prosecutor let the opportunity to do so to pass for some reason.

Another example is that *Bo Xilai* explained that he had hit *Wang Lijun* because of an improper relationship between Wang and *Bogu Kailai.* The court should probe into exactly what type of relationship existed between them, whether it was improper, and what kinds of business transactions occurred during that period. This information may also be related to what actually transpired for *Bogu Kailai* to have killed *Neil Heywood.* However, the court did not pursue this dimension either.

Second, many witnesses who should have appeared in court did not appear, and all of the witnesses who did appear in court were witnesses for the prosecution. No witnesses for the defense appeared, and none of the written evidence laid out in court was favorable to the accused. Also, *Bo Xilai* clearly said in court that he twice applied for *Bogu Kailai* to testify in court, but these applications were denied by the presiding judge because Article 188 of the Criminal Procedural Law stipulates that relatives cannot be forced to testify in court. Of course, it is known that the legal right protected by this regulation is the value of the ethical relationship between relatives, but the public broadcasting of *Bogu*'s testimony on site showed that *Bogu* had already agreed to testify via video. It seemed that whether or not to appear in court was only a technical difference, but her not appearing in court made it impossible to repeatedly confront the many things that touched upon the guilt or innocence of the accused.

Third, the duration of the entire trial was too brief given the complexity of circumstances involved in this case, especially when the trial already exposed some clues which had not been thoroughly investigated by the prosecutors. Fourth, the trial's transparency was somewhat limited. *Bo*'s trial lacked independent observers -- *Bo*'s family, government officials, and a handful of pre-approved journalists were allowed into the courtroom -- while foreign media were excluded. Foreign media were relegated to a hotel across the street, without permission to attend the trial. The information publicly disclosed by the court was likely to have been edited. Some commentators characterized the trial as "selective transparency."[54] In addition, Bo was prevented from using his own lawyers, and it is likely the sentence was probably decided at a higher level of the government and party.[55]

In September 22, 2013 the *Jinan* intermediate People's Court handed down its verdict on the *Bo Xilai*'s case. *Bo* was found guilty on all charges, sentenced to life in prison, and stripped of all political rights for life after being convicted of bribery, embezzlement and the abuse of power. He did appeal to the *Shandong* provincial High Court on both his sentence and conviction. The High Court rejected his appeal and upheld the original verdict. Some commentators thought that *Bo*'s verdict was harsher than expected, and suspected that *Bo*'s denial of guilt and strong self-defense may have broken a deal made during the case, leading to this harsh verdict.[56] It is speculated that the sentence was probably decided at a higher level and that it reflected a political battle which *Bo* lost rather than a case just being targeted for

---

[54] Lai, Alexis, August 27, 2013, Was Bo Xilai's trial in China truly transparent? October 1th, 2013 retrieved from http://www.cnn.com/2013/08/26/world/asia/china-bo-xilai-trial-transparency/index.html

[55] Yang, Sunny, September 22, 2013, Bo Xilai—China Corruption Verdict. October 1th, 2013 retrieved from http://www.usatoday.com/story/news/world/2013/09/21/bo-xilai-china-corruption-verdict/2848003.

[56] Ibid.

corruption.[57] When *Bo* was expelled from the CCP in September of 2012, the decision of the Political Bureau of the CCP Central Committee stated that Bo seriously violated Party discipline, abused his power, made erroneous decisions in the promotion of personnel, received huge bribes, maintained improper sexual relationships with a number of women, and was involved in other crimes. However, in the end *Bo* was ultimately only charged with bribery, embezzlement and abuse of power offenses.

Case 5—Zhou YongKang

<u>Summary</u>

Zhou YongKang, who first started as a technician in the oil and gas industry, later became the senior leader of the Chinese Communist Party for more than ten years. He served as the Minister of Public Security from 2002 to 2007, and was promoted to the Standing Committee of the Politburo (SCP) in 2007. The SCP is the elite seven-member team that makes decisions guiding the entire country. He also was the Secretary of the powerful Central Political and Legal Affairs Commission (*ZhongYangZhengFaWeiYuanHui 中央政法委*) over the period 2007-2012, and he became the top official responsible for China's courts, law enforcement, prosecution agencies, paramilitary forces, and domestic intelligence agencies. *Zhou YongKang* enjoyed a close relationship with *Bo XiLai*. In 2012, following the days of *Bo*'s falling, *Zhou* relinquished the operational control of the Central Political and Legal Affairs Commission due to his broadly known support for and close connection to *Bo XiLai.*[58]

Although *Zhou* retired in November 2012, the corruption investigation on him started in August of 2013. This is the first time that an investigation was initiated against a member of the elite Politburo Standing Committee in China. A number of *Zhou*'s former subordinates with high-ranking positions were investigated and suspended soon afterward. On July 29, 2014 an internal party investigation against *Zhou Yongkang*'s violations of party discipline

---

[57] Ibid.

[58] Anderlini, Jamil, May 14, 2012, Bo ally gives up China security roles, *Financial Times.*

was formally announced.[59] The party investigation concluded that *Zhou* abused his power for the illicit gain of his family, friends, and associates, took "large amounts in bribes personally and through his family and associates; abused his power to further the interests of his family, mistresses, and associates; committed adultery with multiple women, and engaged in the exchange of money and favors for sex; and leaked state and party secrets.[60] Zhou was arrested on December 5, 2014 and was expelled from the Party. In April of 2015, *Zhou Yongkang* was formally charged with abuse of power, bribery, and intentionally leaking state secrets and was sentenced to life in prison.[61] *Zhou*'s trial was not open to the public.

<u>Analysis</u>

First, *Zhou*'s corruption case again shows that corruption and malfeasance in China is not relegated to a few individuals, but is rather an endemic problem. The deep root of this endemic corruption is the Chinese political bureaucracy. *Zhou* had formed a substantial network of collaborators and relied on it for his power and for amassing personal profits. Just as old bureaucrats in different dynasties used their positions in the large government bureaucracy to build up relationship circles and gain profits, he did so on contemporary conditions of governance in today's China. Chinese bureaucrats nowadays are doing the same thing within the party hierarchy and within the government bureaucracy has was commonplace in the past.

Zhou's relationship circles were very comprehensive, featuring four layers (Fewsmith, 2015). First, his immediate family and other

---

[59] Wen, Philip, June 30th, 2014. *The Sydney Morning Herald,* Xi Jinping's purge claims the biggest scalp yet: Zhou Yongkang, October 10th, 2014 retrieved from http://www.smh.com.au/world/xi-jinpings-purge-claims-the-biggest-scalp-yet-zhou-yongkang-20140729-zybsz.

[60] *Xinhua News*, December 6th, 2014. Official Xinhua announcement on the outcome of internal investigation on Zhou Yongkang, December 10th, 2014 retrieved from http://news.xinhuanet.com/politics/2014-12/06/c_1113542222.htm.

[61] *Xinhua News*, April 3, 2015. Zhou Yongkang charged with bribery, abuse of power, intentional disclosure of state secrets. April 3, 2015 Retrieved from http://news.xinhuanet.com/english/2015-04/03/c_134122389.htm.

family members were involved in the corruption by utilizing *Zhou*'s position. Second, the relations were cultivated during *Zhou*'s many years in the oil industry, a sector which has gained huge political power in China. The third layer is composed of *Zhou*'s current and former secretaries. These secretaries had been promoted to high positions in many cases. The fourth layer is the relationships *Zhou* built up during his tenure as the *Sichuan* province party secretary from 1990 to 2002. These circles again indicate a major characteristic of Chinese bureaucracy—namely, officials are not separated from their positions, and they can accumulate personal wealth through work due to a general blurring of distinctions between private and public resources (Will, 2012, p. 10). They use their positions to promote their confidants, build up tight circles of relationships, and gain more power and profits over time. These circles are nurtured within the Chinese bureaucracy, and in time the entire bureaucracy becomes a hotbed of corruption.

Second, overseas media compared this closed trial to *Bo Xilai*'s unusually open trial, and speculated on the reasons behind the difference. Some claimed it as a leap backwards and worried that the rule of law development is regressing in China.[62] Cohen suggested that *Zhou* may have bargained with skill since he is quite familiar with the Chinese legal system.[63] Another reason suggested by Cohen is that the embarrassment to the CCP from an open trial may outweigh any positive publicity and educational value a public trial might offer.[64] No matter what is the real reason, this case shows that the party's interest may override the system and adherence to criminal legal procedure. An unusually open trial can be given to *Bo*'s trial, but an open trial can be

---

[62] Tong, Bao, June 17th, 2015. *Free Asia Radio,* Why Zhou Yongkang's Secret Trial Was a Great Leap Backwards, October 10th, 2015 retrieved from http://www.rfa.org/english/commentaries/baotong/why-zhou-yongkangs-secret-trial-was-a-great-leap-backwards-06172015110317.html.

[63] Cohen, Jeromy, July 7th, 2015. *South China Morning Post,* Why was Zhou Yongkang denied a public trial like Bo Xilai's? August 10th, 2015 retrieved from http://www.scmp.com/comment/insight-opinion/article/1833353/why-was-zhou-yongkang-denied-public-trial-bo-xilais.

[64] Ibid.

declined for another case. The rule of law is only a distant dream if the law is not consistently followed in the criminal justice system.

Third, *Zhou* was the top security official and the secretary of Central Political and Legal Affairs Commission for many years, and his treatment also implies the downgrading position of this commission. The Central Political and Legal Affairs Commission, an important part of the party, controls the justice system. It has high status in the Chinese political hierarchy, and its top official used to be the principal member of the Politburo standing committee, China's highest decision-making organ. The officials of its local branches were also the core members of local governments and party commissions. However, interestingly *Zhou*'s successor was not granted a seat on China's all-powerful Politburo Standing Committee.[65]

The speculation widely made is that this change took place is to avoid having certain members in the committee possess too much power. On the Provincial level, police chiefs are also losing their positions as top officials of regional Political Legal Committees governing the courts, the police and prosecutors, as well as their spots on the party's regional Standing Committees. Although scholars disagree on the reasons behind this change, this change will contribute to the balance of powers in the justice system and will be helpful to get the police under greater legal control.

Case 6—Li Zhuang

<u>Summary</u>

Li Zhuang, a lawyer, was sentenced to eighteen months for perjury after his client, a suspected gangster, reported to the police that *Li* incited him to lie to the court in stating falsely that police officers tortured him during his interrogation. This case attracted the attention of lawyers across China who supported *Li* publicly, and criticized the *Chongqing* government heavily for its action. This case also gave a taste of the distorted "plea bargain" process which takes place in some Chinese criminal cases.

---

[65] *BBC News*, November 22nd, 2012, China leaders reassert control over security portfolio, June 25th, 2014 retrieved from http://www.bbc.com/news/world-asia-china-20422303.

As was discussed in the *Bo Xilai*'s case, *Chongqing*, during the time from 2009 to 2011 when *Bo Xilai* was as the local communist party leader, had undertaken a series of feverish crackdowns on organized crime called the "anti-black" initiative (*da hei, 打黑*) through which *Bo* was able to establish a national reputation and gain promotion to the Politburo of the CCP. During the course of the *da hei* from 2009 to 2011, 4,781 people were arrested, among them known gang members, several police and governmental officials, some judges, and a former deputy police commissioner (Johnson and Loomis, 2013). Among the arrested was *Gong Gangmo*, a local businessman, who was charged with organized crime activities, murder, illegal trading, the purchasing of firearms, drug trafficking, and extortion. *Gong* was detained on June 20, 2009 and *Li Zhuang*, a lawyer specializing in criminal defense from the renowned Beijing *Kangda* Law Firm, was Gong's defense lawyer. *Li Zhuang* and his assistant, *Ma Xiaojun* met Gong on Nov. 24, 26, and Dec. 4. *Li* had arguments with the police officers who insisted on being present during the interviews, and *Gong* told *Li* that he had been intermittently tortured for eight days at their first meeting.[66]

However, on Dec. 10 *Gong* reported to police that *Li* encouraged him to lie in court by testifying that he was tortured during his interrogation. It is believed that *Gong* reached a bargain with the police that this allegation could get him out of the death penalty (Luo &He, 2012; Huang, 2012).[67] *Gong* later claimed that he turned on *Li* because he wanted to gain sufficient credit to avoid the death penalty.[68] *Li* was

---

[66] Lim, Louisa, March 27th, 2012. Abuse Claims Follow Mafia Crackdown in Chinese City, July 27th, 2013 retrieved from http://www.npr.org/2012/03/27/149467544/in-chinas-crime-crackdownclaims-of-abuse4.

[67] Huang, Shiyuan, March 31 2012 'Li Zhuang: Chinese Defense Lawyer Who Was Found Guilty of Suborning Perjury, July 27, 2013 retrieved from http://wrongfulconvictionsblog.org/2012/03/31/li-zhuang-chinese-defense-lawyer-who-was-found-guilty-of-suborning-perjury.

[68] Eberlein, Xunjun, January 5, 2010 Lawyer's Trial Rivets Public and tests Chinese Courts, July 27, 2013 retrieved from

arrested on Dec. 13 for subornation of perjury and was brought to trial before the *Chongqing Jiangbei* Court on Dec. 30. *Li Zhuang* first requested that the *Jiangbei* District People's Court, the Procuracy, and all their associates abstain from the case. His requests were either denied or ignored. *Li* testified that *Gong* had shown him wrist wounds and told him that police had strung him up for eight days, and the written testimony of a medical expert indicated that the bruise on *Gong*'s left wrist was caused by a blunt instrument (Huang, 2012). The *Chongqing* police testified that the *Chongqing* Detention Center's audio and video records showed that *Li* had tried to persuade Gong to give false testimony. However, the prosecutor did not present these records during the trial and the detention center claimed that it has no audio and video equipment. Instead, the prosecutor read written statements of eight witnesses to prove *Li*'s guilt. *Li* requested of the bench that these witnesses appear in court to be cross-examined, but his request was denied once more. On Jan. 8, 2010, *Li* was found guilty and sentenced to two and a half years imprisonment. *Li* firmly denied his guilt and appealed the verdict to the intermediate court.

The second instance hearing was not only open to the public, but it also featured six criminal suspects that included *Gong* and two police officers who appeared in court as witnesses. In addition, the *Chongqing* authorities invited representatives of the People's Congress, the People's Political Consultative Conference and the Beijing Lawyers Association, along with reporters from about 20 media outlets, and faculty and students from local universities to observe the hearing. Surprisingly, *Li* declared that he was guilty in the court hearing (Liu, Liang & Halliday, 2014). On February 9, the *Chongqing* No. 1 Intermediate People's Court upheld the charges from the first trial, but reduced the original sentence from two and an half years to 18 months. Upon hearing the verdict, *Li* exclaim that he was cheated by the bargain made with the Police:

> My earlier admissions were forced. I was forced to do it. The police and procuracy said they'd reduce my sentence to probation if I admitted to [wrongdoing]. They said if I pleaded

---

http://newamericamedia.org/2010/01/lawyers-trial-rivets-public-and-tests-chinese-courts.php.

> guilty, then the second hearing would be an open trial. And still I'm sentenced. If you read my written confession carefully, you would see I was just deceiving the police and procuracy. (Liu, Liang & Halliday, 2014, p9).

Li Zhuang said that his written confession was actually a "hidden poem" in which the first and last Chinese characters of each sentence of *Li*'s confession formed the anagram "[I was] forced to admit guilty to get probation, once released [I would] firmly appeal" (*beibi renzui huanxing, chuqu jianjue shensu, 被逼认罪缓刑, 出去坚决申诉).* Six months after his release from prison, *Li Zhuang* revealed in his blog the story of his confession.[69] As a defense technique, *Li* proposed to a high-ranking public security official after the first trial that he would confess to his crime if the second trial could be opened to the public and he could get probation as the final sentence. This proposal was welcomed by the *Chongqing* authorities who thought that it would mitigate some of the procedural problems which arose during *Li*'s first hearing and change the unfavorable public opinions circulating at the time (Liu, Liang & Halliday, 2014). *Li* said that the authorities involved had promised to let him walk free if he said he was guilty.[70]

Because *Li* did not fully trust the *Chongqing* authorities, he carefully prepared the "hidden poem" while in jail in order to leave a chance to retract. The *Chongqing* authorities also did not keep their promise and gave him an 18-month final sentence (Liu, Liang & Halliday, 2014). This twisted "plea bargain" then went further with new cases. On April 19, 2011 *Li Zhuang*, who was serving his

---

[69]Li Zhuang's blog, December 23th, 2011, The Truth behind Confession. July 27, 2013 retrieved from http://blog.sina.com.cn/s/blog_89aa0dcd0100ze3r.html.

[70] Branigan, Tania 'Chinese lawyer claims he was 'tricked' into confessing to falsifying evidence: Li Zhuang who had vowed to appeal a conviction for falsifying evidence before saying he was guilty claims he was cheated', July 27, 2013 retrieved from the *Guardian*, http://www.theguardian.com/world/2010/feb/10/chinese-lawyer-tricked-pleading-guilty?INTCMP=SRCH.

sentence, was brought to trial before the *Chongqing Jiangbei* Court again and he was charged with enticing a witness to give false testimony in a *Shanghai Xuhui* Court in July 2008 during an embezzlement trial. However, this case should be under the jurisdiction of *Shanghai* rather than *Chongqing* according to jurisdiction law.

The new trial of *Li Zhuang* case was reported in real time on the Internet by both the *Chongqing* media and many lawyers on their micro-blogs. Three days later, the prosecutors unexpectedly dropped the charge against *Li* due to lack of evidence. Many rumors were generated about the reasons behind the withdrawal, and some speculated that the central leadership may actually have exerted influence on the trial, while others thought the *Chongqing* authorities corrected their own mistake to prevent further damages to their reputation (Liu, Liang & Halliday, 2014). No matter which idea is closer to the truth, these speculations indicate that people believe that both central leadership and local administration can have undue influence on judicial system outcomes in China.

Analysis

The *Li Zhuang* case highlights several problems of the current criminal justice system. First, the Western style "plea bargain" is difficult to carry out in China due to the lack of judicial independence and the extent of inappropriate intervention from executive authorities. The bargain could be used to cover real facts rather than enhancing efficiency and achieving justice. Second, the case shows the low status of defense lawyers in the Chinese criminal justice system. Defense lawyers can be easily entrapped given the enforcement of Article 306 of the 1997 Criminal Law providing for the crime of lawyer's perjury. This "Big Stick 306" is used by the procuracy against lawyers often enough that and it discourages many lawyers from collecting their own evidence in criminal cases.

Third, the *Li Zhuang* case also brings attention to the *Chongqing* crackdown campaign in which, *Li Zhuang* has claimed, the confession his client made had been obtained through torture. His claim gains credibility after *Chongqing* police Chief *Wang Lijun*'s case which took place in February of 2012. The evidence which came to light in that case shows that the *Chongqing* crackdown legal proceedings largely ignored both Chinese procedural and substantive law, and that the use of torture was taking place on a major scale.

Despite knowledge of these irregularities, however, little has been done to correct the abuses of power occurring during this crackdown, and others like it. First, the crackdown approach has been used frequently in China to control organized crime and it is usually pushed by executive officials rather than arising from diligently having followed legal procedure. As a result, it is difficult for the courts to correct legal wrongs committed in crackdowns if the political bureaucracy has not decided to do so. Second, criminal cases in China are usually corroborated by the police, by prosecutors, by a Political Committee, by a Party Committee, and by the local administration office; given this multi-stage process it is really difficult to correct wrongful convictions when the courts become aware of them. This specific problem is addressed in the discussion of the next case.

Case 7 and Case 8—Nie Shubin and Wang Shujin

<u>Summary</u>

In cases analyzed thus far it is clear that the courts have demonstrated a lack of independence from the political bureaucracy, and in the next case it will be shown that wrongful convictions are very difficult to correct in major measure due to the lack of judicial independence. *Wang Shujin*, a defendant arrested on charges of raping and killing three women, insisted upon the recognition of his guilt in a fourth murder, but prosecutors have sought to invalidate his confession and affirm his innocence. This forth murder happened in 1994 in which a woman was raped and killed in a corn field in *Shijiazhuang* City, *Hebei* Province, and another man, *Nie Shubin*, was convicted for this crime and duly executed. In 2005, *Wang Shujin* was arrested and confessed to four counts of murder and rape, including that involved in the *Nie Shubin* case. However, this confession did not receive the attention of the procuracy and the court on the first instance trial of *Wang* in 2006.

If it was *Wang Shujin* in fact who raped and killed the woman, *Nie Shubin* was actually grievously wronged. *Wang* made an appeal to the *Hebei* High Court, but the court ruled in 2013 that no evidence exists proving that *Nie*'s case's real murderer is *Wang Shujin*. It took 7 years between the first and second instance trial. *Nie Shubin* was convicted based solely on his confession, and many court observers believe that the confession was likely a forced one. It was reported that *Nie* told a lawyer hired by his family that he was beaten into a confession on his sixth day in jail.[71] *Nie*'s oral confession was the only evidence presented at trial; prosecutors did not produce witnesses or physical evidence such as fingerprints, blood, or semen to prove his guilty.[72]

Wang Shujin has claimed that he was the real murderer, but the courts have repeatedly dismissed Wang's confession and invalidated his multiple appeals. Prosecutors have argued that *Wang Shujin* was able to provide some accurate details about the murder only because he worked in a factory near the corn field, and as a consequence was familiar with the surroundings. The High Court ruled that such evidence cannot prove that *Wang Shujin* committed this murder, and it thus blocks the appeal against the rape and murder conviction of *Nie*. Lawyers familiar with the case have commented that the ruling ignored *Wang*'s confession and numerous matches with the evidence, and feel that it is difficult to find adequate evidence to sustain *Wang*'s guilt or *Nie*'s conviction after 18 years. Furthermore, scholars have argued that the principle of 'innocent until proven guilty' should apply to both the trial of *Wang* and *Nie*. If the court did not convict *Wang* of murder due to lack of evidence now, it should have not convicted *Nie.*[73]

Analysis

There are two plausible reasons that the High Court dismissed *Wang*'s confession. First, the High Court, which was responsible for *Nie Shubin*'s final sentencing, could not possibly rectify its own wrongdoings. Second, a criminal case in China usually involves the police, prosecutors, a political committee, a party committee and the local government administration. All these parties work together and

[71] Du, Jiabao, 7/8/2013, Failing Trust in China's Courts: Is Wang Shujin the Last Straw? October 29th, 2013 retrieved from http://www.tealeafnation.com/2013/07/failing-public-trust-in-chinas-courts/#sthash.otBTn21p.dpuf.

[72] Ibid.

[73] Mao, Lixin, 9/27/2013, October 29th, 2013, retrieved from *Sina weibo*, http://www.weibo.com/p/1005052002687103/weibo?profile_ftype=1&key_word=%E7%8E%8B%E4%B9%A6%E9%87%91&is_search=1#_0.

cooperate with each other in the processing of major crimes. If the conviction was overturned, all of the parties would have to be held accountable and the proceedings of the retrial would pose risks for all parties. It is argued that the root cause of the extreme difficulty of achieving justice in wrongful conviction cases is that China's judicial system is not an independent entity. The judiciary is subordinate to the executive department, and the court and procuratorate act as branches or extensions of the Party and government in many respects (Xu, 2013).[74] Knowledgeable legal scholars have called for the re-trial of *Nie*'s case in order to correct the possible wrong conviction, but more importantly to promote the principle of 'innocent until proven guilty" within the Chinese criminal law process.

If the judiciary lacks independence, it neither could afford an independent, fair and just trial, nor could it correct wrongful convictions because those convictions are in practice collective decisions arising from different agents, including the political bureaucracy. Both the *Nie Shubin* case and the *Wang Shujin* case again show that an independent judiciary is needed to achieve fairness and justice in criminal trials. The influence from the political bureaucracy can be direct intervention through policy and order, and also can be through other channels such as communication media and targeted propaganda. In the next case, how state media can exert an impact on the legal system will be illustrated and discussed.

Case 9—Chen Yongzhou

<u>Summary</u>

In the previous cases it was shown that the political bureaucracy can influence the legal system directly because the judiciary must rely on local executive offices for their funding and public policy guidance. There is also indirect influence arising from the bureaucracy in the form of the state media. In China, major media news services are state-

---

[74] Lawyer Xu Xin's comment which is quoted in Du, Jiabao, July 8th, 2013, Failing Trust in China's Courts: Is Wang Shujin the Last Straw? October 29th, 2013 retrieved from http://www.tealeafnation.com/2013/07/failing-public-trust-in-chinas-courts/#sthash.otBTn21p.dpuf.

owned mouthpieces, and they must follow the direct guidance emanating from the CCP Propaganda Department. State media often plays an important role in major Chinese criminal cases, and it is important to recognize the often adverse effect of sensationalist media coverage propagated by the Propaganda Department.

On October 18, 2013 *Chen Yongzhou*, an imprisoned Chinese journalist, confessed to serious wrongdoing on the state TV. *Chen*, a reporter for the *Guang Dong*-based *New Express Newspaper* was detained by police from *Hunan* Province and was held at a detention center in *Changsha*, *Hunan*, on charges of "damaging the commercial reputation" of *Zoomlion*, which is China's second-largest maker of construction equipment based in *Hunan* province.[75] *Chen* had written a series of articles on *Zoomlion* over the previous 18 months and *Zoomlion* had filed a police report in which it argued that *Chen*'s series of investigative reports alleging financial fraud was incorrect and damaged the company's reputation. *Chen*'s detention raised worries among journalists and media professionals that the police are overstepping their legal jurisdiction in criminalizing civil disputes.[76] The *New Express Newspaper* made two appeals to the police to release *Chen Yongzhou,* using unusually bold front-pages.

However, the *New Express Newspaper* on the third day issued an apology, saying that its response to the investigation was inappropriate and "seriously hurt the credibility of the press."[77] This big turn-around follows a report aired by state-run China Central Television (CCTV) on October 27 showing footage of *Chen Yongzhou* being interrogated by the police in *Changsha*. Dressed in a detention-center vest, handcuffed,

---

[75] Boehler, Patrick October/25th, 2013, HK$3.5 billion, a price too high for gagging journalist Chen Yongzhou? October 29th, 2013 retrieved from http://www.scmp.com/news/china-insider/article/1339724/hk35-billion-price-too-high-gagging-journalist-chen-yongzhou.

[76] *CBC news,* 10/26/2013, Chinese journalist 'confesses' to publishing false reports for money, http://www.cbc.ca/news/world/chinese-journalist-confesses-to-publishing-false-reports-for-money-1.2252802?cmp=rss.

[77] Chinese newspaper apologizes over reporter Chen Yongzhou's Zoomlion stories, October 29th, 2013 retrieved from http://www.smh.com.au/world/chinese-newspaper-apologises-over-reporter-chen-yongzhous-zoomlion-stories-20131028-2wapc.html#ixzz2j8Gz4B2t.

and with his head shaved, *Chen* was heard saying that the information he had released was "absolutely not objective" and that "I'm willing to admit to the crime and repent."[78] This series of events made people suspect that the managers of the *New Express Newspaper* had been pressured to issue the apology and back off its support for its reporter.

It is interesting to note that CCTV was allowed to do their broadcasting from the police detention center; Chinese defense lawyers quite often complain that it is very difficult for them to get permission to meet their defendant clients in these jail settings. It is argued that this broadcast violates the principle of rule of law because the mass media should not intervene into the legal process in such a controversial setting in such a clearly politically motivated way.[79]

Analysis

TV confessions have almost become a way of establishing a public presumption of guilt when the investigation has barely started, and this journalistic practice does not match the principles of criminal justice reform undertaken in recent years (Ford, 2013).[80] It is improper that a state-run TV can broadcast this kind of "confession" when the case is still in a pre-trial process and no court verdict has been rendered. It is essentially conducting a trial by prime media, and thus violating the presumption of innocence as a principle of adjudication. In addition, such media reporting also may leak much evidence to the public before the trial begins, which not even the procuracy and the defense lawyers had the right to disclose. This type of revelations of evidence exerts inappropriate influence on the adjudication procedure (Liu, Liang & Halliday, 2014).

---

[78] Ibid, also see *BBC News*, China reporter Chen Yongzhou 'confesses' on TV, October 29th, 2013 retrieved from http://www.bbc.co.uk/news/world-asia-china-24682523.

[79] Ibid.

[80] Ford, Peter, October 28th 2013, Why China is turning to 'trial by television' in sensitive cases, October 29th, 2013 retrieved from http://www.csmonitor.com/World/Asia-Pacific/2013/1028/Why-China-is-turning-to-trial-by-television-in-sensitive-cases.

Six different people, including *Chen Yongzhou*, have been shown on public TV and have confessed to wrongdoings, although none of them have been charged with any crime.[81] In the past the Chinese police across the country used to parade suspects in the back of open-bed trucks before their public trials. After decades of economic and legal reform, this type of inappropriate public humiliation of the accused takes a new form as television broadcasting. The police and state-run public media, which represents the executive authorities, are functioning as a public "court" to try suspects even before the due process of law begins to establish guilt or innocence.

This case is neither the first time nor the last time that the prime media produced a damaging effect on the public discussion of legal cases and provoked an outcry from the legal profession. For example, in case 5, the *Li Zhuang* case, the *China Youth Daily* had published a lengthy article entitled "The Surprising Exposure of 'Lawyers Falsifying Evidence' in Chongqing's Anti-Black Campaign, Nearly 20 People Arrested"(*China Youth Daily*, December14, 2009) which was mostly based on a standard news brief provided by the *Chongqing* government (Liu, Liang & Halliday, 2014). This article's negative tone described lawyers as being greedy and incapable of doing their jobs, quoting one anonymous Chongqing official who said that many Beijing lawyers were coming to *Chongqing* to seek opportunities for "business" and to uncover "hidden rules" (*qian gui ze, 潜规则*). This article was published just 4 days after *Li*'s arrest and implied that *Li* was guilty, even though *Li* had not yet gone on trial.

Media representatives may justly argue that they have the freedom of the press, but such freedom must be used with responsibility and demonstrate proper regard for the principle of the presumption of innocence of the accused. The defendant should not be a witness against himself or herself before their trial in front of the public mass media. State-owned media have such improper privilege because of the support they receive from the administrative bureaucracy. Besides the mass media, there are several other types of social institutions which gain support from the bureaucracy and they too can exercise influence over the legal process. These other social institutions are discussed in the cases to follow.

---

[81] Ibid.

Case 10, 11 and 12—Yu Qiyi, Chen Qingxia and Xia Junfeng

In these three cases three types of powers which exist beyond the legal system which can exert coercive pressures on the legal process are discussed. These are the internal investigation power of the Chinese Communist Party, the process of local violence against petitioners, and the urban management enforcement process.

Case 10 Yu Qiyi, an Official Died in the *Shuanggui* Process

Summary

In China, if you are a Communist Party member you will get punished if you are against Party discipline even before a legal process begins. The Party disciplinary committee has a complete investigation and punishment process which is not open to outside supervision. As a result, the Party process is beyond the reach of the legal process and extremely coercive measures can take place without recourse to any appeal. In this case, a party member died while involved in the Party's disciplinary process.

Yu Qiyi, Communist Party member and the chief engineer of the state-owned *Wenzhou* Industry Investment Group, died during the *Shuanggui* process. *Shuanggui*, or "dual designations" is a CCP internal disciplinary procedure which entails Party members attending intensive questioning sessions for suspected serious wrongdoing at a designated place for a designated duration. *Yu Qiyi* had been so detained for internal investigations into a land deal since early March of 2013. On the night of April 8, 2013, his head was submerged in a tub of icy water several times by six investigators attempting to extract a confession, and he died in the early hours of April 9. Since his dead body was found to have suffered numerous internal and external injuries, it is possible that he had been tortured in other ways apart from the drowning during his 38 days of detention.[82] These six investigators are Party officials, not the Police; five of them are from the Commission for Discipline Inspection, the Party's watchdog for corruption.

---

[82]Sudworth, John, September 4th, 2013, Chinese official Yu Qiyi 'drowned by investigators. October29th, 2013 retrieved from http://www.bbc.co.uk/news/world-asia-china-23956167.

Analysis

Investigation by Party discipline organs is outside of the formal criminal justice system, and can result in a suspension of all procedural rights (Sapio, 2010). Both the investigated targets and their interrogators are CCP members and are bound by the party's disciplinary code. The whole process and details are mostly kept out of public view. In *Yu Qiyi*'s case, his family was never notified that he was detained. After such investigations the suspect may be turned over to prosecutors along with selected evidence.[83] Besides the local party disciplinary process, local governments also have the power to stop people's petition efforts. The next case will discuss this type of coercive measure, one which is also outside of the formal legal procedure specified in law.

<u>Case 11 Violence against Petitioners</u>

Summary

As has been described above, local governments in China have great executive power, and the local level courts have to rely on them for their funding. As noted as well Chinese people tend to turn to higher authority instead of to the judicial system when their complaints are not addressed at the local level. People usually petition all the way to the petition office in the capital of Beijing, and this is highly annoying to local officials because it reduces their chance of getting promotions. As a result, they always have officers assigned to the task of dissuading those petition-inclined people from petitioning. In this case, a woman was detained for three years after her petition attempt was halted by local officers.

Chen Qingxia, a woman from *Heilongjiang* Province, was stranded in a deserted mortuary for three years by the relevant local department, totally losing her personal freedom after she tried to go to Beijing to appeal to higher authorities to seek justice. *Chen*'s husband, suffering from mental disease, was sent to the local labor camps in 2003 for re-education because he damaged some road barriers in the road. Two

---

[83] *Fox News*, April 17, 2013, Bruised, battered, Chinese official's death spotlights abuses of Communist Party graft probes. 10/31/2013 retrieved from http://www.foxnews.com/world/2013/04/17/bruised-battered-chinese-official-death-spotlights-abuses-communist-party-graft.

months later her husband was set free due to his mental illness. However, *Chen Qingxia* was stunned to find several bruises on her husband's body and his mental ability was worse than before.[84] *Chen* decided to go to Beijing to appeal to higher authorities and seek justice for her husband, just as *Qiuiju* did in the movie noted at the beginning of this chapter. However, *Chen* was forced to go back from Beijing to *Heilongjiang* in 2007 and was sent to re-education through labor for 18 months.[85] In 2010, *Chen* was sent to this mortuary and was locked up. She became paralyzed during her three-year "imprisonment" in the mortuary, which is guarded 24 hours by four staff workers hired by the department. Her 12-year-old son, who was missing during her petition to the Letters and Visits Beijing Office, has not be found.

Analysis

Because the Chinese people have a long-established tradition of appealing to higher authorities to redress injustice, each year numerous people go to Beijing to file their petitions. At the same time, local governments are trying to stop these petitions and force those people back because they will face demotions or other forms of retribution from higher levels of government based on the number of petitioners who come to Beijing. It is not unusual for local governments to intervene in the petition process, abducting the petitioners either before they leave or once they arrive in Beijing. Some of the petitioners will be sent to detention centers or re-education through labor camps.[86] These types of measures are outside of the formal criminal justice system, and petitioning takes place without legal procedures. The 18th CCP Central Committee proclaimed that China would abolish the "re-education through labor" system in November 2013. However, local governments not only have these direct coercive measures at their

---

[84] Zhu Wenjia, January 24, 2013, Woman stranded in deserted mortuary 3 years due to petition. 10/31/2013 retrieved from http://english.sina.com/china/p/2013/0123/552917.html.

[85] Ibid.

[86] Lara Farrar and Kevin Voigt, November 14, 2012, Chinese petitioners claim hotel used as 'black jail'. 10/31/2013 retrieved from http://www.cnn.com/2012/11/14/business/china-hotel-black-jail

disposal, but they also have extensive power through diverse enforcement groups such as the urban management enforcement process. Such extensive power is discussed in the next case.

Case 12 Xia Junfeng and Chengguan (Urban Management Enforceme 城管)

Summary

Urbanization is still developing in China and governments are trying to find effective ways to manage the city development process. *Chengguan* (Urban Management Enforcement, 城管) is one way of achieving the management. However, this group has been authorized to exercise a great deal of power, with little effective supervision. As a result, it has gained notoriety for its often brutal enforcement actions. The following case is an example.

In September 25 of 2013, *Xia Junfeng*, a street vendor, was convicted and executed for killing two city officials. His case raised cries of unfairness in the justice system over Chinese social media. On May 16, 2009, while selling chicken strips, roasted sausages and other snacks with his wife, *Zhang Jing* near a crossroads in *Chenhe* District, in the north-eastern city of *Shenyang (沈阳沉河区)*, *Xia Junfeng* was seized by urban management officers known as *Chengguan (城管)* who enforce the local city's codes. *Xia* was taken to their office and he was severely beaten by those officers. During the course of the beating, *Xia Junfeng* fought back with a small knife he carried in his pocket, stabbing two of the *Chengguans* to death and injuring another. *Xia* said his actions were in self-defense after the two officers began to beat him. The court refused to consider testimony from six witnesses that *Xia* had acted in his own self-defense and convicted him of murder, mostly based on testimony from the *Chengguan.*[87] *Xia* was convicted of intentional homicide and sentenced to death during the first trial in 2009, and the second trial in July of 2011 upheld the verdict of the first trial. The Supreme People's Court in Beijing reviewed the case and approved the death penalty on the morning of September 25, 2013.

---

[87] Jacobs, Andrew, September 25, 2013, Street Vendor's Execution Stokes Anger in China, 10/30/2013 retrieved from http://www.nytimes.com/2013/09/26/world/asia/street-vendors-execution-stirs-anger-in-china.html?_r=0.

Xia's case resonated with the Chinese public because many people have become disgusted over the impunity with which *Chengguan* officers impose local codes on street peddlers – often with excessive violence.[88] Holding a close relationship with the local government, the *Chengguan* is used by the local government to deal with a variety of issues, including urban management, forced demolishment, local sanitation code enforcement, and similar issues arising from rapid urbanization.

Chengguan, the urban management system, was established in 1997 initially to manage the problem of transient street peddlers and vendors. However, *Chengguan* systems actually have no constitutional foundation, and have too often turned into a branch of local executive power. [89] Because no national laws and regulations exist for the C*hengguan* system, it gained unbridled power and has often committed criminal activities in carrying out code enforcement.[90] The *Guangzhou* city government in August of 2010 issued a regulation that C*hengguan* can request police assistance if they anticipate encountering violence when entering unauthorized buildings for investigations or demolition work.[91] In many places, *Chengguang* and the Police are cooperating in such demolition work and related activities.

---

[88] Cao, Xiaxue, September 24th, 2013, China to Execute Xia Junfeng, October 29th, 2013 retrieved from http://chinachange.org/2013/09/24/china-to-execute-xia-junfeng-wednesday-september-25.

[89] Fauna, September 10, 2013, Qingdao City Management Forced Demolition of Military Compound Guard Room Fight, People's Liberation Army Greatly Outnumbered, October 29th, 2013 retrieved from http://www.businessinsider.com/chengguan-brawl-with-pla-over-demolition-2013-9#ixzz2jFAqffsq.

[90] Badkar, Mamta, September 10, 2013, China's Notorious Urban Enforcement Officials Get Into A Brawl With Soldiers Over A Demolition. October 29th, 2013, retrieved from http://www.businessinsider.com/chengguan-brawl-with-pla-over-demolition-2013-9#ixzz2jFAqffsq.

[91] Zheng Caixiong, October 10, 2011, Police set to help chengguan clear illegalstructures. October 29th, 2013 retrieved from http://www.chinadaily.com.cn/china/2011-10/10/content_13858242.htm.

In recent years there have been a series of highly violent confrontations involving *Chengguan*. In July 2013, a watermelon seller in Hunan Province collapsed and died on the street after a *Chengguan* reportedly struck him in the head with a metal weight taken from his scale. *Cui Yingjie,* an unlicensed sausage vendor in Beijing was convicted in 2007 of slashing to death an enforcement official who had seized his cart. The action of the *Chengguan* can even lead to a fight against the army. In September 4, 2013, over a hundred *Chengguan* beseiged a guard room at a military compound in *Qingdao* city, *Shandong* Province, with the intent to forcibly demolish the guard room. A fierce conflict broke out between the two sides, and the army side in the end was unable to resist and was beaten into retreat due to *Chengguan* forces having more people.[92]

Analysis

The *Chengguan* represents an extension of executive power, one which often tramples citizens' rights and whose actions have been labeled as "brutality" in many cases. *Xia Junfeng* won the sympathetic regard from the public and thousands of postings on social media were overwhelmingly are on *Xia*'s side. Nonetheless he was finally executed. It is argued by many legal observers that the verdict was unjust because the *Chengguan* as a social institution has no legal foundation.[93] The support for *Xia* highlights a lack of faith in China's judicial system, which is too heavily weighed against defendants and too often takes into too great account the interests of the state and local officials.[94]

Furthermore, *Xia* was contrasted with *Bogu Kailai*, the wife of *Bo Xilai* whose death sentence was suspended. Some legal observers take note of the different treatment accorded citizens with different backgrounds under the justice system: *Bogu Kailai* was found guilty of murdering *Neil Heywood*, a British businessman, and she got a suspended death penalty which usually will turn into life imprisonment

---

[92] Ibid.

[93] The Guardian news, September 25, 2013, Chinese street vendor executed despite calls for leniency, October 29th, 2013 retrieved from http://www.theguardian.com/world/2013/sep/25/chinese-street-vendor-executed.

[94] Ibid.

after a two-year suspension. A user of the microblogging site said of *Bogu*'s sentence: "The trial indeed shows respect for life, her life. But what kind of people can enjoy such respect. Can *Xia Junfeng* enjoy that?"[95] Suspended death penalty rather than death penalty has been used for a few high-profile officials who committed serious crimes in recent years. The rich and powerful in China normally will not get the death penalty because of their family's connections.[96]

Besides *Chengguan*, other local enforcement systems also exist, for example, the local security team which also holds para police enforcement power. *Ji Zhongxing* was angry because his life was destroyed by a local security team and his years' petition was in vain. On June 28, 2005, *Ji Zhongxing,* who was driving his rickshaw in *Dongguan, Guangdong* Province, was stopped by a local security force known as *zhianduiyuan (治安队),* who demanded a check of his documents. The local security force is employed by the police department to maintain order, including tackling unlicensed vehicles. *Ji* claimed that he was chased by the officials and received a brutal and sustained beating that left him paralyzed in his lower limbs; officials say *Ji* was injured after he fell from his vehicle.[97] *Ji* became a petitioner and went to Beijing to seek justice for the alleged attack. After years of repeated attempts to seek compensation with little success, *Ji* tried to draw attention to his case by detonating a small home-made bomb in Beijing's international airport in July 2013. *Ji* was soon arrested and sentenced to 6 years imprisonment.

Chengguan and *Zhiandui* are seen as para police forces which can commit brutality which is beyond the control of the formal criminal

---

[95] Reals, Tucker, August 20, 2012, Gu Kailai, wife of powerful China politician Bo Xilai avoids execution, which surprises few. October 29th, 2013 retrieved from http://www.cbsnews.com/8301-503543_162-57496452-503543/gu-kailai-wife-of-powerful-china-politician-bo-xilai-avoids-execution-which-surprises-few.

[96] Ibid, Zhang Ming, a political science professor at Beijing's Renmin University, is quoted in this *CBS News*.

[97] Le Dong, October 15, 2013, Ji Zhongxing: From petitioner to bomber, October 29th,/2013 retrieved from http://www.bbc.co.uk/news/world-asia-china-24518450

justice system. They are in fact extensions of executive power and need to be regulated under formal legal procedure. The force local governments use to obstruct petitioners has no legal foundation, and the Party internal discipline process needs to be included in the formal legal procedure as well. From these three cases, we can see each individual could be harmed by extra-legal coercive measures whether he or she is a petitioner, CCP member, or street vendor. The only way to protect the basic rights of citizens is to build an independent justice system wherein no conviction can be made without a fair court trial.

More and more people know the importance of a fair and just judicial system. As those posting on social media correctly observe, anyone could become the victim of an abusive system, just like *Li Zhuang, Nie shubin,* and *Chen Qingxia* if we do not have an independent judicial system upon which we can rely. The judiciary in China is struggling for independence, and it calls for the collective efforts from the whole of Chinese society. Interestingly, the rapid development of the Internet actually provides a stage for this show in the form of the social media. In the next chapter, the impact of social media on the rule of law in China is investigated.

CHAPTER 6

Social Media and the Rule of Law in China

CIVIL SOCIETY AND THE INTERNET

Born within the powerful bureaucracy system, the Chinese judiciary has never really opened up its own ground independently. The Imperial rulers' reform efforts had long been cast in the pattern of an outworn tradition, using law as a ruling tool. Based on this reading of history, it is not difficult to understand the arduous path of legal reform in China. Twelve criminal cases were used to look into the current criminal justice system and examine the struggle of the judicial system against the powerful political bureaucracy. Fortunately, this struggle is not a solo actor effort, and the pursuit of judicial independence is backed up by the Chinese people's dream of justice. Interestingly, legal reform has long neglected the participation of ordinary people due to the yet faint presence of a civil society in the Chinese political arena.

Civil society had been suppressed during thousands years of feudal Imperial dynasties in China. However, the Chinese people are more and more aware of civil and political rights after achieving some measure of economic abundance. Civil society is the nurturing soil for justice. Rousseau, in his book *The Social Contract*, claims that man acted only upon his physical impulses in the state of nature and lacked a sense of justice. During the transition from the state of nature to civil society, the man started to feel a duty to his fellow men, his mental faculties are developed, and his soul is elevated owing to this moral change. As the basis for every social system, the social contract makes the physical differences found in the state of nature insignificant so that all men may be equal by convention and by right.

It has been argued that the sophistication of the Criminal justice system is a way to measure the social development and political liberalism of any country (Karpik, 1998; Pue, 1997). It is argued that legal professionals, especially lawyers trained in criminal law, potentially anchor the key institutions of civil society (Halliday & Liu, 2007). Lawyers need to make their own professional associations self-governing, and if they succeed they can mobilize a profession against the state and/or ally with other groups in civil society to promote the rule of law. Their own profession can variously ally with the judiciary or restrain and critique its actions as circumstances dictate (Halliday & Liu, 2007). The autonomy of the bar can help lawyers confront most directly the coercive and potentially repressive arms of the state as they act in the realm of criminal law. In China, such autonomy on the part of the legal profession has not been realized in general, although some signs of progress are clearly in evidence.

The rapidly expanding use of the Internet and associated social media is creating an unprecedented opportunity to build civil society in China through *virtual public space*, *online community* and *enhanced public surveillance*. The Internet overcomes the barriers of time and place for ongoing communication and the promotion of collective action in a vast country with a very large population. In this regard, the microblog facility platform provides Chinese legal professionals with an unparalleled site for public discourses and the development of a shared professional identity, and also helps form a microcosm of civil society. In this chapter I discuss the prospects for the development of civil society in the era of the Internet, and assess its current impact on movement toward the rule of law. First, I will look into the development of civil society in China. I not only give a survey of current legal activism through the Internet, but also use collected social media data to depict the dynamic interaction taking place among the online legal community in contemporary China.

There are some noteworthy limitations for using this type of data in analyses. First, the microblogs are located within a huge data system, and there are more than 500 million registered users on *Sina Weibo.*[98] My analysis can gather only a small sample of the online legal community. Second, legal professionals express their opinions on social media based on their knowledge and thoughts of the topics, and these opinions are not necessarily correct or based on relevant knowledge. As an observer, I only can do my best to present what I have seen. Even with these serious limitations, however, I believe nonetheless that the observations set forth here based on social media provide a valuable insight into the Chinese legal community in contemporary China. First, legal professionals play an important role in the Chinese legal system, and this type of data provides a new way to study those people who are working in the legal professions in an Internet era. Second, these legal professionals express ideas and opinions through tweets which have a function similar to interview or survey data. This type of data has been rarely used in criminal justice research up to this point, and this book provides a useful template for how greater use could be made of this valuable form of social science evidence.

CHINESE CIVIL SOCEITY IN THE ERA OF THE INTERNET

Civil Society and Public Sphere

The powerful bureaucracy system of China – characteristic of ancient China and the great nation of today – has been depicted in previous chapters, and the question arises whether there is a type of power that can contend against and balance that of the overwhelming bureaucracy. Based on Western experience, a vigorous civil society can indeed hold the state bureaucracy accountable, and in so doing it can promote democracy. According to Rousseau (1754), the origin of civil society itself can be traced to an act of deception, and the advent of private property as a social convention occasioned the beginning of true civil society. He asserts that rather than bend to the whims of an absolute monarch, people should exercise their sovereignty by banding together and creating a public person in the form of the sovereign which promotes the common good. Every person is both a citizen as a

---

[98] February 28th, 2013, Chinese Internet Watch, November 12th 2013 retrieved from http://www.chinainternetwatch.com/1965/overview-of-sina-weibo-2012.

member of the sovereign and is subject to its decisions (Rousseau, 1754). Human societies are grounded in and held together by shared norms and common moral understandings. Why is civil society important? The rights of man are more basic than any political structure, and provide a point of revolutionary leverage from which any state structure may be radically altered (Bellah, 1967). When people join together to form a community, they create a political body with a life and will of its own. This community could be seen as the initiative form of civil society (Rousseau, 1754).

Civil society is an arena in which citizens associate to achieve a range of different purposes, and it has four basic elements: *autonomous individuals*, *autonomous civic associations*, and they can engage in ***more or less organized activities***, in ***public spheres*** (Yang, 2003). Civil society is an important power to restrain individuals who lead the governing state from becoming all-powerful, lest they abuse that power to oppress others for their own benefit (O'Brien, 1999). Although China has a very large population, the civil society dimension of Chinese society has been weak and undeveloped compared to the powerful bureaucracy. Several reasons likely account for this imbalance between weak civil society and powerful bureaucracy in China, viewed both historically and in terms of the present.

First, autonomous individuals and civic associations barely could exist in China during the Imperial era. The lands and people alike belonged to the Emperor in ancient China. Individuals may exercise certain freedoms in their economic activities, but not in their political activities (Hu, 2000). Cities were where bureaucrats resided, and it was unlikely that any strong self-governing organizations could exist in these cities. Although some autonomous associations did appear in urban society in the late *Qing* dynasty, they were actually protected by and often manipulated by the state (Takahashi, 2008). Chinese social organizations are more likely to be seeking to build good mutual relations between the state and the society than to achieve autonomy, and the weakness of civil society contributes to the strength of the state (Takahashi, 2008).

Second, it is difficult to find and gather people in a public sphere to nurture civil activities in a geographically extensive country with a very large population. Public sphere means places outside the immediate control of the state but not entirely contained within the private sphere of the family (Calhoun, 1994, p.190). Public sphere, where the public can discuss, debate and get involved with affairs of the state, plays an important role in realizing democracy (Habermas, 1962). In order for the public sphere to work, the public needs to have opportunities to exchange views; in this regard the right and space to express and exchange their opinions on public affairs represents the most essential aspect of civil society (Habermas, 1962). Chinese public sphere's development during the Imperial era was highly localized rather than reflecting a nationwide network of autonomous associations (Liu, 2011).

After 1949, the state-controlled mass media have been a vehicle of the state, issuing state-oriented publicity rather than providing the underpinnings of a nationwide public sphere (Li, 2003, p. 4). Most scholars would agree that the public sphere in China remains incipient and weak since most social institutions are state-controlled, i.e. most mass media are owned by the state (Yang, 2003). The economic reforms in the 1980s gradually transformed the landscape of the mass media, and to a certain degree the traditional media in China were starting to act as fledgling facilitators of the public sphere (Wang & Bates, 2008). However, the reforms in question did not fully change the nature of the state-oriented mass media which remain state-owned and tightly controlled. The prevalence of the Internet since 1990s is starting to lead to change, however. The Internet breaks into the arena of public discussion and is fostering the development of dynamic online communities. How these communities might be able to nurture a virtual civil society is discussed in the following section.

The Virtual Civil Society

No one can deny that the Internet has brought huge changes to our daily life. The Internet actually arose from a series of government-funded computer networking efforts. The precursor to the Internet began with the U.S. Defense Department's ARPAnet in 1969. Several other public agencies also developed similar networks so that their researchers could communicate and share digital data.[99] In 1981, for example, the

[99] The NSF website has a detailed history of internet, http://www.nsf.gov/news/news_summ.jsp?cntn_id=103050.

National Science Foundation (NSF) provided a grant to establish the Computer Science Network (CSNET) to provide networking services to all university computer scientists. NSF intended to provide much greater access to the high-end computing resources to scientists and engineers around the country from its recently established supercomputer centers. A viable solution would be to link many research universities to these centers and to one another. As a result, NSFNET went online in 1986 and connected the supercomputer centers at 56,000 bits per second—the speed of a typical computer modem today. In a very short time the network became highly congested, and by 1988 its links were upgraded to 1.5 megabits per second. A variety of regional research and education networks were connected to the initial NSFNET backbone, in time extending the Internet's reach throughout the United States.

The creation of NSFNET was the first large-scale implementation of the Internet technologies in a complex environment of many independently operated networks. Throughout the existence of NSFNET, the number of the Internet-connected local computers grew from 2,000 in 1985 to more than 2 million in 1993. To handle the increasing data traffic, in 1991the NSFNET backbone became the very first national 45 megabits/second the Internet network. Tim Berners-Lee and colleagues at CERN, the European Organization for Nuclear Research, in Geneva, Switzerland subsequently launched the World Wide Web in 1991.

From 1993 to 1998, Commercial firms noted the popularity and effectiveness of the growing the Internet and built their own networks. NSF awarded contracts in 1995 for three network access points in order to provide connection points between commercial networks and one routing arbiter in order to ensure an orderly exchange of traffic across the Internet. In addition, NSF signed a cooperative agreement to establish the next-generation, very-high-performance Backbone Network Service. The most visible, and the most contentious, component of the Internet transition was the process of registration of domain names. Domain name registration associates a human-readable character string with the Internet Protocol (IP) addresses, a code of unique identifiers which computers use to locate one another. In 1993, there were 7,500 domain names; a mere five years later, the number of registered domain names had passed 2 million. The year 1998 marked the end of U.S. National Science Foundation's direct role in the Internet, and the network access points and routing arbiter functions were transferred entirely to the commercial sector.

Part of the initial motivation for the creation of the Internet was that of information sharing. In due course communication and social network formation soon become the major motivation of further development. For example, electronic mail became the most significant impact of the innovations, and it provided a new model of how people could communicate with each other; this communication tool greatly changed the nature of collaboration. The success of the Internet is largely attributable to both satisfying basic community needs as well as utilizing the community in an effective way to push the technological infrastructure forward. Commercialization of the Internet involved not only the development of competitive, private network services, but also the development of many commercial products needed for implementing the Internet technology.

When the Internet enters China and connects with 13 billion people it is not easy to predict what kind of surprises it can create. The rapid development of the Internet not only changes personal lives, but also raises a new question—namely, is it possible to create a virtual civil society through online communities in China? If it is, this virtual civil society may come to have a huge impact because it can overcome the barriers of time and space which are important in a geographically vast country with a very large population. The development of online community is the next focus of attention.

Internet and Online Community

Internet usage has expanded more quickly in China than anywhere else in the world. In June 2015, China had 668 million Internet users, and 594 million have access to the internet via their respective smartphones and/or tablets.[100] Social media, as the one of most active parts of the Internet community, is exploding worldwide; China has by far the

---

[100] The China Internet Network Information Center's (CNNIC) 36th China internet development statistics report. October 22nd 2015 retrieved from http://www.baom.com.cn/site2/20150825/4437e67a506917465c2c01.pdf.

world's most active social-media population. A new McKinsey survey of 5,700 the Internet users in China has found that 95 percent of those living in Tier 1, Tier 2, and Tier 3 cities are registered on one or more social-media sites (Chiu, Lin and Silverman, 2012). The radical nature and contested struggles present on China's cyberspace greatly reflect the social changes taking place in China, and in this context social media has pushed the phenomenon of "online activism" to a much higher degree (Yang, 2009).

The Internet has facilitated the environment for what Habermas (1962) has defined as the public sphere, especially for China, and it has wider impact and become a tool to pursue free expression. The public sphere serves as a counterweight to political authority, representing a place somewhere between private individuals and government authorities in which people could meet and have critical debates about public matters. Habermas (1962) saw a vibrant public sphere as a positive force keeping established authorities within bounds because public space discussions can call into question political rulings. These types of discussions can happen physically in face-to-face meetings in coffee houses and cafes and public squares as well as in the media in letters, books, drama, and the arts.

The Internet becomes a new such place within the public sphere, and it allows the "web surfers" to act as consumer and creator of information simultaneously. The Internet actually bears similarities to real-life communication prototypes. In addition, it can also help with more types of social interactions rather than simply having conversations, and can also build new channels of communications between the mass media and the public.

The Internet creates a new social space which is not only informational, but also participatory. This is important for the foundation of a civil society, which requires the widespread participation of people. The Internet can extend the scope of relations in the physical world and can overcome the constraints of time and space. It presents a great potential and provides exciting opportunities to reinvigorate civic engagement in new ways (Tai, 2006, 169-171). Because the Internet is much less constrained by the state than other forms of social interaction, it promises much easier and wider access for people to obtain information, and it assists people to connect with each other and stand up to support political democratization (Liu, 2011).

The most popular the Internet product in China now is social media, which entails web sites for social networking and microblogging through which users create online communities to share information, ideas, personal messages, and other forms of content.[101] In China social media is not only a tool for communication, but has also become both a place of collective opinion expression and seedbed of social forces. Among the hundreds of millions of web users, over 300 million have created individual microblogs. Despite some degree of censorship, the discussions in the Internet forums and social media are more wide-ranging and elaborate than in the conventional media. It is important to note that the Internet has created an unprecedented space for civil discourse in China; it represents a vibrant virtual social space which enables the ongoing efforts to build effective rule of law to resonate throughout the Chinese cyberspace and among its netizens. The social uses of the Internet have fostered public debate and discussion of societal problems, and in the process have created a new associational form—the virtual community (Yang, 2009). Next, a look at the popular social media websites adds some detail to the discussion of the creation of public space in contemporary Chinese society.

Social Network Sites: BBS, Blog and Microblog

There are three types of social media which are popular places to discuss social issues in China. The first one is the Bulletin Board System (BBS) where people from various occupations may reflect on social issues they view as significant and then exchange opinions. The second is that of blogs in which people (including many scholars) write articles on important social issues such as legal reform, major cases and theoretical discussions. The third one is *Weibo* (microblogging) which is more popular than either the web forum or blogs. *Weibo* means "microblogging" in Mandarin. Mainland China's first Bulletin Board System was established in 1994 by the National Research Center for the support of Intelligent Computing Systems (*国家智能计算机研究*

---

[101] Merriam-Webster online dictionary, December 22th retrieved from http://www.merriam-webster.com/dictionary/social%20media.

开发中心). Social network sites, including BBS, blogs, and microblogs have started to emerge since then and have attracted Chinese netizens because of the eye-catching and intercommunicative features available.

The number of Chinese blogs was estimated to be as high as 36.82 million in 2005. By 2010 there were eleven main microblog providers in mainland China (Liu, 2011), and there are 204.32 million microblog users by the end of June 2015. It is argued that microblogs are highly valued by many users as an effective vehicle of communication on which people like to talk about political issues due to China's specific socio-political environment. Because citizens in a collectivist culture are attuned to their collective fates, the collective opinions of Chinese people can serve as a powerful form of oversight pressing the government when individuals acting alone can hardly influence the political process (Lee, 2006). Microblogs actually facilitate a space for collective culture. Microblogs nowadays are very popular, and attract all kinds of people in China.

What has made microblogs so different from other media? First, microblogs are designed to enable individuals to connect with strangers in ways that would not otherwise be possible (Boyd & Ellison, 2007). Because microblogs contain fewer reciprocal relationships compared with other social networks, they are formed based on deeper interests rather than a replication of real worlds (Kwak, Lee, Park & Moon, 2010). Thus, individuals can experience a sense of identification with anyone who shared similar opinions, making the perceived social supports more extensive than other social network sites (W.Wang, 2013). This enlarged social bound among strangers may increase ones' confidence in the capacity of microblogs users as a whole to understand and participate in politics (W.Wang, 2013). Second, the emotional feelings expressed on microblogs can be also contagious, influencing political attitudes among microbloggers, and this *affect* characteristic of the new media has been shown to promote political involvement among average citizens (Barnhust, 2011). Microblogs become a space to enhance the political efficacy of individuals because the more one discusses on microblogs, the more one will obtain factual knowledge about politics, which is followed by increased internal political efficacy (Scheufele, 2000).

Third, microblog communications are instant and spontaneous. Different from traditional social media, the tweets of microblogs can spontaneously involve a large number of people in certain discussions and thereby form a very responsive virtual community. The type of collective political participation facilitated by microblogs is not actualized through collective presences in the same physical places; instead, the participants act in different time, at different venues and have different experiences (Hogan & Quan-Haase, 2010). Fourth, microblogs are easily accessible and relatively inexpensive as compared to traditional media. Even if you do not have a personal computer, Internet cafés, which cost less than $0.5 per hour, are prevalent in most areas of the country.

The 2012 research from the Data Center of China the Internet (DCCI) reports that microblog users account for 88.81% of total Chinese netizens of age 19 or older (DCCI, 2012). The three most popular microblog websites are *Sina Weibo*, *Tencent Weibo and Wangyi Weibo. Weibo* products combine the features of Facebook and Twitter; for instance, users can post personal updates with a 140-character limit, upload photos and videos, and message other users. *Weibo* has more functions than Twitter, such as commenting on others' posts, turning a message into a conversation, and transmitting photographs and other files with posts. *Sina Weibo* introduced a multimedia function a year and a half before Twitter did.

Sina launched *Sina Weibo* on August 14, 2009, and it invited and persuaded many Chinese celebrities to join the platform, leading to its occupying of 56.5% of China's microblogging market that year (DCCI, 2012). Later *Tencent Weibo* was launched on March 5, 2010; *weibo* registered users surpassed 100 million in February 2011. Chinese microblog users' proportion on different *weibo* platforms are shown below: 87.67% of *weibo* users have accounts on *Sina;* 84.69% are *Tencent weibo* users (DCCI, 2012). Among *Weibo* users, 7.74 % have a master degree, 54% have a bachelor degree, and 25.94% have an associate degree (DCCI, 2012). The people in the legal field, including law school professors, lawyers, judges, prosecutors, and police officers mostly have college or above levels of formal education and can proficiently use social media as a highly convenient tool for communication and self-expression. Besides these legal professionals, the general public in recent years also is paying attention to legal cases, especially criminal cases.

Among different types of users on social media, about 14 percent are opinionated users and express their own, often strong, opinions and in many cases build large personal followings after doing so (Chiu, Lin & Silverman, 2012). The legal community belongs to this type of user, and most legal professionals have their own blogs and post discussions on legal issues. The legal community on microblogs usually includes law professors, judges, prosecutors, lawyers, and police officers, and they often respond to each other on diverse legal issues and frequently present their own opinions on those issues.

In order to better understand the online legal community I collected social media posts on hot topics in criminal justice and analyzed their opinions, including those pertaining to legal reform, current law revision, and important criminal cases. The tweets analysis captures an interactive picture of the Chinese legal community. I will use these data to analyze the impact of the microblog communication channel on legal reform in the second part of this chapter, and I will describe the interactions among legal community actors and predict the future trend of legal community development.

During my data collection on social media I found an interesting trend which is closely related to the virtual civil society concept. One important function of civil society is to hold government accountable through active popular surveillance. The virtual civil society is doing just that; the public is watching officials and reporting its observation through Internet space. They often express criticism, gather more evidence through cyber vigilantism, and sometimes organize online legal activism. Next I discuss some pertinent details of public surveillance via the Internet.

Public Surveillance via the Internet

Web—based Criticism

The Internet, as a new medium characterized by interactivity and unlimited information, may provide a particularly efficient, convenient, and widely available forum allowing ordinary people to argue about public affairs and discuss political activity even in the presence of restrictions from government (Wang & Bates, 2008). The Internet also brings transformational revolution to traditional media which now act hand-in-hand with social media to provide an expanded public sphere for social change. In the following section three specific cases are used to characterize this transformation revolution. These three criminal cases all drew substantial attention. The first case, the *Sun Zhigang* incident, turns a new leaf for the traditional media to combine with social media and create unprecedented effects on public surveillance. The second and third cases each involve bringing the online and offline activism together.

Case 1 The Sun Zhigang Incident

The *Sun Zhigang* incident may represent one successful case wherein the traditional media and the new social media combine to bring about a legislative change. *Sun*, a college graduate from Central China Hubei province, worked in an apparel company in the South China city of *Guangzhou*. On March 17, 2003 *Sun* was detained by the police for failing to present his temporary resident card[102] on his way to an Internet café. He was beaten to death some three days later while still in police custody. *Sun*'s death was initially exposed online at *Xici.net*, a popular BBS, and this information inspired the reporters of the *Southern Metropolis News* (*南方都市报, Nanfang Dushi Bao*), a traditional newspaper, to do a thorough and professional investigation (Wang & Bates, 2008). Soon after this newspaper report was published more relevant information came to light, additional in-depth reports were done, and commentaries on the incident were published and circulated on the Internet.

The Internet created an extraordinarily open and healthy platform for the public discussions and debates ensuing, and engaged the public in discussions on the issues of social justice, inequality and constitutionalism. Furthermore, collective opinions were created through this new, powerful channel and became a noticeable influential factor when the government was making public policy (Liu, 2010). In the end, the Premier *Wen Jiabao* signed a decree abolishing the policy known as *Measures for Internment and Deportation of Urban Vagrants and Beggars* (*城市流浪乞讨人员收容遣送办法*, 1982) after a State Council conference on June 20, 2003. This was no doubt an

---

[102] In China, people need to get a temporary resident card if they migrate to areas which are not their officially registered residence.

unprecedented victory with the aid of media, **especially** the new social media (Wang & Bates, 2008; Liu, 2010).

The Internet and new social media have played an important role in this rare case wherein that traditional media opened up for the weak and the powerless to speak out. First, the Internet helps spread the information much more widely and rapidly before the story can be censored. For example, on the first day that *the Southern Metropolis News* published this story online, reader's reactions reached 10,000 within the first few hours; an online memorial page for *Sun Zhigang* attracted more than 10,000 hits in two days (Tai, 2006, p.264-265). Second, the Internet creates a more free space for people to display their opinions and feelings compared to the traditional media. For example, people visited the memorial page with best wishes, comments or donations to Sun's family, and also criticized the police and officials' brutality towards rural residents as lower-class citizens (Tai, 2006: 264). Third, the Internet helps create a national discussion which pushed the legislative change. Many other deaths under detention were exposed and noted by the media and by the public, which in turn led to a widespread offline and online discussion in relation to the patently unconstitutional detention and dispatch system, finally leading to the needed legislative change (Liu, 2011). In this case, public participation was clearly greatly facilitated through online space and communication, presenting a good model of Institutional reform and public policy making through positive interaction between the public and government using new social media (Wang & Bates, 2008).

Case 2 Li Qiaoming

The second case includes not only online surveillance, but also initiated offline activism in which web users also participated in a legal issues investigation. On Jan. 30, 2009, *Li Qiaoming*, a resident of *Yuxi* City, was detained in *Jinning* for felling trees without proper authorization. He was hospitalized on Feb. 8 and died four days later from severe brain injuries. The *Jinning* public security bureau claimed that *Li* was fatally injured while playing hide-and-seek with other inmates, one of whom supposedly reacted angrily when his hiding place was discovered by *Li.*[103] *Li*'s parents and many web users did not believe this official account of the incident which appeared in a local newspaper in the provincial capital of *Kunming* on Feb. 13, 2009. Thousands of netizens responded and opined that *Li* most likely died as a result of police beatings.

Rather than suppress these accusations, The *Yunnan* Provincial Publicity Department posted a notice on major Yunnan-based websites and invited the public to join in the investigation. Out of 1,000 volunteers, a 15-person committee was chosen and the committee visited the crime scene. However, they were not allowed to view surveillance tapes, to examine the autopsy report, nor question the guards. They were also not permitted to interview the prime suspect, *Pu Hua-yong* (*普华永*). After disclosing the identities of the volunteers, netizens later found out that nearly half of the "randomly selected" investigators were current or former employees of the local government or state-run media, including three reporters (including one from *Xinhua News*), four public security and prosecutors' staff personnel.[104] It is the first time in Yunnan, and even in all of China, for netizens to have participated in an official investigation, though the outcome of the case remains uncertain. Such inspections cannot solely rely on passion and idealism, but rather must rely on rational discussion and pragmatic work. This event has again exposed the flaws of the current system and highlighted the need to establish an independent investigation system involving objective expertise.

Case 3 Deng Yujiao

In the first case, traditional media still has taken an important leading function in creating public surveillance and social media steps in at a later point. In this third case, social media already starts to take the major leading role and fully functions as driving force for public

---

[103] *Xinhua News*. China netizens join probe into "hide-and-seek" prison death. November 7, 2013 retrieved from http://news.xinhuanet.com/english/2009-02/20/content_10855443.htm.

[104] Taipeitimes.com. Yunnan police seek to quell criticism with public probe. November7, 2013 retrieved from http://www.taipeitimes.com/News/world/archives/2009/02/26/2003437017.

surveillance. This case opens up new ground for more and more web users to take up the Internet as a tool to express criticism and monitor the actions of bureaucrats and the police.

Deng Yujiao, a young, female pedicurist from Hubei province was charged with murder after stabbing Party official *Deng Guida* (no relation) to death on May 10, 2009 with a pedicure knife in a local hotel where *Deng Guida* had tried to force her to have sex with him and two other officials. After Deng turned herself in to the police, she was initially charged with murder. Deng claimed she acted in self-defense after the official attempted to rape her. *Gan Wu*, a citizen reporter known broadly as The Butcher (*超级低俗屠夫*), was integral to what happened next. He wrote a blog post detailing the night's events and the offenses of the officials involved using human flesh searches.[105] *Deng*'s case then accumulated in excess of four million posts across websites. This case resonated with millions of Chinese fed up with low-level corruption and social injustice, and *Deng* was regarded as a national hero for resisting official abuse of power. As a result of the national outcry, the police released her on bail and put her under house arrest; prosecutors charged her with a lesser offense of "intentional assault" instead of murder.[106] Although government censors 10 days later ordered websites to stop reporting the case,[107]

Deng Yujiao was set free and the murder charges against her dismissed. Some netizens thought that this result should be viewed as a "significant victory of the Chinese Internet users and Chinese democracy" compared to previous similar cases.[108] However, it should be noted that the effect of the netizen's web supervision ultimately depends on the attitude of government. Web-based criticism may be

---

[105] Branigan, Tania, May 27th, 2009. Chinese woman who killed official bailed after online outcry. *The Guardian*. November7, 2013 retrieved rom http://www.theguardian.com/world/2009/may/27/china-bails-deng-yujiao.

[106] Ibid.

[107] May 25, 2009. Chinese Media Bans (Where They Exist). November7th, 2013 retrieved from http://zonaeuropa.com/200905c.brief.htm#011.

[108] Chao, Loretta. June 17th, 2009. China Frees Accused Woman After Protests Online. *The Wall Street Journal*, on November 7th, 2013 retrieved from http://online.wsj.com/news/articles/SB124513141993018119.

used to try to modify or remove a policy where there is division on an issue within the government, but on key issues where there is government unity dissent most likely will be quashed or ignored.[109]

Although the documentation of web-based criticism does not always make for successful changes, Chinese netizens value the power of the Internet and know they can bring about some progress which may not have been possible before. This very knowledge encourages web users to expand their ongoing experiment with online surveillance. Since the Internet has the capacity to handle a high volume of data, netizens find it is a good resource to utilize for monitoring corrupt officials. Next, I discuss how web users often use the Internet as a resource to expose corruption.

<u>Cyber Vigilantism</u>

In 2009 the Internet presented another gift to the Chinese people—namely, the microblog. *Weibo* was launched by *Sina* in that year. The microblog is a popular web tool used by a large populations of Chinese. It is believed that *Weibo* has an inherent micro-impact (微动力, *wei dongli*) because *Weibo* produces power in concentrating the forces of the ordinary people, and ordinary people can engage in social issues with activities take are easy to undertake, such as forwarding and sharing messages even without comments (Liu, 2011). It is suggested that the microblog platform actually provides an effective way to connect different social classes and ordinary people now have a handy tool to express opinions to the government and to leaders in Chinese society (Liu, 2011). Compared to BBS and blogs, microblogs now can exert even more impact on social issues. Using mobile phone applications, microbloggers are able to post information or photos at the scene, reaching their audience in mere seconds. As a result, the microblog platform becomes a big data source where people can search out rich information which provides a natural resource for the corruption watching and monitoring process. What follows are two cases selected to illustrate the microblog vigilantism phenomenon in contemporary China.

---

[109] Ibid.

Case 1 Yang Dacai

Brother Wristwatch, *Yang Dacai*, may be the top example of active microblog vigilantism in 2013. *Yang Dacai*, the former head of the Work Safety Administration in the province of Shaanxi, was sentenced to 14 years in prison after being found guilty of taking bribes and holding a large amount of property for which he cannot account.[110] *Yang* was a nameless official until his pictures were posted on *Weibo* where he was photographed apparently smiling at the scene of a tragic accident that had left 36 dead.[111] This apparent callousness raised the anger of many netizens who quickly conducted a human flesh search and soon it was found that the smiling man was *Yang Dacai*.

The results of this search were reposted over 8,600 times on *Weibo,* and the accusations swiftly evolved from callousness to corruption after people zoomed in on his luxury watch in that photo.[112] Netizens then searched and posted other publicly available photos of *Yang* wearing different watches, one of which cost somewhere between 200,000 and 400,000 *yuan* (about US$30,000 – US$60,000). It was finally found that *Yang* had a collection of at least eleven ultra-high-end timepieces that he could not possibly afford on his public servant's salary.[113] *Yang* was nicknamed “Brother Wristwatch” by the netizens and he was soon removed from his post and an official investigation followed. *Yang* pleaded guilty to charges of taking 250,000 *yuan*

---

[110] Taylor, Adam. September 5, 2013. Chinese Official Who Sparked Anger by Smiling at Fatal Car Crash Smiles as He is sentenced to 14 Years in Prison. November 9th, 2013 retrieved from http://www.businessinsider.com/yang-dacai-smiles-as-sentenced-to-14-years-2013-9#ixzz2kCffs5CY.

[111] Kaiman, Jonathan. September 5th, 2013. China's 'Brother Wristwatch' Yang Dacai jailed for 14 years for corruption. November 9th, 2013 retrieved from http://www.theguardian.com/world/2013/sep/05/china-brother-wristwatch-yang-dacai-sentenced.

[112] Wertime, David. August 27th, 2012. Did a Chinese Safety Official Just Get Caught Smiling at a Horrific Accident Scene? November 9th,, 2013 retrieved from http://www.tealeafnation.com/2012/08/did-a-chinese-safety-official-just-get-caught-smiling-at-a-horrific-accident-scene/#sthash.0ob4EUTX.dpuf.

[113] Ibid.

($40,000) in bribes and having bank deposits of 5.04 million *yuan* ($820,000) from dubious sources.[114]

Case 2 Cai Bin

Another similar story is that of "Uncle Houses," whose wrongdoing surfaced after citizens began posting pictures of his assets, including luxury homes, on the Internet. *Cai Bin*, a mid-level bureaucrat in the southern city of *Guangzhou*, was convicted of taking 2.75 million *yuan* ($450,000) in bribes and the court sentenced him to 11-and-a-half years in jail and fined him 600,000 yuan.[115] *Cai* was said to have accumulated at least 22 properties, even though his known salary was less than $20,000 a year.[116] Since *Cai*'s case, there have been additional reports in the state media of more such "Uncles and Aunts" of property. These later reports involved individuals who were officials from the provinces of *Shandong*, *Guangdong*, and *Zhejiang*; each of them is alleged to have owned in excess of 20 such valuable properties.[117] These cases usually started from *Weibo* postings where those cases were distributed widely, and clearly corrupt officials were exposed by netizens using the human flesh search tool.

---

[114] Chen, Stephen. August 30th, 2013. Time runs out for 'Brother Watch' Yang Dacai. November 9th,, 2013 retrieved from http://www.scmp.com/news/china/article/1300579/chinas-brother-watch-official-goes-trial-graft.

[115] *Fox News*, September 12th, 2013. China's 'Uncle House' given 11 years for bribes: media. November 11, 2013 retrieved from http://www.foxnews.com/world/2013/09/12/china-uncle-house-given-11-years-for-bribes-media.

[116] *China Daily*, October 23, 2012. 'Uncle House' under investigation. November 11, 2013 retrieved fromhttp://www.china.org.cn/china/2012-10/23/content_26875046.htm.

[117] Wang, Xiangwei. December 17th, 2012. Corruption fighters home in on big property owners. November 11, 2013 retrieved from http://www.scmp.com/news/china/article/1106966/corruption-fighters-home-big-property-owners.

Since the microblog has its powerful function, web users can post any picture and video to make very attractive postings to expose corruptive officials. These vivid postings lead to reposting and forwarding to make for extremely quick and broad information transmission. This information technology has led to a number of powerful online movements. There is ascending influence of the virtual civil society in China within which "Chinese vigilantes" organize to criticize and attack social transgressors (Herold, 2008). During the process, online participants collectively find demographic and geographical information of deviant individuals, often with the shared intention to expose, shame and punish them to reinstate legal justice or promote public morality (Cheong & Gong, 2010, p.474).

It is not surprising that the Chinese people have decided to ride on the technological wave to exert their impact on social affairs, on government officials, and on public policies. In the modern era citizens feel it necessary to gain information about public power in order to protect their interests, but the information about public power was rarely available and the state media were not highly reliable (Gao, 2013). Netizens use web *crowdsourcing* and *human flesh searches* to seek camaraderie in justice. They have some degree of trust in a sometimes-untrustworthy governing system to make corrections and sanction corruption. Web-based mass participation can assure them a higher chance of getting the issues redressed than any action they might take as an individual (W.Wang, 2013). Some people claim that the human flesh search can find its similar traits in the 1970s Great Cultural Revolution during which people posted big-character posters to attack others or speak out against injustices (Capone, 2012). The government also is fearful of a high level of cyber vigilantism from the public, and it has reacted accordingly on occasion; we next look into that government reaction.

Official Reaction to Cyber Vigilantism

Facing the prospect of increasing cyber vigilantism from the public, the Chinese government has reacted very quickly, with a mixture of both positive and negative measures. On the one hand, these reactions prove that public cyber vigilantism can have a real impact; on the other hand, the public has learned how to improve their activism during this kind of interaction with the government to minimize negative government reactions. Government reactions have included opening government microblogs and the exercise of greater supervision over online expressions through new legislation and some proactive law enforcement. I discuss each of these governmental reactions below.

Government Microblogs

Facing the prospect of cyber vigilantism from netizens, many governmental institutions have started to open up official microblog accounts and e-government websites in order to utilize the interactive feature of the Internet to interact with citizens (W.Wang, 2013). By the end of March of 2011 there were all together 176,714 government institutional accounts and 63,332 governmental officers' accounts being created (*National School of Administration of E-government Research Center*, 2013). The government microblogs are becoming a new medium for collective opinions to emerge, whereas e-government websites are only an online service platform (Hunter, 1998).

Government microblogs represent significant differences from the traditional government portal, from blogs, and from other forums due to the clearly unique characteristics of microblogs which highlight the personality traits of users and their interaction with each other. All of these traits provide more popular experience with e-governance, and government microblogs attract many people from different social classes to participate in public governance. The government is expanding its service scope effectively via the Internet to reach diverse social groups with more provision for their participation and interaction (Liu & Zheng, 2012).

The Courts, the Police and the Procuracy have started to open up microblog accounts as well, and many judges, prosecutors as well as police officers have also opened their own individual accounts. These government microblogs and individual blogs provide valuable new resources for ordinary people to gather information from and interact with their government. Many high profile criminal case trials have been broadcasted through court microblogs, such as that of *Bo Xilai* in which some very important video evidence was broadly publicized.

The interactions between the government microblogs and netizens are now plentiful. For example, the Police microblogs often receive reports from the public through microblogs including emergency issues, service requests and general questions. Police departments also post information about public safety, traffic, weather, service or information requests. For example, the Shenzhen Police posted a video to show people how to identify the thief on a bus and prevent being a victim of theft.[118]Interestingly, many government microblogs including those of the court, police, and procuracy are expressing increasingly more personality. These microblogs often post meaningful parables, idioms, stories or even jokes to promote good behaviors instead of displaying didacticism. In sum, official microblogs have had some positive effects. In all cases they make information more transparent and they increase communication with the public; hopefully, these improvements can lead these agencies to deliver better public services and be more responsive to citizen needs and preferences.

Supervision of Cyber Expression

The year of 2008 already witnessed the power of *netizens* who helped to disclose a number of high-profile corruption incidents, and produced quick and decisive official actions to punish officials identified by the anonymous online postings (Lye & Yang, 2009). This phenomenon occasioned the expression of positive attitudes regarding social media by China's high level leadership. For example, the Chinese Premier *Wen Jiabao* even participated in a two-hour online chat with netizens in March of 2009 (Lye & Yang, 2009). However, it should be duly noted that genuine reform of the whole bureaucracy system is needed, and that acceptance from several high level leaders is not enough to fully address the major problem of widespread corruption in local government. For example, in March of 2009 *netizens* launched a campaign to ask "officials to declare their assets" and this type of collective opinion has actually raged for years without appropriate responsive government action. The asset declaration concept has been resisted vigorously by most officials in the Chinese bureaucracy, and as a consequence this social media campaign has not reached its goal.[119]

---

[118] November 11th, 2013, retrieved from http://www.weibo.com/mygroups?gid=3641806451417768&wvr=5&leftnav=1.

[119] Wong, Colleen. August 28th, 2013. Enough is Enough! Chinese Officials Must Declare Assets. November 12th, 2013 retrieved from

Furthermore, websites in China may be fined or shut down if they fail to comply with government censorship guidelines. It is reported that approximately 1,000 censors were hired by each individual website under the threat of closure in order to comply with government supervision dictates, and that 20,000–50,000 Internet police (*wang jing, 网警*) and Internet monitors (*wang guanban网管*) exist at all levels of Chinese government (Chen & Ang, 2011). This situation has been characterized as a form of democratic mimicry by which rulers seek to be able to be responsive to collective opinion without being captive of it (Fukuyama, 2012). It has also been found that the censorship program is used to reduce the probability of collective action by technologically clipping social ties whenever any collective movements are in evidence or expected. So, rather than simply suppressing criticism of the state or the Communist Party, the capacity to mobilize collective action is purposefully curtailed by the authorities (King, Pan & Roberts, 2013).

It should be noted, of course, that social media can also have a **dark side**. Social media sometimes also used by criminals to spread rumors and/or make illegal profits. Since August of 2013 police across China have detained a number of suspects and closed several private businesses for fabricating online rumors. For example, two men in Beijing were found to have created and spread online rumors, including false information about a 2011 bullet train accident and about China's most famous Good Samaritan, *Lei Feng* (*雷锋*).[120] On the 9th of September of 2013 the Supreme People's Court and the Supreme People's Procuratorate released the judicial interpretation on the punishment of online rumors and defamation (*最高人民法院、最高人民检察院关于办理利用信息网络实施诽谤等刑事案件适用法律若干问题的解释*). It stipulates that people will face defamation charges if online rumors which they post are viewed by more than 5,000 Internet

---

http://thediplomat.com/china-power/enough-is-enough-chinese-officials-must-declare-assets.

[120] *China Wiki*, November 13th 2013 retrieved from http://wiki.china.org.cn/wiki/index.php/Judicial_interpretation_on_punishment_of_online_rumors_and_defamation.

users or re-posted more than 500 times.[121] Some scholars have argued that this action likely represents a governmental reaction to rising liberal ideas, and some online celebrities have been detained under this judicial interpretation.[122]

<u>Online Legal Activism</u>

Although the government has reacted to public cyber vigilantism in a number of ways, people in China tend to believe that few actual changes in operations and practices have been made, and that sometimes there have been patently negative reactions. Online activists tend to hold the view that more sustained activism is needed. As discussed above, China's Supreme People's Court and Supreme People's Procuratorate issued a new judicial interpretation on sanctioning fines or prison time for those profiting from spreading harmful rumors or deleting posts. Anyone deliberately posting lies, for profit or not, may face up to three years in prison if their posts are shared more than 500 times or viewed by more than 5,000 people.[123] The speaker of the Supreme Court noted that the police have detained people for spreading false information as part of crackdowns on online rumors, but that the lack of detailed guidelines led to inconsistencies in the handling of cases from one province to the next. In making this announcement he promised that netizens who help expose corruption online will not face charges, even if their posts are not 100 percent accurate.[124]

The First Case of Online Rumor Sanctions

The first case of online rumor punishment after this judicial interpretation was announcement involved a teenager, *Yang*, from *Zhangjiachuan* County in north-west *Gansu* province. *Yang* was detained after he questioned the local police force's conduct after a

---

[121] Ibid.

[122] Ibid.

[123] *China Daily*, September 10th, 2013. Judicial move aims at online rumors. November 12th, 2013 retrieved from http://usa.chinadaily.com.cn/china/2013-09/10/content_16955954.htm.

[124] Ibid.

corpse was found outside a karaoke parlor and the police claimed the man died of a head injury after falling from a high place. On September 14, 2013, *Yang* opined on his microblog page that the man had been murdered. He wrote “The karaoke parlor boss is an employee of the court, and there's been a conflict between the police and the masses – they beat up the dead man's family members.”[125] The post was retweeted 962 times and was subsequently deleted. The county court held that *Yang* had "fabricated facts" because the parlor boss was actually a court employee's spouse.

Microblog users reacted to the teenager's detention with thousands of tweets, launching an online campaign for his release by re-tweeting a post bearing the slogan "Save the Child!" more than 10,000 times, adding thousands of comments in the process. Much of the anger was directed at the new judicial interpretation and the perceived bullying of a teenager.[126] Further, people started online searches and found that *Zhangjiachuan*, a state-level, poverty-stricken county, had wasted a great deal of government aid on vanity projects, including the building of luxury office buildings, and the local police chief had bribed his way into his job.[127]

Two activist lawyers, *You Feizhu* and *Wang Shihua*, travelled to *Zhangjiachuan* County and campaigned for the teenager’s release. These two lawyers posted their 72-hour experience with the detention center staff and the police in *Zhangjiachuan* County, and more than 40 prominent lawyers signed a petition calling for Yang’s release. Lawyer *You* kept ongoing contact with the microblog community.[128]

---

[125] Kaiman, Jonathan. September 20th, 2013, China detains teenager over web post amid social media crackdown. November 12th, 2013 retrieved from http://www.theguardian.com/world/2013/sep/20/china-detains-teenage-web-post-crackdown.

[126] Minter, Adam. September 29th, 2013, Where the crime of retweeting can land you in jail. November 12th, 2013 retrieved from http://www.smh.com.au/comment/where-the-crime-of-retweeting-can-land-you-in-jail-20130928-2ul3g.html#ixzz2l1qQUH6B.

[127] Ibid.

[128] *Sina Weibo*, November 12th, 2013 retrieved from http://www.weibo.com/youfeizhu.

You posted tweets saying "the center denied allowing us meeting with *Yang* and they need to ask permit from their leaders… September 22, 10:37am." "We ask officers to request permit from leaders…September 22, 11:03am." Lawyer Chi responded to these tweets with advice "Watch any signatures the police ask to sign…do not sign on empty paper…September 22, 12:44 pm." *You* continued posting "Officer Wang said we can meet *Yang* in 2:30pm this afternoon…September 22, 13:06 pm." "We waited for the morning and afternoon, still no meeting is allowed. But now two police officers from the county police department came and they can meet Yang immediately…We are angry…. September 22, 15:57pm." Two lawyers waited until around 10 pm that day to get the chance to talk with two upper-level officials from the county police department.

At the same time, the online campaign was continuing. Posts about a corruption case that incriminated the police chief in charge of *Yang*'s detention were also circulated online. The pressure from the public pushed the provincial police bureau to cancel the criminal case and change the case filing to one of 7 days administrative detention. *Yang* was released around 1am, September 23rd. This victory raised public optimism for the power of online activism. Lawyer *Zhou Ze* posted on his microblog "If China's netizens unite, who can stop them?"[129]

As a new popular communication tool, online social media have opened up a new era for the Chinese people who expect to ride on the new wave of technology to build a society of justice under the rule of law. There is no doubt that new social media have allowed reformers to make a certain degree of progress, including the development of proactive e-governance and cyber supervision and monitoring of public officials. As I discussed before, more than 70% of the people on the *Sina* microblog have bachelor or associate degrees, and the people in the professional legal field, including law professors, lawyers, judges,

---

[129] Patrick Boehler, September 23rd, 2013. Is a 16-year-old boy's release a victory for netizens in China's internet crackdown? November 12th, 2013 retrieved from http://www.scmp.com/news/china-insider/article/1315878/teenagers-release-rare-victory-chinas-internet-crackdown.

prosecutors, and police officers, mostly have college or above level of formal education and can use social media proficiently as a convenient tool for communication and the expression of their views. Many microblogs are being used by legal professionals, and sometimes their tweets express ideas and concerns about legal reform which are highly insightful. I have followed these legal professionals and use them as a sample to study the online legal community. In the next part of the book, I use the data collected from this sample to do tweets analysis and describe the current state of the Chinese legal community.

MICROBLOGS AND THE ONLINE LEGAL COMMUNITY

As I have illustrated in the cases set forth above the Microblog platform has played a significant role in Chinese society since its development only a short time ago, and many netizens are trying to use it to exert a modicum of supervision over public power. Since criminal justice is a major part of public power, most hot topics on microblogs are about criminal legal issues, a fact which provides good data for this book. There are several noteworthy advantages to the use of data from microblogs. First, the microblogs come from a quite large legal community composed of law professors, judges, prosecutors, lawyers, and police officers. These legal system professionals mostly have a verified status on microblogs, and their postings have validity in representing their respective legal professions. Legal professionals on social media tend to be highly informed and somewhat opinionated users of social media, and often express their own opinions on legal issues and hot topic events with candor and some emotion. I collected blog posts on hot topics concerning criminal justice and analyze their opinions, including those relating to legal reform, current law enforcement practices, and important criminal law cases.

Second, the Microblog platform itself is an interactive community in which people tweet, re-tweet, forward and reply to one another. Different legal professionals often interact with each other on diverse legal issues, including the hot criminal law cases, noteworthy social events, and legal conceptual thoughts. As a result, it is possible to document the current state of mind of the Chinese professional legal community from a study of these interactions. Third, the microblog postings are spontaneous and constitute an active narrative launched by the web users themselves. These postings are what web users want to express, not just the passive response to investigator-composed survey questionnaire items. Without much intervention from investigators, we could observe more fully the free and natural expressions coming from the people who are most directly engaged in the rule of law issues confronting contemporary Chinese society. From the many microblog tweets I collected, one major category pertains to the discussion of legislation and public policy. A second major category of tweets is more directly related to the interactions taking place among legal professions in China today.

Legal Discussions on Microblogs

It is admittedly somewhat difficult to categorize the legal discussions on microblogs in China because their content tends to be rather broad, and often the tweets touch upon various aspects of the legal system. I have, nonetheless, grouped these tweets under the headings of "hot topics," "informational tweets," and "emotional tweets." I list each such topic separately below.

Hot Topics

One type of legal discussion includes commentaries and observations on hot topics in the legal system, topics which attracted many responses. Some such topics have been discussed offline in daily life for a long time, but a more unified pattern of opinion can be documented via a study of microblogs.

Topics of Procuracy Supervision

A discussion of the supervisory power of the procuracy which was initiated on November 7th of 2013 was re-tweeted 263 times and received 80 individual responses.[130] This original microblog started by a judge (@汉德法官) observed the following: "We need to establish an independent judicial system in order to build the rule of law, and the supervision power of the procuracy will become the target of reform." In response villyy observed "The first step on the problem in China is

---

[130] *Sina Weibo*, November 1, 2013 retrieved from http://www.weibo.com/1552302990/AhCKWhELo

to separate legal cases from the letter and visit system…rule of law is a long way to go…" A lawyer (姚燕倩律师)said in her/his own microblog: "Let's start from urbanization which produces the sense of rule, and nurture citizens…it makes more sense to talk about rule of law in an urbanized society." Another participant in the commentary 今天立夏_observed the following: "Rule of law may have more than one way to go, judicial independence is not a religion with no doubt. It is not necessarily that judicial independence must exclude supervision." Scholar *You* (@学者游伟) next observed: "The multiple roles of procuracy must be changed, otherwise the supervision function cannot be implemented well." @南方的熊888888 said in response: "How can the procuracy supervise the trial when it is one part of the trial? It is funny that a player becomes the judge of the match. I heard a criminal case once, and the prosecutor opposed because the judge allowed the defense lawyer to talk a little more. Is the procuracy supervision supposed to restrict the defense, right?"

A prosecutor (常州检察院巢琨宇) responded with this remark: "Both judge and prosecutor are servant of law, not the master." A one-time prosecutor and now judge @Penaljudge said "I hate that people repeatedly try to prove the supervision power of procuracy, and this is the reason now I take a career as a judge." 山寨检控官在福建 noted the following: "Procuracy supervision is learned from USSR (Union of Socialist Soviet Republics) and should have been abolished. The key is the independence of Judge without which no judicial independence will exist. Work hard, folks." It seems that most people agree that judicial independence is the key in legal reform, and even prosecutors themselves have provided no solid support for the continuation of procuracy supervision.

Topics of Judicial Independence

Another topic, that of the goal of judicial independence, has also been discussed for a long time offline, but people tend to be braver when they express their opinion online. From their tweets we can see that the goal of judicial Independence has been agreed upon by most people. On October 6th of 2012 Professor of Law and lawyer *He Bin* posted a tweet on *Sina Weibo* and commented on a *People's Daily*'s article which praised the Supreme Court for its consistent resistance to the wrong ideas of Judicial Independence as a “Western” thing. His original post said in this regard that “Judicial independence exists in Japan, South Korea and India…Taiwan, and Hong Kong and Macao of our country also have judicial independence. Is judicial independence a Western idea or a worldwide idea?”[131] His original post got **3,299 responses** and was **re-tweeted 9,810 times**. Most people, including scholars and lawyers, agreed to build Judicial Independence and listed reasons derived from history, from sound legal theories and from practice alike. 韓青子said in this regard “Is Marxism not also from the Western Countries?” Scholar *Xie* (谢佑平) said along these lines: “There is no justice if there is no judicial independence.” He further commented “Marx himself actually promoted judicial independence.” 可可先生observed that “…the *People's Daily* represents a certain interest group. Judicial independence is not good to serve this group…” 范忠信 said “the non-independent judicial system is an organ to implement the order of upper-level officials.” Lawyer *Long* (龙元富律师) made the following remark regarding the Western origins of the concept: “judicial independence does not belong to the West only…it belongs to China...the administration of justice is the terminal tool to solve conflicts among human beings…independence is the nature of the administration of justice.” 绿水青山总关情said in support: “ It is difficult to get justice if there is no judicial independence. The justice will be disturbed if it is not independent. Judges only can serve upward if it is not independent, rather than serve law and facts…It is common sense, no matter the West or East…People do Letters and Visits instead of resorting to lawsuits because of no justice in the administration of justice.”

Ordinary people mostly posted stinging comments regarding this problem. 道德如是说 said “It will be easier to say that judicial independence belongs to places outside of mainland and we here need the rule of man.” 黄东 Sir said “It is socialism with Chinese characteristics.” 湖边静思 said in this regard “The ‘West’ is a political concept…equals to the enemy…we oppose everything that our enemy support!” 傻菇粮 said relatedly: “Why do good things always belong to

---

[131] *Sina Weibo*, November 1, 2013 retrieved from http://www.weibo.com/1215031834/yF9pCsC0K?type=repost.

the West? Why? …" Some people posted angry comments such as 谭奥航 who said the following: "I have been sick about the *People's Daily*…Where is the dignity of law? Isn't our country building rule of law? Or is it rule of man? Rule of officers? Rule of Brothers Wristwatch? " 雁城在南方 said "How can the interests of a party ride over the rights of country…and people, enjoy all benefits without any obligations… " Only a few people disagreed. 注疏哲dw said in opposition "Judicial transparence is good. Independence, how to explain it...It is just crying from another interest group…"

Some people's thoughts were quite insightful, indeed. For example, 郑秀军said: "When we talk about the judicial independence, we should talk more how to gain this independence. Whether the qualification of our judges can take this responsibility and meet the criteria? We could realize the judicial independence earlier if all of us are thinking, promoting and working hard!" Scholar Chen (陈泰和-民决团) argued that "It was nice to see so many people support judicial independence and this proved that rule of law has been promoted in people's minds. However, I am worried…that it will be a fake independence if the judicial independence is based on the Continental law which many scholars agree with." He explained further "I proposed that judicial independence must take the form of jury which take control of the court and this is the really scientific independence." Another comment from @柳刀叶 stated the following: "Justice could not exist even with judicial independence. Let's remember the inquisition during the medieval period…the inquisition was one of the darkest judicial places." BAOGANGSHENG said in this regard: "No need to call for judicial independence, and there is better way to check and balance. Let the administration of justice under the Political Consultative Conference and all chief justices have to be non-communist party legal professionals."

Some people provided specific suggestions. For example, scholar Zhou (周永坤微博) suggested: the following: "the administration of justice should be independent on different level…supervision should not exist because it will compete for the authority…"[132] This particular

[132] *Sina Weibo*, November 12th, 2013 retrieved from http://www.weibo.com/2927612341/AhY3zlKuG.

post was re-tweeted 238 times and received 64 responses. People from different professions posted their comments. Lawyer *D* (地道法律英语) observed the following: "It is too narrow to define supervision like you did…" Judge *Yi* (一生不读报) noted: "It means no supervision from outside power, avoiding the intervention. The internal discipline procedure can prevent and detect wrong cases and correct them…" Lawyer *Zhu* (朱中华律师-国际国内工程律师) suggested the following steps: "List all the court decision documents outside the courts and publish them online permanently, let the society judge their work…(make) judges publicize their property and income…" The original blogger *Zhou* further commented that "the judicial independence should be the independence of the judge, not the independence of the court." Judge Z disagreed: "The independence of court is the foundation of judicial independence; it is too early to talk about judicial independence since the court has not been independent." Journalist *Ye* (叶竹盛) noted: "supervision should exist in certain ways, for example, judges can be elected…media can monitor…but these (forms of) supervision should not disrupt judicial independence…."

Informational Tweets

The second group of tweets selected as illustrative are primarily informational, providing legal knowledge, reflections and ideas suggested for reflection. These tweets were written primarily by legal professionals dealing with criminal cases daily, and reflect the thinking of lawyers who have deep understanding about the criminal justice system and the law of criminal procedure. These tweets on the one hand can reflect the quality of legal professionals, and on the other hand they disclose certain problems in the system calling for study and drafting of solutions.

First, for some more complicated issues microblogs lack the space to elaborate and mostly play the role of information dissemination. In a tweet posted on August 24 in 2012 by lawyer Mao (ID on microblogs is 刑诉毛立新) worry was expressed about the tentative Supreme Court judicial interpretation that the courts can punish lawyers if they act against court orders or propose justice administration organs to cancel lawyers' practice certificate.[133] This tweet received 160 responses and was re-tweeted 539 times. Many people responded to express similar concern and to articulate criticism. Some doubt this interpretation is legal. @alxonC said "Is this interpretation against law?" 湖边问道人 said "It is difficult for some Judges to make something lawful since they do not understand law." Microbloger @倚亭览书said in this regard: "I am surprised to know that the Chief Justice of the Supreme Court has no law degree." A lawyer 贾军武律师 said that in his opinion "The Court punishing lawyers exceeds its judicial power."

Second, some legal professionals use long tweets to offer reflections on the criminal justice system. For example, in recent years more judges and prosecutors have advanced degrees in law and have started to reflect on the legal system. In terms of the limited judicial capacity in the courts, Prosecutor *Li* 检察官李小萌offered this analysis: "We have non-judicial officials in the courts and judges also take many social responsibilities besides judicial jobs…" Judge *Q* 倾城 observed: "I found that the procuracies always protest no matter the court decisions are just or not, because they have to protest certain number of cases every year to complete the required quota …" 深客法缘 observed the following: "Having served the court almost 20 years and having had more than 10 intern students so far…hope they all read more classical law books and will not serve as judges unless they love this career very much…it is difficult and burdensome to tell them why…"[134] He further commented thusly: "The administrative style of judicial system and bureaucratization are the obstruction to judicial independence…it is wrong to use executive system to hold judges accountable…"[135]

---

[133] *Sina Weibo*, November 1, 2013 retrieved from http://www.weibo.com/2002687103/yyBncDSDG?type=repost.

[134] *Sina Weibo*, November 12th, 2013 retrieved from http://www.weibo.com/p/1005051898426140/weibo?is_search=0&visible=0&is_tag=0&profile_ftype=1&page=40#feedtop.

[135] Ibid.

Third, lawyers were more concerned about the practice environment. Lawyer *Zhou* (@周泽律师) worried openly that "this may become another big stick to hit on lawyers." Lawyer *Gan* (@甘元春律师) said "If this becomes true, lawyers become the ears of the Deaf." Lawyer *Zhang* (@律师张国华) claimed further that "judicial interpretation cannot exist if it is against law." Lawyer *Xu* (@徐宗新) noted the following: "Lawyers cannot abuse their power…the public power cannot abuse either, the abuse of public power has worse results." Lawyer *Cui* (@崔小平律师) added this noteworthy thought: "This is trying to get rid of all righteous lawyers and make them become decoration. Once lawyers become decoration, abuse of power will be rampant, how can citizens' rights exist then?"

Lawyers expressed their frequent confusions in working with courts, the procuracy and the police. Lawyer *Zhu* (朱明勇律师) posted on January 25, 2013 to complain that: "What kind of lawyers can help the defendants? You even cannot enter the court, no one lets you check the case file, and the case already exceeded the time limit. This is the current criminal defense with Chinese characteristics."[136] Lawyer *Mo* (鼎凌所-莫梦觉律师) responded that "I feel that it is more useful to be '*Sike*' lawyers who fight for the justice until death." Lawyer *Zhang* said "One of my cases has been sent back to trial, but the original court said that they did not find this case, and the secondary trial court did not have this case either. Soon after I found this case went to a local procuracy of another city…no one really knows why the provincial procuracy changed the jurisdiction…" Lawyer *F* said that "If the lawyer brings an order from the higher lever leaders, the court will welcome the lawyer sincerely." Lawyer *Xu* dee1976 许小状 said in this regard: "The worse is that you were trained not to make hard time with the police, procuracy and court before you enter the profession, and the criminal defense is expected to cooperate with them to deal with the defendants…" He further observed that "…We lawyers are even less capable than the security guard in front of the court."

---

[136] *Sina Weibo*, November 12th, 2013 retrieved from http://www.weibo.com/1264080891/zg9CEASUo.

Emotional Tweets

The first type of emotional tweets express strong opinions. These tweets usually are focused on prevalent hot topics during a fixed period of time, especially when big events happen. For example, lawyer *Zhu* (朱孝顶律师) posted a tweet on August 18, 2012 claiming that he was beaten and then thrown out of the provincial high court in *Shandong* province on August 17th.[137] Since August 18th, Zhu tweeted on this issue using the title "Yelling once each day!" on his microblog calling out every day for an apology from the court. After 155 days no apology had yet been given.

Scholar *Xu* (徐昕) repeatedly posted a tweet on the "*Nie Shubin*" case once every day and calls for the justice for *Nie*. His original tweet posted on February 22nd, 2013 was re-tweeted **354,902 times** and received **35,313 comments**.[138] Many people across the country responded that *Nie* has been wronged and that the court should redress his case. As I discussed at some length in the preceding chapter, the *Hebei* high court officials steadfastly maintain their decision and insist that the evidence cannot prove that *Nie* is innocent. This type of "Yelling once each day!" has been used a great deal by lawyers and scholars posting on Microblogs to call for justice and promote the legal redress of issues they feel strongly about. The lawyers who are insisting on the "redressing of certain injustice" are given the name of "*Sike*" lawyer, a term which literally means fight for justice until death.

The second type of emotional tweets entail releasing one's anger, expressing disappointment, or expressing profound sadness. For example, @一口馍 said "It seems that we only can rely on media and microblogs to prevent this from coming true." @狐狸懒懒 said that "Fortunately, I did not choose law as my major." Lawyer *Wang* (王绍涛律师) "In many judges' eyes, lawyers are not necessary." Lawyer *Guo* (郭爱律师) posed the provocative question: "If the court can punish a lawyer directly, can they punish the prosecutors?" Another Lawyer *Zhang* (@张锦宏律师) ridiculed the notion of sanctioning lawyers by observing: "The interpretation should be stricter and get rid

---

[137] November 12th, 2013 retrieved from http://t.qq.com/p/t/201046066188190.

[138] *Sina Weibo*, November 12th, 2013 retrieved from http://www.weibo.com/1701401324/zkj4ce2kC?type=repost.

of the legal defending system, let us all go back home and sell sweet potatoes." Some lawyers also proposed certain solutions with clear emotion: some proposed the use of constitutional review over judicial interpretation to correct the abuse of judicial power (@律师张国华); some supported the idea that China's lawyers' guild should send its opinion report to the National People's Congress and Ministry of Justice (@江净律师). Although there were 160 responses to this tweet, most were releasing anger as opposed to expressing clear opinions.

There are grounds for optimism regarding seeing more and more people, even non-legal professionals and lay persons, start to participate in online discussions on legal system issues. Their participation not only provides a foundation for potential legal system reform, but also serves to draw broader attention into the goals of legal reform and movement toward the rule of law. Legal professionals, the pioneers for legal reform in the physical world, are also taking the lead in online discussions in the social media. However, it is clear that they do have diverse backgrounds and often disagree with one another. How do they communicate and interact with each other on microblogs? What kind of issues are they interested in discussing? The following analysis will show the state of the current Chinese criminal law community actively interacting via microblogs.

Legal Community on the Microblogs

The Chinese professional legal community includes a large number of lawyers, judges, law professors, prosecutors, police and legal scholars. Different from their counterparts in Western countries, Chinese legal professionals were all government employees before legal reform. These people were considered "in the system" and they were permitted to switch jobs within the larger system. After 30 years of legal reform, lawyers are gradually being separated from the civil service system, while judges, prosecutors and the police are still civil servants in the bureaucratic system. It is understandable that there is conflict between lawyers who are largely "out of the system" and those judges, prosecutors and police who are "in the system."

Lawyers' and scholars' microblog accounts are more like reflecting their true identities, while the accounts of judges and prosecutors tend to be posted while using fictitious names. For example, they use terms such as "One judge" or "Small judge" or "A judge in local court," etc. This fact may show that lawyers and scholars have more career freedom to express their personal views. Compared to prosecutors and police officers, legal scholars, judges and lawyers more often discuss legal issues on microblogs. Prosecutors are relatively silent on hot topic discussions, and their own tweets mostly transmit some aspect of legal knowledge. The 12 tweets I collected from police officers either disseminate knowledge on how to prevent victimization or accidents, or involve the distribution of risk-involved event warnings.

Judge *vs.* Lawyer

It is not unusual that judges and lawyers argue against each other on some of the microblogs. Judge *H* (汉德法官) posted a tweet to Scholar *He* (何兵) saying that he has criticized too much about court work without knowing the facts, and hopes he can post his future tweets more cautiously.[139] This tweet was re-tweeted 1,026 times and received 645 responses. *He* (何兵) responded: "Should you be more specific? Do not know how you have so much superiority…" Many people said that there is freedom of speech and different opinions should be allowed to exist. 假装是法官 said in this regard: "we should support *He* since too few scholars can speak up…you can tell the specific points that he did not speak well and let people discuss…" 帅帅的流氓兔 further commented: "Judge *H* has superiority since he is in the system…" Lawyer *Q* (喬老爺) pointed out "some courts even ruled without facts, how can you require other people do…" Some people thought that Judge *H* represented important figures from court to warn *He* since his speech threatens the interests of judges.

Lawyer *Yun* (云之南爨水流) observed as follows in this regard: "Lawyers have better credentials than judges." Lawyer *Wei* (开诚律师) 魏家林said in this regard: "the court should reflect on its culture and mindset, and get rid of judicial corruption…" Lawyer *Q* (青石律师) noted the following: "The problem now is not that lawyers do not

[139] *Sina Weibo*, November 12th, 2013 retrieved from http://www.weibo.com/1552302990/yFcEMiZZQ#_rnd1384819848615.

respect judges, actually most lawyers obey the arbitrary judges too much." Lawyer *W* 伍雷 said: "Only real judges rather than the accomplice should be respected." Judge *Y* (Yanlipingfaguan) said in his own defense: "I always respect lawyers…what if judges' rights are intruded?" Another judge (倾城) pointed out that the fight between lawyers and judges are useless and only lead to less trust in justice. Legal scholar and lawyer Xu (徐昕) said: "All legal professionals need do reflection…as a part-time lawyer, I hope lawyers can respect judges to the most degree." Lawyer *Si* (斯伟江) observed in this regard: "Legal professionals cannot reach agreement because there is a hand behind judges. Lawyers can criticize this hand, but judges cannot. It will get better if judges start saying no to this hand one day." Lawyer *Yan* 腌小鱼儿said: "hope all judges know that judges should take on more responsibilities in building judicial authority and credibility."

In August of 2013 four senior Shanghai judges were suspended from their posts after evidence emerged that they had hired prostitutes, and this scandal drew multiple criticisms from lawyers on microblogs. Lawyer *Chi* posted on August 8, 2013 that one judge had not been suspended because he got drunk after the prostitutes came. She asked, "Can we people continue to feed these alcoholic guys as judges? Let them roll back home and plant sweet potatoes!"[140] The second sentence is a rather common saying in China and means that civil servants should serve the public well, otherwise they should go home to plant and sell sweet potatoes. This tweet was re-tweeted **9,611** times, and received **2,078 responses**. Most posts ridiculed those judges and opined that they should be fired. Lawyer *Yang* (杨名跨律师): "Alcohol saved him…is that court so dirty?" Lawyer *Xiong* (熊代英律师) commented: "A judge like this still got protected, and I see the root is officials shield one another…" SYU之微博看世界observed: "We change nothing except for complaining, because all other civil servants who have not been found out are the same…"

I am not pessimistic in the least about these arguments between judges and lawyers. Healthy debating can reveal truth, and ultimately help improve progress toward the rule of law. The terminal goal of

---

[140] *Sina Weibo*, November 12th, 2013 retrieved from http://www.weibo.com/1935084477/A3KcAk0JH.

judges and lawyers alike is ultimately the same – namely, to achieve justice. The road to the rule of law and judicial independence will witness much more lively debate and many more contentious issues, but it is a source of optimism to see the microblog social media platform being used to frame and sustain discussion within China's legal community.

Lawyer *vs.* Lawyer

Besides the professional conflicts between judges and lawyers arising from role conflicts and organizational perspectives, lawyers of diverse background also have conflicts with each other. Some lawyers used to work "in the system" and have now switched over to private legal practice. Others went to legal practice directly after passing the bar exam. Interestingly, these previous "in the system" lawyers are more able to gain success since they have wider connections than do their counterparts without such experience. For example, lawyer *Chen* (陈有西) is a quite well known lawyer who has taken an important role in several high profile lawsuits filed to help deserving weak groups. He used to work in a provincial police bureau, served on the provincial political and legal committee and provincial high court, and then switched to be a private practice lawyer. He posted a tweet on *Sina Weibo* saying that "Many lawyers do not know lawyers also have professional titles which are reviewed by the government. I here show you all the files from the government entitled 'Confer 21 people (including Chen himself) who obtain the high level professional titles of lawyers and greffier.'" [141] *Chen*'s proud tweet received 242 responses, most of which are doubts and criticism.

Lawyer *Lü* (吕峰律师) said that "the professional titles are not good for the growth of lawyers' independent personality and professionalism." Lawyer *Si* (斯伟江) commented "I heard that the first level lawyer used to be like high level engineer and was qualified to buy a sleeping berth on the train. Now, anyone can buy it with money. I think this lawyer review system should have been abolished." Lawyer *Xing* (邢建民律师) criticized *Chen* in these terms: "Having an

---

[141] *Sina Weibo*, November 12th, 2013 retrieved from http://www.weibo.com/1803570001/yCO9Ayt8D#_rnd1384388398567.

unceasing affection for professional titles, pleased with his past experience as a government bureaucrat, he is actually fond of the old bureaucracy system." lawyer *Li* (李律师在上海) said "If you mind professional titles that much, go back to being a government employee again. If we want to build judicial independence, lawyers have to be independent first. "

These disagreements among lawyers are not negative in the least because the fact that this sharing of differences of opinion is occurring means that Chinese lawyers are seeking out a professional identity after being separated from the state system. It also shows that the profession of "lawyering" is becoming more mature and independent, so lawyers can play a more effective role in promoting justice and the rule of law. It would be wrong to say that the profession of lawyer lacks solidarity moreover; there are many moments when we can see Chinese lawyers unite on microblogs promoting the value of legal activism. There are many examples about the solidarity of Chinese lawyers that could be reported from the microblog tweets collected for this book.

I have discussed the case of *Li Zhuang* in chapter 5, and this case can be cited as the start for Chinese lawyers to group together to protect their own profession's rights. In the *Li Zhuang* case, 12 lawyers provide free legal assistance to help *Li Zhuang*, a criminal defense lawyer who was charged with perjury. In addition, during the first case of the online rumor I discussed in the first part of this chapter, many lawyers from diverse areas of China united online to support the two lawyers who were working on the spot.

Another example of solidarity in the legal profession is that of the *Beihai* lawyer perjury case. On June 13, 2011 four lawyers who were defense counsel in a murder trial in *Behai* were detained by police on charges of "witness tampering" (妨害作证罪) under Article 306 of China's Criminal Law. Many lawyers in China volunteered to form a special group to provide help, and a six-lawyer defense group was formed on June 26 and set for *Beihai* to provide legal assistance to the detained lawyers and their defendants.

This event was broadcasted on lawyers' microblogs to release information instantly and called for more support. Lawyers from around the country participated in this event actively, following and forwarding tweets, after responding with their own suggestions. After

48 hours the local police were forced to release three detained lawyers, all except for lawyer *Yang Zaixin*. *Yang* then was detained in jail for a period of 9 months, changing to residential surveillance for a period, and then released on bail. On February 7, 2013 the perjury case was dismissed and attorney *Yang* was proven innocent. During these 15 months many Chinese lawyers paid continuous close attention to *Yang*'s case, and posted microblogs almost every day to call for the release of *Yang*. Chinese lawyers have to continue to speak out and act boldly, both for their clients and for themselves. Although they may have some conflicts among themselves sometimes, their solidarity as a group is inevitable.

Prosecutors

Compared to either judges or lawyers, prosecutors writing on microblogs are relatively quiet. Prosecutors rarely argue with other legal professionals, and they rarely discuss hot topics in criminal justice. Most of them post legal knowledge on their microblogs. For example, prosecutor *Leng* (冷月检察官) tweeted in order to clarify the misunderstanding of why the procuracy lodge protests against court judgments and said this in regard to this issue: "Prosecutors protest against court judgments based on objective facts…the procuracy also protests if the court convicted the innocent people…." Another prosecutor *Ma* (检察官马草原) persistently posts legal knowledge on his microblogs. For example, he wrote "It is depressing to be asked that 'procuracy is also court, right?' I have to tell them over and over again that the court is part of the state judiciary, and procuracy takes charge of legal supervision …it seems that we need to promote more legal knowledge..."

Some prosecutors dared to express their opinions. For example, Prosecutor *Yang* (检察官杨斌) said "although I belong to the system…I live based on my knowledge and capabilities…law is my King."[142] Her tweet received 65 responses and was re-tweeted 255 times. Most people are positive, though some people think that she is

[142] *Sina Weibo*, November 12th, 2013 retrieved from http://www.weibo.com/p/1005052184287602/weibo?is_search=0&visible=0&is_tag=0&profile_ftype=1&page=16#feedtop.

predisposed to using high-flown words. She also wrote: "Now I am not that excited when corruptive officials are found out and sent prosecuted…I do not mean to sympathize with them…I am feeling that it is useless to catch several corrupt officials if the system which nurtures the evils cannot be removed..."[143] *Yang* quit her job in 2015 and decided to be a lawyer.[144]

It is not difficult to explain why the different types of legal professionals behave differently on the social media. Prosecutors and police officers are less likely to post strong opinions because their organizational structures are highly hierarchical and bureaucratic, featuring strict management control. Court organization in China is no less bureaucratic, so judges rarely write posts to criticize the system within which they operate. Instead, they debate with lawyers who often criticize the courts and judges. On the one hand, this debate shows the unfortunate lack of understanding between different legal professions and documents the pressure lawyers feel from the bureaucracy during their practice. They can do little about it other than complain and debate with judges online. On the other hand, the Internet provides a space for legal professionals to discuss and get involved in the rough journey ahead to the rule of law. Comprehensive discussion and open debate can help reach common understanding, and thus lay a solid foundation for future legal system reform.

The Internet has clearly brought progressive changes to Chinese society, both in the physical world and in the minds of people. First, the Internet has facilitated the formation of an online community which provides the foundation of a national public space. Second, the Internet has provided the possibility and space for a form of open public surveillance. Third, the Internet, especially the new powerful social

---

[143] *Sina Weibo*, January 2nd, 2014 retrieved from http://www.weibo.com/p/1005052184287602/weibo?profile_ftype=1&key_word=%E6%88%91%E7%8E%B0%E5%9C%A8%E5%AF%B9%E8%B4%AA%E5%AE%98%E8%90%BD%E9%A9%AC%EF%BC%8C%E4%B9%9F%E4%B8%8D%E4%BC%9A%E6%8B%8D%E6%89%8B%E7%A7%B0%E5%BF%AB%E4%BA%86&is_search=1#_0.

[144] *Sina Weibo*, January 2nd, 2016 retrieved from http://weibo.com/u/2184287602?is_all=1#_rnd1451850579176.

media aspect of it, gets both legal professions and members of the general public involved in active discussion of the legal system, and facilitates legal activism. There is a great potential for the new social media and the Internet to take up an important role in Chinese legal system reform.

However, it should be noted that the online community ultimately needs to have the support of "the real world" in the end, and that virtual legal activism alone is not enough to bring about comprehensive change. Through the online discussions and public arguments we have reviewed here it possible to see the issues that arise among Chinese legal professions and associated interests groups. It is clear that legal professionals from diverse career paths, personal backgrounds, and regions of the country may have different opinions on legal issues and concepts, but active debate and discussion is much better than silence for stimulating progress toward the rule of law. The virtual public space online is facilitating these national-scope discussions needed to promote the development of civil society and prepare it for deep democratic changes in the future.

CHAPTER 7

Conclusion: The Rule of Bureaucracy

BACKGROUND

In this book I have drawn upon four different types of evidence, including those of history, current criminal court structures and processes, case studies and social media interaction among legal professionals. It is argued that it is necessary to look into the impact of the bureaucratic system on the society to understand Chinese courts and the criminal justice system which evolved in China. For this purpose, I review the thousands of years of Chinese history to explore the deep roots of the pervasive Mandarin bureaucracy, and then I examine the current status of Chinese courts and the criminal justice system using twelve illustrative criminal cases. Then I go beyond the physical setting to investigate the social network and the online legal community. I examine this arena for insight into the battle between bureaucracy and rising civil society, exploring its impact on courts and the criminal justice system.

China's government is facing many Promethean challenges now, such as restructuring the economic system, responding to the increasing scope of social demands, reducing the endemic corruption present, and controlling the horrendous environmental pollution brought on by rapid economic growth. In order to complete these tasks a well-grounded legal system is absolutely essential. Some highly critical scholars have argued that there is no real legal system in the country and the judicial system is too closely tied to the political system in China to act as a neutral arbiter of disputes (Lubman, 1999). Lubman (2012) also has argued that all Chinese legal and adjudicative institutions, especially those dealing with criminal law, are too closely tied to the political system, a fact which serves to prevent actions inimical to its interests.

Chinese Bureaucracy

Western people may find it is quite confusing when they check the status of Chinese courts. On the one hand, the Chinese judiciary is formally separated from the executive branch with its own system provided for in the Constitution. On the other hand, the judiciary has to follow orders from both the party and the government, and the courts need to report directly to the national legislature, the National People's Congress (NPC) on its performance. It would be most appropriate to conceptualize the judiciary in China as a part of a huge government bureaucracy situated entirely under the executive branch of government. The courts in China are merely a conflict resolution tool; they are **not** the independent judiciary found in Western societies. The cases processed in Chinese courts do not necessarily go forward by legal criteria exclusively; the function and structure of Chinese courts also are not the same as those of their counterparts in Western societies. For most of Chinese history a highly centralized and heavily bureaucratized political system controlled the whole country, including the government, the law, and the economy. To understand Chinese law and courts in China we have to appreciate the nation's rather unique history and culture, especially with respect to the Chinese Mandarin form of bureaucracy.

The Chinese Mandarin bureaucracy differs markedly from the well-known Weberian legal-rational form of bureaucracy common to the West (Whyte, 1973). Mandarin, a word of Portuguese origin, first was used in a Portuguese report about China referring to higher-level officials in Imperial China (Ferguson, 1902). A Mandarin bureaucracy is a formal organization composed of officials who are generalists, one in which recruitment to office is based on open and competitive examinations; the training of officials is geared towards serving the public. The job environment offers relative immunity from most social, political and occupational pressures (Khator, 1997). It features a heavy emphasis on philosophical and literary training for service, and a person attains high office by virtue of his degree of educational achievement rather than specialized knowledge of the office. This education system bred strict obedience of all officials, reverence toward the King or Emperor at the top of the hierarchy from whom all authority flows, and an arrogant attitude toward the people (Jumper, 1957).

Chinese Mandarin bureaucracy used an open, competitive, written national examination system to select generalist officials; these exams were based primarily upon knowledge of the Confucian classics (Riggs, 1997). It was not important whether officials possessed any technical knowledge or commanded the skills of a particular position. This is opposite to the Weberian bureaucracy where the best matching of person to positional needs was the goal of recruitment. Although the source of power for a Mandarin bureaucrat is still expertise and knowledge, the specialized knowledge of these bureaucrats was that of the administrative process and skills working with people. After gathering administrative expertise, the Mandarin officials become indispensable to rulers and powerful players themselves in the political system (Khator, 1997).

Recruitment through open examinations may give bureaucrats a certain degree of neutrality compared to political appointees. However, this system requires little accountability on the part of the Mandarin bureaucrats. Their own performance is measured by the degree to which implementation has been carried out rather than the degree to which goals have been met (Khator, 1997). They can earn promotion after launching policies or projects even if those actions turn out poorly over the long run. In addition, these Mandarin bureaucrats were poorly paid by the state, and a tradition arose where "gifts" (referred to as "going through the back door" or to "using *guanxi*") were an accepted mode of business for influencing decision-makers (Dellapenna, 2005, p.370). It is not surprising to witness much abusive use of power, widespread influence peddling, and outright corruption arise in such a Mandarin bureaucracy system.

Unfortunately, the Chinese judiciary was created within such a bureaucratized system, and it has been part of this system for thousands of years. The Chinese judiciary never got an opportunity to build its independent identity. Compared to the American way of operating the criminal justice system through the use of a highly decentralized and fragmented set of federal, state, county, and municipal agencies, the criminal justice system in China is under the control of a highly centralized hierarchy. In order to understand that system we have to delve into the historical background of courts in China. The current research starts with a discussion of the long history of Chinese bureaucracy and the origin of law in China, and explores the significant impact of Chinese bureaucracy on the legal system and criminal courts (Chapter 1and 3). Two important factors associated with Chinese bureaucracy were discussed, one being that of feudalism and the other being that of Confucianism.

Chinese History

Feudalism

As early as 1045 B.C., the ancient Chinese state already had a legal bureau inside the government to take on judicial functions (Li, 2008). Starting in the Qin dynasty (221B.C.), a penal-oriented legal system and bureaucratized political apparatus were gradually developed throughout the Chinese Imperial era. A top-down, highly centralized hierarchical bureaucracy was established with the Emperor on the top, and the bureaucracy wholly controlled the politics, law and economy of the entire country. The judiciary was part of the governmental agencies and the chief executive officials took charge of the executive, legislative and judicial powers (Park, 2010; He, 2005; Alford, 1984). During this process of the ongoing institutionalization of Imperial governance two cultural factors gave shape to public affairs and institutional development; one is that of feudalism, and the other is that of Confucianism. It can be said that feudalism laid a foundation for a powerful bureaucracy in China, and that the philosophy of Confucianism provided content and principles for this bureaucratic system.

As with other types of feudalism across the world, Chinese feudalism also started with the distribution of the land. The King or Emperor had ownership of all land, and divided that land among a hierarchy of nobles who then became seigneurs (Sills, 1968). Through the succession principle, land was divided again among sons of seigneurs and many politically self-sufficient patrimonial units were formed. The seigneur granted peasants use of his land and his protection in return for personal services and for dues (or taxes).

Feudalism involved not only the division of land, but also a strategy to build "patriarchal authority" (Weber, 1957, p.375-376). The central government tried to attain absolute authority through feudal relationships and obligations. In practice, however, the division of land ownership actually helped local powers to arise and fight for more land among themselves, and occasionally with the ruler.

In order to attain maximal effective control, the central government had to rely on a functional bureaucracy composed of elites and officials with a focus on rank gained through obedience. These officials were arrayed in a line of ranks from top to the bottom, and collectively constituted a hierarchical Mandarin system. This highly centralized system was used by the Emperor and central government to monitor local lords and their underlings. This Mandarin bureaucracy system was maintained during the nation's long history and continuously resisted social changes. Such a powerful bureaucratic structure can manage social turmoil through systematic social control for a long time, but when major governmental change is needed to accommodate great social change it can become a strong obstacle to needed social reform. It follows that a comprehensive social change or reform such as adoption of the rule or law, judicial independence and democracy reform has to start with systematic alteration of this bureaucratic structure with deep historical Mandarin roots.

Confucianism

Although feudalism can physically help to build a centralized kingdom, that kingdom needs philosophic support to inculcate this control into people's way of thinking and acting. Around 12th century BC, the kingdom of *Zhou* already had a series of *li* (rites) (Liu, 1998). *li* (Rites) were used to regulate the relations between the *Zhou* King and local nobles. However, the collapse of the Zhou dynasty saw the decline of *li*. Confucius was fascinated by *Zhou li (Rites of the Zhou)* and he tried to compile the spirit of *li* into a type of philosophy which would be applicable to all people and to all human relationships (Creel, 1949; Liu, 1998). His theories were incorporated into a school—Confucianism. Confucianism was adopted by Imperial dynasties and helped stabilize the structure of Chinese society and all human social relationships through moral education and the inculcation of values derived from Confucian thought.

The "rites" in Confucianism locate people in structured individual relationships with specific duties prescribed to each other. In particular, five Bonds can be formed: ruler to ruled, father to son, husband to wife, elder brother to younger brother, and friend to friend. Juniors owe their seniors reverence, seniors have corresponding duties of benevolence and concern toward juniors; husbands need to show ongoing benevolence towards their wives and the wives need to respect their husbands in return; the ruled need to obey orders from the ruler, and the ruler grants protection to the ruled. The social norms and people's minds in ancient China were guided by Confucianism, a philosophy which has served as China's state ideology from the early *Han* dynasty until the collapse of the *Qing* dynasty and advent of the Republic of China in 1911 (MacCormack, 1996a).

During the *Zhou* dynasty the state bureaucracy gradually started taking shape with the initiation of feudalism in the background. Imperial officials needed to pass comprehensive examinations which were based on knowledge of Confucian classics. These scholar-officials did not need to demonstrate command of technical or legal knowledge to adjudicate legal cases. In addition, Confucianism holds that "law" is equivalent to punitive punishment, a tool of ruling, rather than a repository of rights to be protected through rules and due process. The criminal law was used as a reining tool by the Imperial bureaucracy system (Park, 2010; He, 2005; Alford, 1984).

Confucianism-based examinations actually produced a class of bureaucrats, the Mandarins, who enjoyed incomparable prestige from their formal positions in a state bureaucracy hierarchy. This tentacular bureaucracy carried out and controlled all the functions of the state and oversaw all activities of social life, permitting very limited social space to ordinary people (Balazs, 1971). In this Mandarin bureaucratic system the county official was only subject to the supervision of higher government rather than responding to the public over whom they held a responsibility to govern. There was no separation of powers or checks and balances; the executive bureaucrats held absolute power including political, judicial and economic power (He, 2005; Alford, 1984; Cohen, 1968).

In dealing with a criminal case, these bureaucrats were both police and judges, and they accumulated evidence, evaluated the evidence, rendered a judgment, and passed sentence. The litigation business was banned, and the legal profession had no space to grow. It is understandable that many justice rules and theories could not be developed, such as Rules of Evidence, Neutrality and passive jurisdiction, rights of parties, etc. (Gelatt, 1982; Cohen, 1968). The profession of lawyer was roundly condemned in ancient China. An independent judiciary could not be established during Chinese Imperial history due to the lack of support from established groups of independent legal professionals.

Furthermore, the highly centralized government bureaucracy, holding all the military, legislative, judicial, executive and taxation powers, posed a very powerful obstacle to legal system reform. On the one hand, the bureaucrats in place wished to maintain their status of absolute authority (Ai, 2004). On the other hand, ordinary people dreamed of becoming bureaucrats through examinations themselves, and they also did not expect the existing legal system ever to change (Ai, 2004). This conception of bureaucracy has penetrated into the social culture of Chinese society and continues to permeate daily life. If you ask kids in China what they want to do after growing up, the answer would be "become a bureaucrat!" It is not far from the truth to say that there is a seed of bureaucratic culture in the heart of each Chinese person. To build an upright government and neutral and independent justice system, it is necessary to uproot this addiction to bureaucracy culture.

Current State of Court and Analysis

The current state of courts and the contemporary criminal justice system is discussed in Chapter 4. Looking through the modern window, I found that neither the revolution of 1911 nor that of 1949 significantly changed the nature of Chinese courts. Owing to the deeply-rooted bureaucratic tradition and Chinese culture, the Chinese judiciary remained as an element of the executive branch of government during thousands years no matter under the Imperial court, the nationalist party or the socialist state. After 66 years, a comprehensive socialist legal system has been constructed with over 230 laws and more than 600 regulations. About 3,500 courts were established nationwide (Liang, 2008). However, little in the way of judicial independence or rule of law is in evidence.

However, with ongoing modernization, rapid economic development, and the globalization of commerce China's court caseload is continuously increasing while the number of judges has not increased accordingly. The need for greater court capacity is clear, and the need for a more professionalized judiciary is increasingly recognized among informed publics. In order to deal with large amount of cases brought to the court, however, the administrationization of the court trial process is being used as a temporizing coping mechanism instead of moving ahead forcefully to the enhanced professionalization of courts. The administrationization of court trial refers to the replacement of the legalistic content of the judicial system with executive goals, structures, approaches, principles and effects, thereby causing the judicial system to operate in an executive mode characteristic of any bureaucracy (Long and Yuan, 2014).

Within the centralized hierarchical state bureaucracy the courts are led by the committees of the CCP of the corresponding districts, and judges are cadres who are selected, trained and managed by the Party. It is fair to say, however, that Chinese judicial officials are nonetheless ever so gradually becoming professionally more distinctive. Compared to earlier times in 1970s when most judges were recruited from the army or the police, more and more judges these days have received formal legal education with either a bachelor or graduate degree. Appointments of judges, especially high-ranking officials, are under the charge of the Party's local committees located in the areas of the courts. A great majority of China's judges are CCP cadre and therefore are subject to the discipline of the party organizations within and outside the court, as well as subject to the discipline of the judicial hierarchy where CCP influence increases as one moves up the hierarchy. Also, the courts have largely been financed completely by local government rather than supported by the central government, a fact which explains their over-responsiveness to local pressures in carrying out their adjudicative duties.

Western scholars may misunderstand some terms used in the Chinese legal system due to the presence of translation difficulties. For example, “judge” in Chinese is written as "*shenpan yuan (审判员)*" and "*faguan (法官),*" literally meaning "adjudication person" and "legal official" which evokes the image of a Western style judge (Cohen, 2014). Similarly, the "judicial system," literally not only means the courts but also includes the police as well as the procuracy. Although many justices in China nowadays dress upon in black robes instead of their previous very military-type uniforms, they still operate as adjudicators without independent judicial power rather than acting like their independent counterparts in most of the countries of the West. Chinese judges are actually civil servants working within a vast state bureaucracy, and they are subject to an ongoing general cadre evaluation system which evaluates their performance (Cohen, 2014). There is scarcely a hint of judicial independence in how they carry out their work.

The court is also highly bureaucratized inside. First, the court divisions have become more and more explicit and complicated, such that there is a case-filing division, an administrative division, a juvenile division, an intellectual property division, etc. In addition, some divisions themselves have branches. Second, the people’s courts also have set up many offices, including an administration office, a human resource office, a supervision office, a facility center, a veteran cadre office, etc. All levels of the court have corresponding CCP branches. The numbers of staff personnel working in the courts has increased dramatically, growing from 59,000 in 1978 to over 300,000 in 2008 (Liu, 2009). The high degree of job specialization in the people’s court may well enhance judicial power by expanding the organizational capacity on the courts. However, this same hyper-division of labor may also cause internal problems in the court itself, including functional overlapping and some degree of overstaffing. More divisions need more staff and more funds for support at a time when the courts do not have abundant funding resources.

The current bureaucratized judicial system does not support an independent and powerful judiciary, and the judicial system is tightly under the leadership of party and government. Local government leaders can dominate the judiciary through financial measures, and the court’s internal managerial system also operates to reduce judicial independence. Judges are actually civil servants of a vast government bureaucracy subject to a general cadre evaluation system and the administrationization of court trials in a pursuit of efficiency has further reduced their social status. Courts in China have become primarily a tool for conflict resolution, leaving judges without much of a sense of independent legal spirit.

Analysis and Limitation

In Chapter 2, the methods used for conducting a study leading to this book are set forth. As is the case with other research on Chinese law, the current research has had to face many challenges. First, the organization and bureaucracy of the criminal court is mainly closed to outsiders. Second, bureaucratization is an abstract concept and is difficult to operationalize through empirical measures. Third, bureaucratization is a process that has to be understood in a dynamic way rather than being conceptualized through static measures or numbers. Considering all these challenges, the current study uses both case studies and social media analysis as its main methods to provide a vivid and dynamic depiction of the Chinese criminal justice and the work of the courts.

Twelve criminal cases were chosen which received nationwide attention to craft qualitative analyses. The information pertaining to these cases was collected from the national news websites. Each of the twelve cases has a quite clear connection to the bureaucratization phenomenon. In Chapter 5, I analyzed these cases and show how they illustrate a range of issues regarding the impact of the Chinese bureaucracy on courts and the criminal justice system. Given the widely recognized limitations of the courts, ordinary people tend appeal to higher executive authorities instead of going to court to seek justice. Unfortunately, the hierarchical bureaucracy provides an ideal organizational environment to nurture absolute power and deviance from the law; "close" mutual collaboration relationships abound among criminal justice agents acting without much evidence of accountability; there is frequent intervention into the criminal justice process from officials exercising executive power.

Some have argued that an independent judiciary is a Western idea, and doubt whether it should be a model for every country, especially those countries with very different cultural heritage. I have to honestly admit that I do not know if this is the case. However, the case studies presented in this research show that the long history of bureaucracy has formed the Chinese mind-set of relying on executive authority for justice rather than pursuing justice through courts. The judiciary in China currently lacks the independence and strength to distribute justice, and a judiciary without independence can neither achieve justice nor assure people's confidence in justice. A rule of bureaucracy rather than the rule of law exists in the Chinese criminal justice system.

Legal reform in Chinese history has emphasized certain leading politicians instead of calling for the participation of ordinary people due to the lack of a mature civil society. Today, Chinese people are more and more aware of civil and political rights after achieving a modicum of economic abundance. The criminal justice system, an important part of social development, has become a subject of increasingly broad interest in China's newly rising civil society. In order to show this special arena in Chinese society, I systematically collected social media data for this research, including microblogs, blogs and forum discussions. In Chapter 6 I use these data to analyze the impact of social media on Chinese society and on legal system reform. Even though the highly centralized bureaucracy is indeed very powerful, the rapid development of modern information and communication technology presents certain challenges to its continued dominance. China already has more than 668 million Internet users, and China has the most active social-media population in the world. Many of them are netizens engaging in civil activism supportive of judicial independence and the rule of law.

The Internet overcomes the barriers of time and place for the communication of information and organization of collective action in a geographical vast country with a very large population. Electronic communication entails an aspect of freedom of expression and openness in the sharing of ideas. It is bringing new social change in China, and has pushed "online activism" to a high degree. Social media in China is more and more becoming both a reflection of public opinion and seedbed of nascent social forces. The Internet has facilitated the formation of an important online community which provides the foundation of a national public space. It has shown the possibility for developing an open public surveillance capacity within Chinese society. In addition, the Internet, especially the new social media aspects of it, gets both legal professionals and the general public involved in legal discussion and even legal activism on occasion. The social media not only provides Chinese legal professionals with an unparalleled site for public discourses and the development of professional identity, but also helps form the microcosm of a civil society.

The Internet creates a new social space which is not only informational, but also participatory. This produces a vibrant public sphere as a positive force helping to keep authorities within proper bounds. The prevalence of the Internet in China is vast. It is not only a tool for virtually instantaneous communication, but also has become both a place of collective opinion expression and a seedbed of social development with its hundreds of millions of web users. The three public surveillance cases which are analyzed here illustrate how the Internet can bring transformational qualities to traditional media and provide an important public sphere for the promotion of social change. It can be used to initiate drives for legislative change, it can monitor the abuse of official power, and it can be used to push for justice in specific cases and the rule of law as a long term goal of reform. The two cyber vigilantism cases discussed show that the Internet provides a space for ordinary people to congregate their individual micro-impacts to achieve influence and push for progress. For example, the process of re-tweeting and posting can disclose more issues and impose pressure upon those engaged in the abuse power and corruption. One may argue that this process may only create small bits of power and it use takes a long time before major change occurs; this may well be so, however it is also the case that many tiny efforts can make a big difference over the long run.

The expanding reach of the Internet is creating an important opportunity for people to discuss social issues and congregate public opinions. It also helps to build civil society through its virtual public space, through its great capacity for online community formation, and through its capacity for facilitating public surveillance. The Internet overcomes the barriers of time and place for the rapid communication of messages and the organization of collective action in a vast country with a very large population. Both the legal professionals and many ordinary people with high interest pay attention to legal issues discussed in Internet forums. They quite frequently choose to discuss legal issues on diverse online social media, including the legal web forums, blogs and microblogs. This Internet-based power may be not recognized by traditional political scholars, but it cannot be denied that this virtual congregation could produce an unparalleled social movement under the right circumstances. The development of civil society in the era of the Internet will definitely impose its impact on movement toward the rule of law in China.

There is an active legal community on Internet social networks which includes law professors, judges, prosecutors, lawyers, and police officers. They engage in legal discussions, react to each other on legal issues, and present their own opinions. The legal professions could potentially anchor institutions of civil society, and their opinions could present a clearer picture of current civil engagement in China. From the data collected from microblogs, it is clear that legal professionals are leading discussions on legal reform, debating controversial issues, and often call for support to take action against injustice through legal advocacy. The legal community in China is just beginning to pursue its professional identity. They have not yet organized as a tight-knit powerful group due to their diverse backgrounds and internal conflicts. However, these comprehensive discussions and ongoing debates can help lead to the reaching of common understandings, and in time lay a solid foundation for future legal reform.

There are limitations associated with the methods employed in this research. For the twelve case studies used in Chapter 5, the sample of cases selected may not be highly representative. The criminal cases are complicated, and it was not possible to obtain all the information for each case. The analyses presented could be biased and incomplete. For the social media data used in Chapter 6, there are many challenges. First, the sampling of data is not representative. It is clearly impossible to follow all information on the social media considering the huge volume of data in the Internet database. Also, it is not possible to constantly monitor social media; some insightful tweets may have been missed. The analyses presented here may represent only a small part of the online community. Second, legal professionals often express their opinions on social media based on their knowledge and thoughts of the topics, and these opinions are not necessarily correct.

Even with these limitations, this research presented here could be viewed as a valuable contribution to the research literature. First, this book explores the important relationship between Chinese bureaucracy and the law. Although a good deal of research has been done on either bureaucracy or law in China, only very limited scholarship has sought to reveal their inter-relationship. Second, social media data were used in this research in addition to the traditional case study method. These observations based on social media could be valuable since little prior research has used this particular method of research. People express ideas and opinions through tweets which have a function similar to the interview or survey questionnaire. Although it is difficult to predict what the ultimate impact of the Internet will be on Chinese society, the vibrant online activism present in China carries great potential for change toward a rule of law distant goal. In addition, legal professionals play an important role in the Chinese legal system, and social media data provide a new way to study those people who are working in legal professions in an Internet era.

OBSERVATIONS

In this book, many topics have been discussed, but the major issues stressed are the impact of the Mandarin bureaucracy legacy on courts and the criminal justice system in China. I argue that understanding Chinese courts and judiciary has to be based on knowledge of the history and culture of China. From Chinese history, I look into the thousands of years of development of Mandarin bureaucracy and examine its profound influence on Chinese society. Through the window of modern Chinese society, I still see the impact of the Mandarin bureaucracy legacy on the country's judiciary and courts. Mandarin bureaucracy has permeated the culture and life style of Chinese society; it is deeply rooted in the mindset of the people.

The cases I used in this book present the struggle of contemporary Chinese courts working in the context of a deeply-rooted bureaucracy-centered culture. Legal reforms made in recent years have clearly occasioned some progress, and this is indeed encouraging. However, it would clearly be premature to draw ultimate conclusions regarding

China's ongoing effort on the part of its legal community to promote a distinctive type of independent judicial decision-making. Nonetheless, it is not too early to make a few informed observations on the basis of the evidence presented in this book.

First, the continuing influence of Mandarin bureaucracy cannot be ignored. It would be very difficult to understand Chinese bureaucracy from a purely Western viewpoint. Bureaucracy in Western modern society has been a relatively positive and largely beneficial social institution, and Weberian theories even connect it in a favorable way with modern democracy. However, Mandarin bureaucracy in China cannot deny its link to the autocratic centralization of state power and lack of sufficient provision for an independent judiciary. Furthermore, the Mandarin bureaucracy nurtures a culture of bureaucracy that is taken for granted to be perpetual. Developed over the course of thousands of years, it undoubtedly presents a huge barrier inhibiting progressive change and delaying needed reform. A successful legal reform has to take this into consideration and find an appropriate solution.

Second, as noted above it is necessary to study the Chinese judicial system from an historical and cultural perspective in order to understand why it remains so very different from that of many other countries. Without a contextual analysis, any critique of the current system is weak and may be made in vain. Some scholars expect that China could change quickly and follow the same steps as Western countries. I would say this expectation may be unrealistic if we look back to a long history laden with a deep brand of bureaucratization. Even it was possible to change the Mandarin bureaucracy system in a relatively short period through political reform, it would take a great deal of time to change people's thinking and alter the highly bureaucratized popular culture. In addition, the complex of Chinese legal reform may be beyond our imagination due to the mix of Confucian traditions and the influences present from both continental European and Anglo-American legal system models.

Third, the criminal justice system is the most vibrant part of the Chinese legal reform arena. For thousands of years, the criminal justice system had been used as a ruling tool, and its use in this way has permeated deeply into almost every perspective of Chinese governance.

The criminal justice system also represents the forces of civilization and social development. The economic reforms creating a socialist market economy and increasing modernization call for a more mature criminal justice system. This is needed in order to protect the rights of people and their civil society organizations. Over the course of the last three decades certain improvements have been made in legislation and adjudication to protect human rights, punish crime, and deter the abuse of power. However, these changes have not yet led to the Chinese judiciary being fully separated from the political bureaucracy, and it still lacks an independent status within Chinese society.

Fourth, China's vast population, with the help of an increasingly prevalent Internet, has increasingly voiced a demand for greater fairness and justice in the country's legal system. The Internet has become a potential space for elements of civil society to initiate group formation and develop influence. Although it is too early to predict ultimate outcomes, it definitely has had two noteworthy results so far. First, it pushes the government to pursue consistent legal reform in order to build popular confidence in the courts and the Chinese criminal justice system. So the legal reform will continue, even though the movement could be rather slow. Second, and maybe the most important, the vibrant discussion and congregating achieved through the Internet is a good way to change the people's mindset and enlighten citizens' intellect. With this continuous discussion taking place over an extended period we may expect that the negative impact of the Mandarin bureaucracy cultural obstacle could be reduced little-by-little over time.

Appendix

Timeline of Chinese History

Xia Dynasty			2070-1600 B.C.
Shang Dynasty			1600-1046 B.C.
Zhou Dynasty		Western Zhou	1046-771 B.C.
		Eastern Zhou	770-256 B.C.
		Spring and Autumn Period	770-476 B.C.
		Warring States Period	475-221 B.C.
Qin Dynasty			221-206 B.C.
Han Dynasty		Western Han	206 B.C.-A.D. 25
		Eastern Han	25-220
Three Kingdoms		Wei	220-265
		Shu Han	221-263
		Wu	222-280
Western Jin Dynasty			265-317
Eastern Jin Dynasty			317-420
Northern and Southern Dynasties	Southern Dynasties	Song	420-479
		Qi	479-502
		Liang	502-557
		Chen	557-589
	Northern Dynasties	Northern Wei	386-534
		Eastern Wei	534-550
		Northern Qi	550-577
		Western Wei	535-556
		Northern Zhou	557-581
Sui Dynasty			581-618
Tang Dynasty			618-907

Five Dynasties	Later Liang	907-923
	Later Tang	923-936
	Later Jin	936-947
	Later Han	947-950
	Later Zhou	951-960
Song Dynasty	Northern Song	960-1127
	Southern Song	1127-1279
Liao Dynasty		907-1125
Jin Dynasty		1115-1234
Yuan Dynasty		1206-1368
Ming Dynasty		1368-1644
Qing Dynasty		1616-1911
Republic of China		1912-1949
People's Republic of China		Founded on October 1, 1949

January 14, 2016 retrieved from People Net
http://en.people.cn/aboutchina/history.html

Bibliography

Adams, R. M. (1966). *The evolution of urban society.* Chicago: Aldine.

Adams, R. M. (1978). Strategies of maximization, stability and resilience in Mesopotamian society, settlement, and agriculture. *Proceedings of the American Philosophical Society, 122,* 329-335.

Ai, Y. M. (2004). Why did the attempt to modernise the legal system in late Qing China fail? A Sino-Japanese Comparative Study, *Bond Law Review, 16* (1), 69-92.

Alford, W. P. (1984). Of arsenic and old laws: Looking anew at criminal justice in late imperial China. *California Law Review*, 1180-1256.

Andy, S. (2007). *China briefing business guide: Mergers and acquisition law in China.* Kowloon, Hong Kong: Asia Briefing Media.

Balazs, E. (1964). *Chinese civilization and bureaucracy: Variations on a theme.* (H. M. Wright, Trans.). New Haven: Yale University Press.

Balazs, E. (1971).The bureaucratic society of imperial China. In M. T. Dalby (Eds.), *Bureaucracy in Historical Perspective* (pp.27-31). New York: Scott Foresman.

Barnhust, K. G. (2011). The new "media affect" and the crisis of representation for political communication. *The International Journal of Press/Politics*, 1940161211415666.

Bellah, R. N. (1967). Civil religion in America. *Journal of the American Academy of Arts and Sciences, 96*(1), 1-21.

Berman, H. J. & Whiting,V. R. (1980). Impressions of Cuban law. *American Society of Comparative Law, 28,* (3), 475-486.

Bodde, D. (1963). Basic concepts of Chinese law: The genesis and evolution of legal thought in traditional China. *Proceedings of the American Philosophical Society, 107,* 375—398.

Bodde, D. & Morris, C. (1967). *Law in imperial China: Exemplified by*

190 Ch'ing dynasty cases. Cambridge: Harvard University Press.

Bodde, D. (2014). *Essays on Chinese civilization.* Princeton, NJ: Princeton University Press.

Boyd, D. M., & Ellison, N. B. (2007). Social network sites: Definition, history, and scholarship. *Journal of Computer-Mediated Communication, 13*, 210–230.

Brockman, R. H. (1980). Commercial contract law in late nineteenth-century Taiwan. In J. A. Cohen, R. R. Edwards & F. C. Chen (Eds.), *Essays on China's legal tradition* (pp. 76-136). Princeton, NJ: Princeton University Press.

Burke, M. E., Cutshaw, K. A. & Krishna, R. (2006). The legal systems in India-China: A comparative perspective. *Indian Journal of Economics and Business, Special Issue China & India,* 1-27.

Butler, W. E. (1983). *The Legal System of the Chinese Soviet Republic, 1931-1934*. Dobbs Ferry, NY: Transnational Publishers.

Cabestan, J. (2005). The political and practical obstacles to the reform of the judiciary and the establishment of a rule of law in China. *Journal of Chinese Political Science, 10* (1), 43-64.

Calhoun, C. (1994). *Neither Gods nor emperors.* Berkeley: University of California Press.

Cao, D. (2004). *Chinese law: A language perspective.* Hants, England: Ashgate Publishing.

Capone, V. (2012). *The human flesh search engine: Democracy, censorship, and political participation in twenty-first century China.* Retrieved from http://scholarworks.umb.edu/ghc/2012/panel3/3.

CCP Central Committee. (1991). *Several Opinions of the Central Committee of the Communist Party of China on the Strengthening of the Leadership over the State Legislative Work,* Document Number 8.

Chen, A. H-Y. (1992). *An introduction to the legal system of the People's Republic of China.* Singapore: Butterworths Asia.

Chen, W. (2010). Retrospection and perspective: Chinese criminal procedure law (1979–2009). *Frontiers of Law in China, 5* (4), 510-531.

Chen, X. & Ang, P. H. (2011). Internet police in China: Regulation, scope and myths. In D. Herold & P.Marolt. (Eds.), *Online Society in China: Creating, Celebrating, and Instrumentalising the Online Carnival* (pp. 40–52), New York: Routledge.

Cheong, P.H. & Gong, J. (2010). Cyber vigilantism, transmedia collective intelligence, and civic participation. *Chinese Journal of Communication, 3* (4), 471-487.

Chiu, C., Lin, D. & Silverman, A. (2012). *China's social-media boom.* Retrieved from http://www.mckinseychina.com/wp-content/uploads/2012/04/McKinsey-Chinas-Social-Media-Boom.pdf.

Chiu, H. (1992). *China's criminal justice system and the trial of pro-democracy dissidents.* University of Maryland Paper Series in Contemporary Asian Studies

Ch'ü, T'. (1961). *Law and society in traditional China.* The Hague: Mouton and Co.

Ch'ü, T'. (1962). Local government in China under the Ch'ing. *Harvard East Asian Studies,* 9, 361. Cambridge, Mass: Harvard University Press.

Clark, G. J, (2008). An introduction to the legal profession in China in the year 2008. *Suffolk University Law Review,* 41, 833-850.

Cohen, J. A. (1968). *The criminal process in the People's Republic of China, 1949-1963.* Cambridge: Harvard University Press.

Cohen, J. A. (1969). The Chinese communist party and judicial independence: 1949-1959. *Harvard Law Review, 82* (5), 967-1006.

Cohen, Jerome. (2014). *Struggling for justice: China's courts and the challenge of reform.* Retrieved from http://www.worldpoliticsreview.com/articles/13495/struggling-for-justice-chinas-courts-and-the-challenge-of-reform.

Come, P. (1997). Legal system reforms promise substantive-but limited-improvement, *China Law & Practice*, 29, 31-34.

Crank, J. (2003) Institutional theory of police: A review of the state of the art. *Policing: An International Journal of Police Strategies & Management, 26* (2), 186-207.

Creel, H. G. (1949). *Confucius, the man and the myth.* New York: John Day.

Creel, H. G. (1964). The beginning of bureaucracy in China: The Origins of The Hsien. *Journal of Asian Studies, 22,* 162-163.

Curran, D. J. (1998). Economic reform, the floating population, and crime. *Journal of Contemporary Criminal Justice, 14* (3), 262–280.

Dai, J. (2009). On several problems in legal transplantation. *Journal of Politics and Law, 2* (3), 107-109.

Data Center of China Internet (DCCI). (2012). *Bluebook of China Weibo.* Retrieved from http://www.dcci.com.cn/media/download/529592d3f496e761b42c2462925f88ec505d.pdf.

Dellapenna, J. W. (2005). A few words on law and the environment in China. *TEMP Journal of Science, Technology and Environmental Law, 24,* 367-373.

Deutscher, I. (1969). Roots of bureaucracy. *Socialist Register, 6,* 9-28.

Diamant, N. J. Lubman, S. B. and O'Brien, K. J. (2005). *Engaging the law in China: tate, society, and possibilities for justice.* Stanford: Stanford University Press.

Ding, S. (1956). *Jiaguwen suo jian shizu jiqi zhidu* (The clans and their institutions found in oracle). Beijing: Science Press.

Dobinson, I. (2002). The criminal law of the People's Republic of China *(*1997*):* Real Change *or* Rhetoric*? Pacific Rim Law & Policy Journal, 11* (1), 1-62.

Durkheim, E. (1893/1984) (W. Halls, Trans.). *The division of labor in society.* New York: The Free Press.

Durkheim, E. (1897/1951). *Suicide: A study in sociology* (J. Spaulding and G. Simpson, Trans.). New York: The Free Press.

Eberhard, W. (1970). *Conquerors and Rulers Social Forces in Medieval China.* Brill Archive.

Engels, F. (1972). *Origins of the family, private property, and the state.* London: Pathfinder Press.

Epstein, E. J. (1994). Legal documents and materials on administrative detention in the People's Republic of China. *Chinese Law and Government Series,* Armonk, N.Y.: M.E. Sharpe.

Epstein, M. (2009). Making a case: Characterizing the filial son. In R. E. Hegel & K. Carlitz (Eds.), *Writing and law in late imperial China: Crime, conflict, and judgment* (pp. 27-43). Seattle: University of Washington Press.

Erie, M. S., (2003). Through culture and its disciplines: Human rights and the institutionalization of law in China. *Cornell Law Faculty Working Papers,* 13.

Feng, X. (2007). Shanganning bianqu gaodeng fayuan zai yanan shiqi de sifashijian (Shaanxi-Gansu-Ningxia border region Supreme Court legal practice in YananTimes). *People's Court Daily.* Retrieved from http://oldfyb2009.chinacourt.org/public/detail.php?id=109879

Fei, X. (1992). *From the soil: The foundations of Chinese society.* Berkeley: University of California Press.

Ferguson, D. (1902). *Letters from Portuguese captives in Canton, written in*

1534 & 1536: With an introduction on Portuguese intercourse with China in the first half of the sixteenth century. Bombay: Educ. Steam Press, Byculla.

Fewsmith, J. (2015). China leadership monitor. *Hoover Institution Online Publications,* Winter, 46. Retrieved from http://www.hoover.org/research/chinas-political-ecology-and-fight-against-corruption.

Finer, S. E. (1997).*The history of government from the earlier times: Ancient Monarchies and Empires,* Oxford: Oxford University Press.

Fiss, O. (1983). *The Bureaucratization of the judiciary.* New Haven: Yale Law School Faculty Scholarship Series.

Ford, P. (2013). Why China is turning to 'trial by television' in sensitive cases. Retrieved from http://www.csmonitor.com/World/Asia-Pacific/2013/1028/Why-China-is-turning-to-trial-by-television-in-sensitive-cases.

Fu, H. (2011). Institutionalizing criminal process in China. In G. Yu, (Eds.). *The development of the Chinese Legal System: Change and Challenges* (pp.26-48). New York: Routledge.

Fukuyama, F. (2012). The patterns of history. *Journal of Democracy, 23* (1), 14-26.

Gao, L. (2013). *The human flesh search engine in China: A case oriented approach to understanding online collective action* (Unpublished dissertation). Loughborough, UK: Loughboroough University.

Gelatt, T. A. (1982). The People's Republic of China and the presumption of innocence. *Criminal Law. & Criminology, 73*, 259-316.

Gonzalez, E. (1983). *Cuba's political structure: Institutional development of a revolutionary state.* Unpublished paper presented at the International Conference on "Cuba in the Eighties", Bonn, Germany,

Goode, L. (2009). Social news, citizen journalism and democracy. *New Media & Society, 11*, (8), 1287-1305.

Grafflin, D. (1990). Reinventing China: Pseudobureaucracy in the early southern dynasties. In A. E. Dien (Eds.), *State and Society in Early Medieval China.* Stanford: Stanford University Press.

Gray, J. H. (1972). *China: A history of the laws, manners and customs of the people.* New York: Barnes & Noble Books.

Habermas, J. (1962/1989). *The structural transformation of the public sphere: An inquiry into a category of Bourgeois society.* Cambridge: Polity Press.

Hall, R. H. (1963).The concept of bureaucracy: An empirical assessment.

American Journal of Sociology, 69 (1), 32-40.

Halliday, T. C., & Liu, S., (2007). Birth of a liberal moment? Looking through a one-way mirror at lawyers' defense of criminal defendants in China. In T. C. Halliday, L. Karpik, & M. M. Feeley (Eds.), *Fighting for Political Freedom: Comparative Studies of the Legal Complex and Political Liberalism* (pp. 65–107). Oxford: Hart Publishing.

Haque, M. S. (1997). Incongruity between bureaucracy and society in developing nations: A critique. *Peace & Change*, 22 (4), 432-462.

Hegel, R. E. (2007). Writing and law: An introduction. In writing and law in late imperial China. In R. E. Hegel & K.Carlitz (Eds.), *Writing and law in late imperial China: Crime, conflict, and judgment* (pp. 3-23). Seattle: University of Washington Press.

Hegel, R. E. (2009).*True crimes in eighteenth-century China: Twenty case histories*. Seattle: University of Washington Press.

He, N. (2013). *Chinese criminal trials: A comprehensive empirical inquiry.* New York: Springer.

He, X. (2009). Court finance and court responses to judicial reforms: A tale of two Chinese courts. *Law and Policy*, 31(4), 463-486.

He, W. (2005). Judicial system and governance in traditional China, paper presented at the *Canada-China Governance Dialogue Seminar*, Ottawa, Canada.

Hecht, J. (1996). *Opening to reform? An analysis of China's revised criminal procedure law*. New York: Lawyers Committee for Human Rights.

Herold, D. K. (2008). Development of a civic society online? Internet vigilantism and state control in Chinese cyberspace. *Asia Journal of Global Studies, 2* (1), 26-37.

Hogan, B., & Quan-Haase, A. (2010). Persistence and change in social media: A framework of social practice. *Bulletin of Science, Technology and Society*, *30* (5), 309-315.

Horowitz, S. A. & Schnabel, A. (2004). *Human rights and societies in transition: Causes, consequences, responses.* New York: United Nations University Press.

Hsu, C. & Linduff, K. M. (1988). *Western Chou civilization*. New Haven: Yale University Press.

Hsu,C. (1966). Some working notes on the western Chou government. *Zhongyang yanjiuyuan lishi yuyan yanjiusuo jikan (The season journal of central institute of historical language*), 36, 513-524.

Hsu, I. C. Y. (2000). *The rise of modern china (*6th ed). New York: Oxford University Press.

Hu, J. (2007). *Three supremacies doctrine.* The Three Supremacies Doctrine first appeared in Hu, Jintao's speech at his meeting with the representatives of the National Conference on Politics and Law and senior judges and prosecutors, Beijing. Retrieved from http://news.xinhuanet.com/newscenter/2007-12/25/content 7312439.htm.

Hu, S. (2000). *Explaining Chinese democratization.* Westport, CT: Praeger.

Huang, S. (1985). Tongqi mingwen Yi Yu Ze de diwang jiqi yu Wuguo de guanxi (The bronze inscriptions Yi Yu Ze's king and the relations with Wu Kingdom). *Kaoguxu (ZazhiArcheology Journal), 5,* 98-I102.

Huang, P. C. (1996). *Civil justice in China: Representation and practice in the Qing.* Stanford: Stanford University Press.

Huang, S. (2012). 'Li Zhuang: Chinese Defense Lawyer Who Was Found Guilty of Suborning Perjury. Retrieved from http://wrongfulconvictionsblog.org/2012/03/31/li-zhuang-chinese-defense-lawyer-who-was-found-guilty-of-suborning-perjury.

Hucker, C. O. (1966). *The* censorial system of Ming China. Stanford: Stanford University Press.

Hunter, C. D. (1998). *The internet and the public sphere: Revitalization or decay?* Retrieved from http://neuage.org/phd/vc/67-Internet_and_the_Public_Sphere.htm.

Huntington, S. P. (1968). *Political order in a changing society.* New Haven: Yale University Press.

International Herald Tribune. (2005). *The enlightenment from the ratio of officials to civilians in the U.S. As 1:15 (美国官民比例1 : 15的启示).* Retrieved from http://news.sina.com.cn/c/2005-03-14/13316079907.shtml.

Jiang, Y. (2005). *The great Ming code: Da Ming Lü.* Seattle: University of Washington Press.

Jenkins, H. (2006). *Convergence culture: Where old and new media collide.* NY: New York University Press.

Jenner, W.J.F. (1992).*The tyranny of history: The roots of China's crisis.* London: Penguin Press.

Jones, W. (2003).Trying to understand the Current Chinese Legal System, In S. Hsu (Eds.), *Understanding China's Legal System,* (pp. 40-41). New York: New York University Press.

Johnson, V. R. and Loomis, S. C. (2013). The rule of law in China and the prosecution of Li Zhuang. *The Chinese Journal of Comparative Law, 1*(1)66-83.

Johnston, R.J. (1986). Individual freedom and the world economy. In R.J. Johnston & P.J. Taylor (Eds.), *A World in Crisis?* (pp.176-182). New York: Basil Blackwell.

Jumper, R. (1957). Mandarin bureaucracy and politics in South Viet Nam. *Pacific Affairs: An International Review of Asia and the Pacific, 31*(1), 47-58.

Karpik, L. (1998). Builders of liberal society: French lawyers and politics in T.C. Halliday & L. Karpik (Eds.), *Lawyers and the rise of western political liberalism: Europe and North America from the eighteenth to twentieth centuries*. Oxford: Oxford University Press.

Keeton, G. W. (1937). The Progress of Law Reform in China. *Journal of Comparative Legislation and International Law, 19* (4) 197-211.

Keith, R. C. (1994). *China's struggle for the rule of law.* New York, N.Y.: St. Martin's Press.

Keith, R. C., Lin, Z., & Hou, S. (2013). *China's Supreme Court*. New York: Routledge.

Khator, R. (1997). Professionalism in bureaucracy: Some comparisons based on the Indian case. In A. Farazmand (Eds.), *Modern Systems of Government: Exploring the Role of Bureaucrats and Politicians* (pp. 74-94). Thousand Oaks, CA: SAGE Publications, Inc.

Kim, C. (1987). The modern Chinese legal system, *Tulane Law Review. 61*, 1413-1452.

King, G., Pan, J. & Roberts, M. (2013). How censorship in China allows government criticism but silences collective expression? *American Political Science Review, 107(2),* 1-18.

Kwak, H., Lee, C., Park, H., & Moon, S. (2010). *What is twitter: A social network or a news media. Proceedings from the 19th International Conference on the World Wide Web* (pp. 591-600). New York: ACM.

Ladany, L. (1992). Law and legality in China. London: Hurst & Co.

LaPalombara, J. (1963). *Bureaucracy and political development.* Princeton: Princeton University Press.

Lattimore, O. (1951). *Inner Asian frontiers of China.* New York: Capital.

Lau, D. C. (1963). *Lao Tzu Tao Te Ching*. Harmondsworth: Penguin Books.

Lee, F. (2006). Collective efficacy, support for democratization, and political participation in Hong Kong. *International Journal of Public Opinion*

Research, 18 (3), 297-317.

Legge, J. (Trans.) (1960). *The Chinese classics* (5 vols.) (reprint), Hong Kong: Hong Kong University Press.

Leng, S. & Chiu, H. (1985). *Criminal justice in post-Mao China.* Albany: SUNY Press.

Leng, S. (1982). Crime and punishment in post-Mao China, criminal law: Some preliminary observations. *Criminal Law & Criminology, 73, 204-206.*

Leng, S. (1967). *Justice in communist China: A survey of the judicial system of the Chinese People's Republic.* New York: Oceana Publications, Inc.,

Li, F. (2008). *Bureaucracy and the state in early China: Governing the western Zhou.* Cambridge: Cambridge University Press.

Li, G. (1989). *Shen Jiaben yu Zhongguo xiandaihua (Shen Jiaben and the modernization of China).* Beijing: Guangming Ribao.

Li, Q. (2011). State capacity, democratic principle, and constitutional order. In X. Huang, (Eds.). *The institutional dynamics of China's great transformation* (pp.152-160). New York: Routledge.

Li, Y. & Yang, M. (2004). Liang Botai he zhonghuasuweiai gongheguo sifazhidu zhijianshe (Botai Liang and Chinese Soviet Republic Judiciary System Development). *Journal of the Party School of the Central Committee of the Chinese Communist Party.* Retrieved from http://www.cnki.com.cn/Article/CJFDTotal-ZGXB200403014.HTM.

Li, Z. (2003).Will the internet form the public sphere in China? Paper presented at the International Conference on Politics and Information Systems: Technologies and Applications, Orlando, FL, USA. Retrieved at http://www.iiisci.org/journal/CV$/sci/pdfs/P637454.pdf.

Liang, B. (2008). *The changing Chinese legal system, 1978-Present: Centralization of power and rationalization of the legal system.* New York: Routledge.

Liao, K. (1983). Independent administration of justice and the PRC legal system. *Chinese Law and Government, 16* (2-3), 123-152.

Lin, J. (1998). Qindai Falü Zhidu Chu Tan. In Zhongguo Falü Shi Xue Hui (Eds.) FALÜ SHI LUNCONG, An initial inquiry into the Qin dynasty legal system (Appraisals of Chinese Legal History). Beijing: Chinese History Society.

Lin, R. (1995). *The acceptance of influence of Roman law: Collected in the Roman law, China law and the codification of civil law.* Beijing: China University of Politics and Law Press.

Liu, J. (2005). Crime patterns during the market transition in china. *The British Journal of Criminology*, *45* (5), 613-633.

Liu, J. (2009). Re-conceptualizing crime patterns during modernization. In E.W. Plywaczewski (Eds.), *Current Problems of the Penal Law and Criminology*. Bialystok: Temida Press.

Liu, L. (2011). *Public sphere, politics and the internet in mainland China.* Unpublished Thesis. Oslo: University of Oslo.

Liu, S. & Halliday, T. C. (2009). Recursivity in legal change: Lawyers and reforms of China's criminal procedure law. *Law & Social Inquiry, 34* (4), 911-950.

Liu, S. & Halliday, T. C. (2011). Political liberalism and political embeddedness: Understanding politics in the work of Chinese criminal defense lawyers. *Law & Society Review, 45 (4),* 831-865.

Liu, S., Liang, L. & Halliday, T. C. (2014). The trial of Li Zhuang: Chinese lawyers' collective action against populism. *Asian Journal of Law and Society, 1,* 1-33.

Liu, X. & Zheng, L. (2012). Government official microblogs: An effective platform for facilitating inclusive governance. Paper presented in ICEGOV '12, October, 2012, Albany, New York.

Liu, Y. (1998). *Origins of Chinese law: Penal and administrative law in its early development.* New York: Oxford University Press

Liu, Y. G. (2009). Chinese legal tradition and its modernization. David C. Lam Institute for East-West Studies (LEWI) Working Paper Series, Hong Kong.

Lo, C.W.H. (1995). *China's legal awakening: Legal theory and criminal justice in Deng's Era.* Hong Kong: Hong Kong University Press.

Long, Z. & Yuan, J. (2014). Curbing the trend towards the "administrationization" of courts under the background of deepening the reform. *The Legal Study (Faxue Yanjiu),* 2014 (1), 36-38.

Lotverit, T. (1973). Chinese Communism 1931-1934: Experience in Civil government. *Lund Studentlitterature.* 106-144.

Lu, H., & Drass, K. A. (2002). Transience and the disposition of theft cases in China. *Justice Quarterly, 19,* 69–96.

Lu, H., Liu, J., & Crowther, A. (2006). Female criminal victimization and criminal justice response in China. *British Journal of Criminology, 46,* 859–874.

Lu, H., & Liang, B. (2008). Legal responses to trafficking in narcotics and other narcotic offenses in China. *International Criminal Justice Review, 18* (2), 212-228.

Lu, H., & Miethe, T. D. (2002). Legal representation and criminal processing in China. *British Journal of Criminology, 42,* 267–280.

Lu, H. & Miethe, T. D. (2003). Confessions and criminal case disposition in China. *Law & Society Review, 37* (3), 549-578.

Lubman, S. (1999). *Bird in a cage: Legal reform in China after Mao.* Stanford: Stanford University Press.

Lubman, S. (2012). China's criminal procedure law: Good, bad and ugly. China Realtime Report (Mar. 21, 2012 at 9:11 p.m.). Retrieved from http://blogs.wsj.com/chinarealtime/2012/03/21/chinas-criminal-procedure-law-good-bad-and-ugly.

Luo J.Q. & He X. (2012). In Bo Xilai's City, A legacy of backstabbing. *Caixin.* Retrieved from http://english.caixin.com/2012-12-07/100470022.html.

Luo, W. (2000). The amended criminal procedure law and the criminal court rules of the People's Republic of China: with English translation, introduction, and annotation. Buffalo, N.Y.: W.S. Hein.

Lye, L. F. & Yang, Y. (2009). The Chinese leadership and the internet. *EAI Background Brief, 467*, 1-17. Retrieved from http://www.eai.nus.edu.sg/BB467.pdf.

Ma, Y. (2000). A research note on the history of the Chinese police. *International Journal of Comparative and Applied Criminal Justice, 24* (1), 115-123.

Macauley, M. (1998). *Social power and legal culture: Litigation masters in late imperial China.* Stanford: Stanford University Press,

MacCormack, G. (1990). *Traditional Chinese penal law.* Edinburgh: Edinburgh University Press.

MacCormack, G. (1996a). *The spirit of traditional Chinese law.* Athens: University of Georgia Press.

MacCormack, G. (1996b). Religion and law in traditional China, in A. Watston (Eds). *Law, Morality, and Religion: Global Perspectives* (pp. 95-110). Berkeley: Robbins Collection Publications, School of Law, University of California.

Maine, H. (1930). *Ancient Law* (reprint), Oxford: Oxford University Press.

McConville, M., Choongh, S, Choy, P., Wan, D., Chui, E., Hong, W., Dobinson, I. & Jones, C. (2011). *Criminal justice in China: An empirical inquiry.* Cheltenham, UK, and Northampton, MA: Edward Elgar Publishing.

McConville, M. (Ed.). (2013). *Comparative perspectives on criminal justice in China*. Edward Elgar Publishing.

McKnight, B. E. (1997). Punishments in traditional China: From family, to group, to state. In R. M. Andrews, (Eds.), *Perspectives on Punishment: An Interdisciplinary Exploration* (pp.9-15.). New York: Peter Lang.

McKnight, B. E. & Liu, J. T.C. (1999). The enlightened judgments: Ch'ing-ming Chi. *The Sung Dynasty Collection.* New York: SUNY.

Meng, C. (1931). Modern judicial reform in China. *China Weekly Review, 55 (6), 235-237.*

Metzger, T. A. (1973). *The internal organization* of *Ch'ing bureaucracy*: *Legal, normative; and communication aspects*. Cambridge: Harvard University Press.

Meyer, J. & Rowan, B. (1977). Institutionalized organizations: Formal structure as myth and ceremony. *American Journal of Sociology, 83* (2), 340-363.

Michels, R. (1962). *Political parties, study of Oligarchic system*. Illinois: Free Press.

Moore, Jr. B. (1966). *Origins of dictatorship and democracy: Lord and peasant in the making of the modern world.* Boston: Beacon Press.

Muhlhahn, Klaus (2009). *Criminal justice in China: A history*. Cambridge, MA: Harvard University.

National School of Administration of E-government Research Center. (2013). *2012 Zhong guo zheng wu wei bo yan jiu bao gao* (2012 Chinese government micro-blog Assessment Report). Retrieved from http://www.egovernment.gov.cn.

O'Brien, R. (1999). *Civil society, the public sphere and the internet*. December 17th, 2012 retrieved from http://www.web.net/~robrien/papers/civsoc.html.

Office of the State Council of China. (2008). *White paper on the rule of law in China*. Retrieved from http://www.chinadaily.com.cn/china/2008-02/28/content_6494029.htm.

Park,Y. D. (2006). King Sejong's confucian rule by law: Focusing on the relationship between law and rule by benevolence. *The Review of Korean Studies*, 9(3), 103-131.

Park, S. (2010). Law and literature in late imperial China and choson Korea. *Sungkyun Journal of East Asian Studies, 10* (2), 229-250.

Peerenboom, R. (2005). What have we learned about law and development? Describing, predicting, and assessing legal reforms in China. *Michigan*

Journal of International Law, 27, 823-871.

Peerenboom, R. (2008). *China modernizes: Threat to the west or model for the rest?* Cambridge: Oxford University Press.

Peking University Law Department. (1980). *Collection of constitutional materials (II).* Beijing: Peking University Press.

Posner, Richard. (1995). *Overcoming law*. Cambridge: Harvard University Press.

Posner, R. (2005). Judicial behavior and performance: An economic approach. *Florida State University Law Review,* 32, 1259-1279.

Pue, W.W. (1997). Lawyers and political liberalism in eighteenth- and nineteenth-century England. In T.C. Halliday and L Karpik (Eds.), *Lawyers and the Rise of Western Political Liberalism: Europe and North America from the Eighteenth to Twentieth Centuries.* Oxford: Oxford University Press.

Pugh, D. S., Hickson, D. J., Hinings, C. R. & Turner, C. (1968). Dimensions of organization structure. *Administrative Science Quarterly, 13 (1),* 65-105.

Qiao, X. (2005).Who controls China's Courts? http://www.hrichina.org/sites/default/files/PDFs/CRF.2.2005/2.2005-RS-Courts.pdf.

Quigley, H. S. (1926). Extraterritoriality in China. *American Journal of International Law, 20* (1), 46-68.

Quigley, J. (1992). The Romanist character of Soviet law, in F. J.M. Feldbrugge (Eds.), *The Emancipation of Soviet Law,* 27-43, Netherlands: Brill

Reclus, E. (1891). *Evolution and revolution.* London: W. Reeves.

Ren, X. (1997). *Tradition of the law and law of the tradition.* Westport, CT: Greenwood Press.

Riggs, F. W. (1997). Modernity and bureaucracy. *Public Administration Review, 57* (4), 347-353.

Rousseau, J. J. (1754). *A dissertation on the origin and foundation of the inequality of mankind and is it authorised by natural law?* Holland: Marc-Michel Rey.

Rojek, D. G. (1996). Changing directions of Chinese social control. In C. B. Fields, & R. H. Moore Jr. (Eds.), *Comparative Criminal Justice: Traditional and Nontraditional Systems of Law and Control* (pp. 234–249). Prospect Heights, IL: Waveland.

Rowe, W. T. (2010). *China's last empire: The great Qing.* Cambridge: Harvard

University Press.

Salas, L. (1983). The judicial system of post-revolutionary Cuba, *NOVA Law Journal, 8,* 43- 44.

Sapio, F. (2010). *Sovereign power and the law in China.* Leiden: Koninklijke Brill NV.

Schafer, E. H. (1967). *Ancient China. Great ages of man: A history of the world's cultures*. NY: Time Life Books.

Scheufele, D. A. (2000). Agenda-setting, priming, and framing revisited: Another look at cognitive effects of political communication. *Mass Communication & Society, 3* (2&3), 297-316.

Shen, Z. (2004). *Jurisprudence* (2nd ed.). Higher Education Press, Beijing

Shiga, S. (1974). Criminal procedure in the Ch'ing dynasty, with emphasis on its administrative character and some allusion to its historical antecedents. *Memoirs of the Research Department, Toyo Bunko*, 32(1974), 1-45.

Shih, Chih-yu. (1999). *Collective democracy: Political and legal reform in China*. Hong Kong: The Chinese University Press.

Shizuka, S. (1954). In no ozoku to seiji no keitai (The political structure of Yin royal family). *Kodaigaku (The Study of Ancient Times), 3,* 1, 19-44.

Sills, D. (1968). *International encyclopedia of the social sciences.* New York: Macmillan.

Skosey, L. A. (1996). *The legal system and legal tradition of the Western Zhou (CA. 1045-771 BCE)*. Doctoral dissertation, University of Chicago, Department of East Asian Languages and Civilizations.

Soy, S. K. (1997). *The case study as a research method.* Unpublished paper. Austin: The University of Texas.

Strauss, J. C. (1998). *Strong institutions in weak polities: State building in republican China, 1927-1940*. Cambridge: Oxford University Press.

Subramaniam, V. (2009). Indian Legacy of Bureaucracy and Administration.In A. Farazmand (Eds.), *Bureaucracy and Administration.* Boca Raton: CRC Press.

Susumu, F. (1993) Min-Shin jidai no shoshi to sosho seido, (Pettifoggers and the system of filing complaints during the Ming and Qing periods). In Umehara Kaoru (Eds.). *Chugoku kinsei no hosei to shakai (Legal systems and society in modern China).* Kyoto: Kyoto Daigaku Jinbun Kagaku Kenkyujo.

Szeftel, M. (1956). Aspects of feudalism in Russian history. In R. Coulborn (Eds.), *Feudalism in History* (pp.167-182). Princeton: Princeton

University Press.

Tai, Z. (2006). *The internet in China: Cyberspace and civil society*. New York: Routledge Curzon.

Takahashi, N. (2008). In search of a historical perspective on "civil society" China. In Chiharu Takenaka, Nobuo Takahashi, Nobuto Yamamoto (Eds.). *Gendai Ajia Kenkyu2-Shimin Shakai* (pp. 35-56). Tokyo: Keio University Press.

Trevaskes, S. (2001). *The culture of criminal court work in China: A study of grassroots justice in Baotou, Inner Mongolia*. Unpublished PhD thesis. Queensland: Griffith University.

Trevaskes, S. (2003). Public sentencing rallies in China: The symbolizing of punishment and justice in a socialist state. *Crime Law and Social Change, 39*(4), 359-382.

Trevaskes, S. (2004). Propaganda work in Chinese courts. *Punishment & Society-International Journal of Penology, 6* (1), 5-21.

Trevaskes, S. (2007). *Courts and criminal justice in China*. Lanham MD: Lexington Press.

Trevaskes, S. (2010). *Policing serious crime in China: from'strike hard'to'kill fewer'* (Vol. 35). New York: Routledge.

Turack, D. C. (1999). The new Chinese criminal justice system. *Cardozo Journal of International and Comparative Law, 7 (*49), 50-51.

Valdes, N. P. (1976). Revolution and institutionalization in Cuba. *Cuban Study, 6, 1-16.*

Wang, C.G. (2008). From the rule of man to the rule of law. In D. Cai, & C.

Wang, (Eds.), *China's Journey toward the Rule of Law: Legal Reform, 1978-2008* (pp. 6-8). Leiden: Brill.

Wang, C.Z. and Bates, B. (2008). *Online public sphere and democracy in China*. Retrieved from http://web.cci.utk.edu/~bates/papers/iamcr08-wang-bates-publics.pdf.

Wang, H-C. (1983). *Han-shu Pu-chu (汉书补注). Beijing:* Zhong Hua Shu Ju.

Wang, J. C. 1999. *Contemporary Chinese politics: An introduction* (6th ed.). Upper Saddle River, NJ: Prentice Hall.

Wang M. (1995). Xingshi beigaoren quanli yanjiu" (Research on the Rights of Criminal Defendants). In X. Yong (Eds.), *Zou xiang quanli de shidai: Zhongguo gongmin quanli fazhan yanjiu* (Toward a Time of Rights: A Perspective of the Çivil Rights Development in China) (pp. 500-550). Beijing: Zhongguo zhengfa daxue chubanshe.

Wang, P. (2013). The rise of the Red Mafia in China: A case study of organised crime and corruption in Chongqing. *Trends in Organized Crime 16, 1,* 49–73.

Wang, S.J, (2009). President of the supreme people's court of China. *Adhering to the Guiding Principle of the "Three Supremacies"- and Driving to Achieve the New Development of the Court Work.* Speech at the National Teleconference of People's Courts. Retrieved from http://www.court.gov.cn/html/article/200912/21/1557.shtml.

Wang, W.X. (2013). *The influence of Weibo political participations on the political efficacies of Weibo users*. Unpublished Dissertation. London: London School of Economics and Political Science.

Wang Y.C. (1949). An outline of the central government of the Former Han Dynasty. *Harvard Journal of Asiatic Studies, 12 (*1/2), 134-187.

Wang, Z.M. (2006). The Roman law tradition and its future development in China. *Frontiers of Law of China, 1*, 72–78.

Watson, A. (1987).The evolution of law: Continued. *Law and History Review*, *5* (2), 537-570.

Weber, M. (1958). Bureaucracy. In Gerth and Mills, (Eds.). *From Max Weber: Essays in Sociology.* London: Oxford University Press.

Weber, M. (1978). Economy and society: An outline of interpretive sociology. (2 vols.). G. Roth, & C. Wittich, (Eds.). (translated by several scholars). Berkeley: University of California Press.

Whyte, M. K. (1973). Bureaucracy and modernization in China: The Maoist Critique. *American Sociological Review, 38* (2), 149-163.

Will, P-É. (2012). China: Back to the imperial sense of the state? *La Vie des idées.* Retrieved from http://www.booksandideas.net/IMG/pdf/20120217_PEW.pdf.

Windrow, H. (2006). A short history of law, norms, and social control in imperial China. *Asian-Pacific Law and Policy, 7,* 244-301.

Wittfogel. K. A. (1957). *Oriental despotism: A comparative study of total power*. New Haven: Yale University Press.

Woo, M. (1999). Law and discretion in the contemporary Chinese courts. *Pacific Rim Law & Policy Journal*, *8* (3), 581-616.

Wu, B.G. (2008). *Stick to the path of political development of socialism with Chinese characteristics and strive to upgrade the work of the National People's Congress to a new level.* Speech at the First Assembly Meeting of the 11th National Congress as the Chairman of National People's Congress of China. *Retrieved from* http://politics.people.com.cn/GB/1024/7129950.html.

Wu, K-C. (1982). *The Chinese heritage*. *New* York: Crown Publishers.

Wu, Z. & Li, S. (2007). A general introduction to jurisprudence. *University Textbook Series 53.* Beijing: Law Press.

Wu, Z. (2009). No rhyme or reason to China's rule of law. *Asia Times*. Retrieved from http://atimes.com/atimes/China/KA14Ad01.htm.

Xiao, Q. (2011). The battle for the Chinese internet. *Journal of Democracy 22* (2), 47-61.

Xia, M. (1998). China's National People's Congress: Institutional transformation in the process of regime transition (1978-98), *Journal of Legislative Study, 4,* 103-129.

Xin, C.Y. (1999). *Chinese legal system and current legal reform*. Beijing: Law Press.

Xu, M. Q. (1985). *Zhongguo jianyu shi (A History of Chinese Prison).* Beijing: Qunzhong chubanshe.

Xu, X. Q. (1997). The fate of judicial independence in Republican China, 1912-1937. *China Quarterly,* 149, 1-28.

Xu, X.Q. (2008). *Trial of modernity: Judicial reform in early twentieth-century China, 1901-37*. Stanford: Stanford University Press.

Xue, M. (1986). *Zhongguo jianyu shi (A history of Chinese prisons).* Beijing: Qunzhong chubanshe.

Yang, G. B. (2003). The internet and the rise of a transnational Chinese cultural sphere. *Media, Culture & Society, 25* (4), 469-490.

Yang, G. B. (2009). *The power of the internet in China: Citizen activism online.* New York: Columbia University Press.

Yang, H. (1930). *Zhongguo falü fazhan shi (A history of the development of Chinese laws).* Shangwu yinshuguan, Shanghai.

Yang, K. (1984). Xi Zhou zhongyang zhengquan jigou pouxi (西周中央政权剖析). *Li Shi Yan Jiu, 1,* 78-91.

Yang, K. (1999). *Xi Zhou Shi (西周史).*Shanghai: Shanghai Renmin Publisher.

Yi, M. (2010). Chinese people's three dreams. *The Study Review, 11,* 54-55.

Yin, R. K. (1984). *Case study research: Design and methods.* Newbury Park, CA: Sage.

Younkins, E. W. (2000). The evolution of law. *The Quebecois libre, 65*. Montreal.

Yu, P. (2006). *Administrative model v. adjudication model the impact of administrative detention in the criminal process of the People's Republic of China.* Unpublished Dissertation. Seattle: University of Washington.

Yu, X.Z. (2001). Legal pragmatism in the People's Republic of China. *Journal of Chinese Law, 3, reprinted in* P. Keller (Eds.), *Chinese Law and Legal Theory.* Burlington, VT: Ashgate.

Zeldin, W. (2012). *China: Amendment of criminal procedure law.* Retrieved from http://www.loc.gov/lawweb/servlet/lloc_news?disp3_l205403080_ text.

Zhang, J. F. (1999). *Evolution of the Chinese Legal Civilization.* Beijing: China University of Law and Politics Press.

Zhang, L, Messner, S. F. and Liu, J. (2008). A critical review of recent literature on crime and criminal justice in China: Research findings, challenges, and prospects. Introduction to a special issue of *Crime, Law and Social Change: An International Journal,* 50,125-130.

Zhang, M. (2010).The socialist legal system with Chinese characteristics: China's discourse for the rule of law and a bitter experience. *Temple International and Comparative Law Journal, 24,* 1-64.

Zhang, Y. (2014). *Bureaucracy and law: A study of the Chinese criminal courts and social media.* Unpublished dissertation. Boston: Northeastern University.

Zhao, E. (2003). *The history of Qing. Criminal Law (清史稿, 1-4 刑法志).* Beijing: Press of Zhong Hua Shu Ju (中华书局).

Zhao, B. & Bao, S. (1995).The present and future of criminal law reform in China. *Journal of Chinese Comparative Law, 1* (1) 133-156.

Zhong, H., Hu, M., & Liang, B. (2011). Public opinions on criminal trials in China: A comparative study of Chinese college students in the PRC and Hong Kong. *Asian Journal of Criminology*, *6*, 191-205.

Zhu, J.W. (Eds). (2007). *Zhongguo falü fazhan paogao (1979–2004)* [*China Legal Development Report (1979–2004)*]. Beijing: China Renmin University Press.

Zihe, X. (滋贺秀三). (1993). Study on Qing's county court trial (清代州县衙门诉讼的若干研究心得) translated by Yao, Rongyi (姚荣涛译), in *Japanese Scholars' studies on Chinese History Selection, 8 (日本学者研究中国史论著选译, 第8 卷)*. Beijing: Press of Zhong Hua Shu Ju (中华书局).

List of Documents

Falü pinglun, (1927). No. 185, p. 17.
Falüpinglun, No. 215 (14 August 1927), p. 8.
Falü pinglun, (1929). Vol. 6, No. 43, pp. 16-17
Falü pinglun, (1929).Vol. 6, No. 31, pp. 36-37.
Falü pinglun, (1929).Vol. 6, No. 34, pp. 3-8.
Faling zhoukan, No. 87-90 (1932), p. 1.
Sifa gongbao, No. 18 (1935), pp. 17-18.
Sifa gongbao, No. 74 (5 November 1935), p. 8.
Sifa gongbao, No. 83 (20 December 1935), pp. 46-47.
Sifa xingzheng gongbao (Bulletin of Judicial Administration), (1932). No. 2, p. 53.
Wang,Chengzhi, Zhonghua sifa wenti, p. 50.
Zhengfu Gongbao (Government Bulletin), (1913). No.33, p.280.
Zhengfu Gongbao (Government Bulletin), (1914). No.777.
Zhengfu Gongbao (Government Bulletin), (1915). No.974.
Zhengfu Gongbao (Government Bulletin), (1918). No.851.
Zhengfu Gongbao (Government Bulletin), (1927). No.4986.
Zhenfu gongbao fenlei huibian (Government Bulletin compiled in categories), No. 36, 11.
Zhonghua falü zazhi, Vol. 5, Nos. 8-9 (September 1934), pp. 73-74.
Zhonghua Faxue Zazhi. (Journal of Chinese Legal Studies), 2, 252-253; Falü Pinglun (Law Review), 8, 21, 8-9
Zhonghua Renmin Gongheguo Falü Huibian (Compiled Legislations): 1981-1983. (1985). Falü Chubanshe.

Index